Debating Higher Education: Philosophical Perspectives

Volume 11

Series Editors

Ronald Barnett, Institute of Education, University College London, London, UK

Søren S. E. Bengtsen, Danish School of Education (DPU), Aarhus University, Aarhus, Denmark

Assistant Editor

Tessa DeLaquil, Center for International Higher Education, Boston College, Chestnut Hill, MA, USA

Debating Higher Education: Philosophical Perspectives is a new book series launched by Springer and is motivated by two considerations.

Higher education has become a huge matter globally, both politically and socially, commanding massive resources, national and cross-national decision-making, and the hopes of many. In parallel, over the last four decades or so, there has been a growing interest in the academic literature in grappling with technical issues in and around higher education. In particular, work has developed drawing on philosophical perspectives and social theory. This is evident right across the world, especially in the journal literature and in research students' doctoral theses. In effect, we have witnessed the formation of a new sub-discipline, a shorthand of which is 'the philosophy of higher education', and which includes perspectives drawn not only from philosophy and social theory but also feminism, ethics, geopolitics, learning theory, and organizational studies.

Through this book series – the first of its kind – the editors want to encourage the further development of this literature. We are keen to promote lively volumes which are informed about changing practices and policy frameworks in higher education and which engage seriously and deeply with matters of public interest, and are written in an accessible style.

Books will take a variety of forms, and will include both sole-authored and multi-authored formats. Importantly, each volume will have a dialogical flavour, engaging explicitly in dialogue with contemporary debates and their contending positions and, where practicable, especially in volumes with many contributors, will themselves exemplify dialogue.

The editors are keen that the series is open to many approaches. We wish to include work that focuses directly on the university as a social institution and on higher education as an educational process; on the idea of the university and on higher education as a sector with political and policy frameworks; on students and learning, and on academics and academic knowledge; and on curricula and pedagogy, and on research and knowledge processes.

Volumes will examine policy and practical issues including, for example, internationalisation, higher education as a set of 'public goods', access and fairness, and the digital era and learning as well as more conceptual and theoretical issues such as academic freedom, ethics, wellbeing, and the philosophy of social organizations.

The editors very much welcome informal inquiries at any time.

Ronald Barnett, UCL Institute of Education – ron.barnett@ucl.ac.uk Søren S.E. Bengtsen, Aarhus University – ssbe@tdm.au.dk

Nuraan Davids

Academic Citizenship, Identity, Knowledge, and Vulnerability

Nuraan Davids
Stellenbosch University
Stellenbosch, South Africa

ISSN 2366-2573 ISSN 2366-2581 (electronic)
Debating Higher Education: Philosophical Perspectives
ISBN 978-981-99-6900-5 ISBN 978-981-99-6901-2 (eBook)
https://doi.org/10.1007/978-981-99-6901-2

© The Editor(s) (if applicable) and The Author(s), under exclusive license to Springer Nature Singapore Pte Ltd. 2023

This work is subject to copyright. All rights are solely and exclusively licensed by the Publisher, whether the whole or part of the material is concerned, specifically the rights of translation, reprinting, reuse of illustrations, recitation, broadcasting, reproduction on microfilms or in any other physical way, and transmission or information storage and retrieval, electronic adaptation, computer software, or by similar or dissimilar methodology now known or hereafter developed.

The use of general descriptive names, registered names, trademarks, service marks, etc. in this publication does not imply, even in the absence of a specific statement, that such names are exempt from the relevant protective laws and regulations and therefore free for general use.

The publisher, the authors, and the editors are safe to assume that the advice and information in this book are believed to be true and accurate at the date of publication. Neither the publisher nor the authors or the editors give a warranty, expressed or implied, with respect to the material contained herein or for any errors or omissions that may have been made. The publisher remains neutral with regard to jurisdictional claims in published maps and institutional affiliations.

This Springer imprint is published by the registered company Springer Nature Singapore Pte Ltd.
The registered company address is: 152 Beach Road, #21-01/04 Gateway East, Singapore 189721, Singapore

Contents

1	**Academic Conundrums**	1
	1.1 Setting the Scene	1
	1.2 Academics, Identity, and Citizenship	2
	1.3 Academic Citizenship and Vulnerability	6
	1.4 Motivation for This Book	8
	1.5 Organisation of the Book	11
	References	14

Part I Identity, Citizenship, and Vulnerability

2	**Academic Identities and Citizenship**	19
	2.1 Citizenship and Professionalism	20
	2.2 Academic Citizenship	22
	2.3 Identity, Recognition, and Participation	24
	2.4 Contestations	27
	2.5 Erosion and Disengagement	30
	2.6 Key Considerations of Chapter	32
	References	32
3	**Academic Citizenship as an Agonistic Space**	35
	3.1 Agonism as Expressions of Pluralism and Disagreement	36
	3.2 Competing Truths and Academic Freedom	38
	3.3 Research, Knowledge and Democratic Dissensus	40
	3.4 Criticality of Agonism for Academic Citizenship	42
	3.5 Key Considerations of Chapter	44
	References	45
4	**Identities, Citizenships, and Vulnerabilities**	47
	4.1 Intersections Between Identity, Citizenship, and Vulnerability	48
	4.2 The (In)visibility of Vulnerability	50
	4.3 Institutional Power and Vulnerability	53

	4.4	Academic Vulnerability as Openness	56
	4.5	Key Considerations of Chapter	59
	References		59
5	**Diversity as Vulnerability**		**61**
	5.1	(Mis)recognition	62
	5.2	Paradoxical Effects of *Doing* Diversity	64
	5.3	Negotiation, and Vulnerability	68
	5.4	Diversity and Dialogue	71
	5.5	Key Considerations of Chapter	73
	References		73

Part II   Academic Citizenship, Knowledge, and Curiosity

6	**Academics as Embodiments of Knowledge**		**79**
	6.1	Othering and Erasure	79
	6.2	Knowledge and Academic Citizenship	82
	6.3	Knowledge as Embodiment	85
	6.4	Academic Citizenship as Activism	89
	6.5	Key Considerations of Chapter	91
	References		92
7	**Academic Citizenship as Curiosity**		**95**
	7.1	Why Curiosity Matters	95
	7.2	Curiosity as Care	99
	7.3	Curiosity and 'Unfinishedness'	101
	7.4	Curiosity for Liberatory Academic Citizenship	104
	7.5	Key Considerations of Chapter	106
	References		106
8	**The Vulnerability of Unlearning**		**109**
	8.1	Experience and Learning	110
	8.2	Learning to Unlearn	114
	8.3	Learning *from*	117
	8.4	Key Considerations of Chapter	120
	References		120

Part III   Identity and Citizenship as Transformation

9	**Identity and Transformation**		**125**
	9.1	Transformation as (Mis)representation	125
	9.2	The Risks for Academic Citizenship	129
	9.3	Academic Identities and Institutional Transformation	133
	9.4	Key Considerations of Chapter	137
	References		137

10	**Stories as Reclamations of Knowledge**	141
	10.1 Why Stories Matter	142
	10.2 Academic Citizenship as Lived and Storied	144
	10.3 Key Considerations of Chapter	155
	References	156
11	**Responsibility and Being *Other*-Wise**	157
	11.1 That's How the Light Gets in	157
	11.2 Responsibility and not Being 'Purely Academic'	159
	11.3 Epistemic Bubbles and (Dis)entanglement	163
	11.4 Key Considerations of Chapter	166
	References	167
12	**Concluding Reflections: Academic Citizenship, Collegiality, and Trust**	169
	12.1 Collegiality	170
	12.2 Trust, and Trustworthiness	173
	12.3 Key Considerations of Book	175
	References	176

Chapter 1
Academic Conundrums

1.1 Setting the Scene

Much has been written on the roles and responsibilities which shape academic citizenship, with Macfarlane and Burg (2018:3), describing it as a 'set of attitudes and activities connected to internal and external service work supporting the infrastructure of academic life and the wider civic mission of the university.' Minimal attention, however, has been given to who these citizens are and what their citizenship experiences entail. Importantly, and underscoring the motivation of this book, is that universities are not homogenous institutions, dedicated merely to knowledge production. They are constituted by different kinds of academics, who, depending on their identities and the knowledge they bring, experience, or are subjected to different kinds of citizenship. The seemingly homogenous descriptor of academic citizenship has yet to be peeled back for interrogation. Beneath professional appointments and designations are multiple identities, histories, perspectives, perceptions, experiences, and truths. While some academics stand inside of the institutional culture their universities and its power dynamics, others do not.

This book seeks to bring into question the idea of academic citizenship as a homogenous and inclusive space. It seeks to show that even when academics occupy similar positions, or hold similar professional standings, their citizenship and implied notions of participation, inclusion, recognition, and belonging is largely pre-determined by who they are personally, rather than what they do professionally. As a result, not only do academics experience different kinds of citizenship, but they live through different sets of vulnerabilities. And hence, the arising questions: Who are the academics who constitute the citizenship of universities? What does this citizenship imply not only for their ensuing rights, responsibilities, but for their sense of belonging? Who are the producers of knowledge which establish and sustain the power dynamics of the university? What kinds of knowledge are valued and foregrounded, and whose are discounted? And by implication, who are the academics, who stand outside of these structures, and on what basis are they relegated to the peripheries of institutions? Why should universities attend to the citizenship of their academics? Why does academic citizenship matter, if at all?

1.2 Academics, Identity, and Citizenship

On the surface, academics' responsibilities centre on the pillars of teaching and writing. Just beneath these surfaces are a myriad other roles and tasks, which can include any of the following: student supervision; serving on departmental, faculty, programme and university committees; undertaking leadership and management roles within the university; acting as a peer reviewer for an academic journal, publisher or funding body; working as an external examiner of dissertations or moderator of university modules or programmes; fulfilling editorial roles for journals or books; organising a conference for a professional or academic society; writing grant proposals, evaluating peers as they seek promotion; as well as serving on external advisory panels, committees and societies. Once assigned a title or position, there is an unspoken initiation into an academic citizenship, which is limited to a list of performative criteria, with seemingly scant regard for considerations of who academics are, or indeed what the university is about beyond its academic imperatives.

There is a steadily emerging body of literature on academics' experiences in higher education (Barnett & Di Napoli, 2008; Clegg, 2008; Fitzmaurice, 2013; Nixon, 2001), as there is on notions of academic citizenship (Harris, 2005; Macfarlane, 2005; Macfarlane & Burg, 2018; Merton, 1947a, 1947b; Nixon, 2008; Nørgård & Bengtsen, 2016). On the one hand, there are differentiations between 'early career' or 'first career' academics, who enter the academe upon completion of their PhDs, and 'second career academics', who enter the academy after occupying other professional designations. Herman et al (2021) maintain that while 'early career academics' have been the subject of many educational developers' inquiries (see Fitzmaurice, 2013; Sutherland, 2017), less is known about 'second career academics' or how to support them.

On the other hand, there are differentiations between academic citizens as 'locals' or 'cosmopolitans' (Merton, 1947a, 1947b). 'Locals' are viewed as loyal, long serving members of staff, with implicit knowledge of their respective institutions, and are more teaching-focused (Macfarlane, 2005). Whereas 'cosmopolitans' are seen as more closely connected with members of their disciplinary community outside their institution and are more likely to prioritise research. In this regard, more attention is given to internationalisation—understood as a 'trend or policies to increase border-crossing knowledge transfer and various related activities as well as possibly understood as a trend and policy to increase the similarity of higher education across countries (often also called 'globalisation')' (Teichler, 2015: 7). Whether academics choose to prioritise certain responsibilities or how they choose to define themselves is often as dependent on academic positions as it is on the internal dynamics of faculties and departments. Typically, early career academics might find themselves carrying heavier teaching loads than more established professors, who might have heavier research responsibilities.

Closely tied to 'cosmopolitan' academics, is yet another enactment of academic citizenship, namely academic mobility, or academic migration (Teichler, 2015). Driven by an emphasis on internalisation, academic mobility, explains Teicher (2015: 7), is considered as 'very important for academic progress in general, for international understanding, comparative analysis and as a counterbalance to parochial thinking in general.' As a result, it is common for postgraduates and academics to seek new opportunities in the form of specific programmes, postdoctoral fellowships, or appointments. While a significant feature of higher education and considered as valuable for knowledge exchange and professional development, academic mobility might not be voluntary or motivated by an agenda to establish an international academic reputation. Other factors which play a role include the increasing managerialist and cost-cutting paradigms of higher education institutions, which have put into play a growing trend of contract posts, thereby creating not only job insecurity, but also forcing especially early career academics to seek employment in contexts in which they might not necessarily enjoy full professional or personal recognition (Dmitrishin & Viñas-Bardolet, 2021).

Additionally, universities are not immune to external factors, which might influence the shape and scope of universities—with growing fears among academics that their independence and authority are under threat from state interventions (Beck & Young, 2005). In South Africa, which serves as a background to this book, the higher education landscape has undergone a series of reform measures, necessitated by a transition from an apartheid-based differentiated system to a 'single, national co-ordinated system that would ensure diversity in its organisational form and the institutional landscape, mix of institutional missions and programmes commensurate with national and regional needs in social, cultural and economic development' (DoE, 1997: 2.3). A 'single, national co-ordinated system' implied not only the merging of certain historically advantaged ('white') and historically disadvantaged ('black') institutions but included a commitment to the government's socio-economic transformation policy of employment equity, specifically, an 'Organizational Culture mind shift to accommodate previously disadvantaged groups namely black people, women and people with disabilities' (DHET, 2019: 6).

For many academics (including myself), appointed at historically 'white' universities, the challenge of becoming an academic involves not only 'a cognitive and emotive process' (Fitzmaurice, 2013: 613), but a perpetual struggle of recognition, participation, and inclusion. The post-apartheid emphasis on employment equity mirrors that of the massification of students from historically disadvantaged backgrounds. Increasing student enrolment is viewed as critical to the diversification and democratisation not only to higher education in South Africa, but to society. Ironically, massification has shown little evidence of tackling social inequalities of access and participation—inequalities in terms of access and success persist even in participation systems (Hornsby & Osman, 2014; Marginson, 2016). Instead, students struggle to find points of resonance at what they experience as deeply alienating spaces—not unlike some academics, who often describe themselves as imposters in their own departments or faculties.

While driven by different political demands, the South African higher education landscape is not unique in its challenges with a changing system. Barnett and Di Napoli (2008) report that a changing UK university system, which saw the end of the binary system (between traditional, elite institutions, and the polytechnics), the growth of the audit and quality regimes, not only created fractures in the system, but brought into question academic identities and senses of self. In this regard, academics 'whose traditional sense of identity might have been framed by the notion of 'academic freedom', were obliged to rethink their roles in higher education. Wider phenomena such as massification, accountability and marketisation aided these dislocations of identity' (Barnett & Di Napoli, 2008: 3). To Barnett and Di Napoli (2008), changes in the UK university system created spaces for the emergence of new and wider identities as well as voices in redefining the nature and scope of higher education.

Hence, while it indeed might be the case that the changing nature of universities provides a broader range of opportunities for the expression and recognition of their identities (Delanty, 2008), it is hard to shrug off the predominant focus on on what academics *do* (or not), rather than who they are. In other words, there is a preferred focus on the 'academic' characterisation, and not on the 'citizenship', even as Barnett (2000: 256) argues that 'what it means to be 'an academic' is by no means given but is a matter of dynamic relationships between social and epistemological interests and structures.' This concern notwithstanding, does the silence in the literature suggest that the commonly encountered controversies in citizenship are limited to the public sphere, and do not trickle into academic citizenship? Or is there a presumption that academics are better equipped and willing to navigate the uneven terrains of citizenships? Both speculations seem misplaced considering the growing research on the disparate experiences of women, who face intersectional nodes of discrimination, including race, ethnicity, culture, and religion.

According to Bosniak (2006), the contention that citizenship itself can represent an axis of subordination means citizenship is experienced unequally and un-equitably. Anecdotal evidence suggests that this same axis of subordination and discrimination prevails within academic citizenship. That universality of equality remains restricted by the setting in which it is expected to operate, (Mohanty & Tandon, 2006), implies not only that those institutions do not exist in isolation, but that 'what you actually are obliged to look at is more and more framing' (Spivak & Grosz, 1990: 5). As such, institutional experiences within the university have to be explored by taking account of the broader centre-periphery construction outside of the university. More specifically, as Spivak et al., (1990: 40–41) observe, 'there is nothing that is central. The centre is always constituted in terms of its own marginality… in terms of the hegemonic historical narrative, certain peoples have always been asked to cathect the margins so others can be defined as central.'

Bhattacharya (2016: 310), for example, shares that as an Indian or 'brown' woman in formal or non-formal spaces at an American university, she has 'repeatedly been relegated to the roles of the exotic Other or the Third-World broker, or someone

1.2 Academics, Identity, and Citizenship

whose scholarship can be dismissed unless presented with appropriate *citational privileging*.' She emphasises the common occurrence of 'women of color' 'being denied tenure because her work is too radical, too angry, too anecdotal, too driven by "ethnic" theories, too far from mainstream scholarship in her field, and therefore irrelevant and lacking in scholarly impact' (Bhattacharya, 2016: 310). Unsurprisingly therefore, in the United States, 'women of color' are underrepresented in tenured and full professorships in American colleges and universities (Alcalde & Subramaniam, 2020); 'black' and ethnic minority women academics have not attained the progressive benefits that have accrued to white women in the wake of gender equality initiatives and directives (Jones, 2006; Oforiwaa & Afful-Broni, 2014). This trend seemingly extends into leadership roles: women are not simply denied top leadership opportunities at the culmination of a long career, but rather such opportunities seem to disappear at various points along their trajectories (Alcalde & Subramaniam, 2020). A South African study found that 'there are concerns about unrepresentative demography mostly demonstrating that minorities are not proportionately represented in senior positions' (Sadiq et al., 2019: 424).

To date, irrespective of geopolitical and institutional contexts and histories, responses to the diversity inherent to universities are predominantly framed in languages of performativity, and visual redress (Ahmed, 2006; Bhopal & Pitkin, 2020; Doharty et al., 2021)—intent on portraying universities as anti-racist and embracing diversity. Apparent, is a preoccupation with the optics of diversity and its representation, rather than any concerted efforts to understand the lived experiences of academics. There is seemingly scant consideration of the importance of recognising and understanding the identities of academics in relation to what they do.

To Taylor (1994: 33), identity is who we are, where we have come from and serves as the background to our interests, our values, our tastes, our opinions, as well as our aspirations. Identity provides us with our distinctive humanity. Taylor (1994: 30) asserts that there is 'a certain way of being human that is my way'. Humans can only live their lives in a way they have come to understand; their identity, how they conceive themselves, is what gives shape to their unique identities. When they are prevented from being true to who they are—through misrecognition or discrimination—they miss being what being human is for them (Taylor, 1994). In turn, Mendieta (2008: 407) describes identity as a 'social locus' of how individuals position themselves within a particular context. Depending on how an individual negotiates the influences of her 'social locus'—whether imaginary or not—the social space is continually shifting and transforming (Mendieta, 2008). Mendieta (2008: 412) contends that if identity is influenced by a constantly changing 'social topography', then identities must be understood as 'fragile negotiations' with their respective 'social topography.'

The implications for universities exceed that of the marginalising effects and vulnerabilities of minority group academics. Belonging, argues Yuval-Davis (2011), is not just about social locations and constructions of individual and collective identities and attachments; it also is concerned with the ways these are assessed and valued by the self and others. A failure to find belonging in academic citizenship brings into contestation the idea of this citizenship as much as it does the role and responsibility of universities in cultivating spaces for diverse formations and expressions of being—for academics, students, administrators, and governors, alike (Davids, 2022).

1.3 Academic Citizenship and Vulnerability

While due attention might be given to mentoring new appointments into specific roles and expectations, such as, teaching, writing, and supervising—it is questionable whether careful thought is given to what it means to be an academic citizen. Careful examination will reveal that underscoring most academic responsibilities are presumptions of informed commentary, especially on peers. Academics are required to review, assess, evaluate, rate and moderate not only their peers' writing and proposals, but their academic achievements in relation to appointments and promotions. Academics are increasingly expected to prove their worth through standardised performative and competitive measures (Jackson, 2018; Peseta et al., 2017). Apparent from the implicit functioning of the academic sphere is, on the one hand, an extensive reliance on peer appraisal and estimation, and on the other hand, a willingness to being open to critique and assessment. From the outset academics are initiated into dyadic cycles of seemingly seamless expectations—shifting roles between author and reviewer, supervisor and examiner, and presenter and respondent. Critical to these expectations, however, is an unrelenting acceptance that whatever academics state, write, teach, present, or supervise, must be subjected to critique. Most academics understand this. They understand the, at times, scathing experiences, of bad and harsh reviews or the occasional insulting student evaluations. There are certain shared understandings (perhaps, even support) about an academic citizenship, which is not only unafraid of subjecting itself to assessment and analysis but recognises the implicit vulnerability of the profession.

These shared understandings notwithstanding, there are, however certain unexplored discriminations about what it means to be a citizen of the academy, which are shrouded in the silence of unspoken experiences, and speak to an exposure of vulnerabilities. The contained competitive nature of academic citizenship serves to curtail reflection or discussion on what this perpetual competing state might mean for individuals. The implicit acceptance of an 'academic' environment seems to render it off limits to expressions of vulnerability, despite the explicit demands on academics to make themselves vulnerable. There are good reasons for academics being told to have 'thick skins' if they are to survive, let alone flourish in the academy. It is not only that academics are subjected to different kinds of appraisal, or that some academics encounter callous reviews more often than others. More importantly, different academics experience different kinds of vulnerabilities, both in terms of who they are, and the kinds of knowledge they produce. Even within these differences there are intricate experiences. There are the tangible and more easily understood sets of experiences which differentiate between early career and established academics, for example, as well as between those who have tenure and those who do not. Less perceptible, are the differences experienced by academics based on their gender, race, culture, nationality, ethnicity, religion, or sexuality.

Vulnerability is typically understood as an openness or a susceptibility to being hurt or harmed. Cautions against showing vulnerability often stem from concerns about showing weakness or revealing too much of oneself. In turn, the descriptor of vulnerability is often attached to individuals or groups, who are considered as being at risk. For example, certain students, because of financial constraints, are described as vulnerable, because they are at risk of dropping out. And of course, in instances like these, measures are necessary to offset these risks. Concomitantly, being less vulnerable, implies being safe from risk or harm. Philosophically, however, vulnerability is not necessarily a deficit, and in education, it can be conceived as valuable (Jackson, 2018). While Gilson (2014: 309) propagates an 'epistemic vulnerability' as a precondition for learning, and an openness 'to not knowing', Palmer (2017: 8) describes teaching as a 'daily exercise in vulnerability', and an exploration of authenticity.

For Gilson (2014), vulnerability is not limited to being open to the unknown, it also involves venturing ideas and feelings, even if it means being wrong, so that learning might unfold. In this regard, vulnerability is seen as enabling learning, whereas invulnerability stifles learning. 'Women of color' reports Bhattacharya (2016), are often subjected to subtle forms of marginalisation, which include academic bullying and isolation. Creating secret, safe spaces in which these women can share their stories and be vulnerable, allows them to interrogate the intersectionality of their experiences as academics from diverse racial, religious, cultural, or sexual identities. Stories, as Ellis et al. (2011) note, are complex, constitutive, meaningful phenomena that introduce unique ways of thinking and feeling and assist individuals in making sense of themselves and others. (Bhattacharya, 2016: 310) neither sees these spaces only as protests against oppressive structures, nor the women as existing in 'narratives of victimization'.

Stated differently, it cannot be presumed, as Butler (2016) argues, that if women or minorities seek to establish themselves as vulnerable, they unwittingly or wittingly seek to establish a protected status subject to a paternalistic set of powers that must safeguard the vulnerable (those deemed as weak and in need of protection). Rather, explains Bhattacharya (2016), by connecting with each other, and by finding themselves in each other's stories, some of the women have discovered the strength that can be found in vulnerability. A similar view is advanced by Butler (2016: 21), who conceives of vulnerability as an indication of a 'broader condition of dependency and interdependency which changes the dominant ontological understanding of the embodied subject'.

The argument here, and as it in this book, is twofold. Firstly, a focus on the benefits of vulnerability can lead to deeper understandings and engagements with and of the other. Secondly, however, the benefits should not be understood as minimising or placating the lived experiences of certain academics. That is, the fact that certain groups of academics are more vulnerable than others by virtue of who they are, rather than what they do, should not be an acceptable norm. Spivak et al. (1990) caution that the more vulnerable individuals are, the more they must negotiate. It is helpful, therefore, to understand vulnerability as having both benign and malignant aspects (Jackson, 2018). Normalising a place for vulnerability in higher education, argues Jackson (2018: 234), 'can be done to decrease rather than increase harm, depending on the circulation and distribution of vulnerability: that is, *who* in the group is more and less vulnerable, and in what respects.' Specifically, she continues, when some perspectives and experiences are normalised while others are not, those with minority views are vulnerable to misrecognition of their concerns. Yet, states Jackson (2018), when those with normalised views develop vulnerability, they can learn from others so that social justice can be enhanced.

1.4 Motivation for This Book

The purpose of this book is not only to delve into who academics are, and how they come to embody their academic citizenship, if at all. It is also about stepping into the unexplored constructions of how knowledge is used in the deployment of valuing some forms of academic citizenship, while devaluing others. In this regard, it is hard to ignore not only the contested and vulnerable terrain of academic citizenship, but the necessity of unpacking the agonistic space of the university which both sustains and benefits from these contestations and vulnerabilities.

The inherent disagreements and conflicts, embedded in diverse histories, perspectives and truths,—described by Chantal Mouffe (2014) as 'agonistic pluralism'—are not undesirable phenomena to be overcome by democratic consensus, but rather as constitutive of politics, and hence academic citizenship. At work, are multiple intersections between personal identities and professional dispositions, institutional cultures and discourses and a deployment of a language of transformation, which seemingly produces requisite policies, without compulsions of action. Consequently, there are profoundly more complex factors influencing 'academic disengagement' (Macfarlane & Burg, 2018) or erosion, than the effects of performativity on the nature of modern academic life; the political disenfranchisement of academics, as they are excluded from practical roles in institutional governance; or the shift away from a collegial to a more bureaucratic and managerial culture (MacFarlane, 2005).

What, therefore, is necessary to transform academic citizenship as an imperative for transforming universities into spaces of diverse thinking and being? What kinds of academic citizenship are essential for producing knowledge which question and disrupt normative ideas about the world and its people, rather than pandering to systems of knowledge, which reproduces itself?

These thematic explorations are underscored and influenced by a postcolonial vantage point, interested in unblocking and opening spaces, thoughts, and voices of reimagined embodiments and expressions of academic citizenship, as well as hitherto silenced and discounted forms of knowledge and being. Santos (2021) explains that postcolonialism, decoloniality, epistemologies of the South are three primary ways of critically approaching the consequences of European colonialism in contemporary social, political, and cultural ways of thinking and acting. Epistemologies of the South, continues Santos (2021), do not only denounce the cognitive and ontological destruction caused by coloniality. They also insist on the possibility of inter-knowledge and intercultural translation, thereby bringing into question the plasticity of the sociological categorisation of the Global South and the Global North (Santos, 2014). The main objective of postcolonialism, explains Andreotti, is to address the epistemic violence of colonialism and the interrogation of European cultural supremacy in the subjugation of different peoples and knowledges in colonial and neocolonial contexts' (Andreotti, 2010). To this end, postcolonialism seeks to develop a different paradigm in which identities are no longer starkly oppositional or exclusively singular but defined by their intricate and mutual relations with others (Young, 2009).

Postcolonialism, therefore, begins from its own counter-knowledges, and from the diversity of its cultural experiences. It offers a language of and for those who have no place, who seem not to belong, of those whose knowledges and histories are not allowed to count (Young, 2009). In this way, states Peters (2019: 143), 'postcolonial studies takes its place with other disciplines within the academy to analyze the politics of knowledge in terms of power relationships that dominated the colonial university system including questions of elite formations, identity and the construction of the colonial subject, and the formation of the canon'. For Mbembe, however, postcolonialism and postcolonial studies are far from constituting a system, because it is largely being constructed as it unfolds. As such, it offers a fragmented way of thinking, which, according to Mbembe, is both a strength and a weakness. Irrespective of how one chooses to frame postcolonialism, learning to navigate different epistemologies, can be a useful strategy for the emergence of better relationships and for addressing material and cultural inequalities (Andreotti et al., 2011)—which is ultimately, what this book is asking its readers to do.

Following these explications of postcolonialism, and in support of disrupting the inscribed binaries between whose knowledge and citizenship matters, and whose does not, I draw on an array of theorists—some of whom sit comfortably in the discourses of post-colonial theory, and some who might not necessarily be inclined see their work as such. The intentions, however, remain intact: to show that different kinds of knowledge are necessary for both the building and questioning of theory; the more expansive our immersion into knowledge, the greater the capacities and opportunities for unlearning and relearning. Bhabha (1999) reminds us that theory can help us to break the continuity and the consensus of common sense, and to interrupt the dominating strategies of generalisation so that we might look beyond and learn that other logics of signification exist.

As manifestations of these other logics are the profound stories from academics, located at various universities (South Africa, USA, Hong Kong, and the Philippines). Hartman (2008: 11) describes stories 'as a form of compensation or even as reparations'; and as restorative, not only in the sense of filling in the missing pieces or words, but in terms of restoring dignity and justice. Our lives, and hence our stories, are not self-contained. Instead, we all exist in a complex web of human relationships (Arendt, 1958), which make it impossible for individuals to describe themselves without taking into account others. Identity is not only constructed in dialogue (that is between the individual and others, or the collective), but the dialogical construction of identity is both reflective and constitutive—'It is not individual or collective, but involves both, in an in-between state of 'becoming,' in which processes of identity construction, authorisation, and contestation take place' (Yuval-Davis, 2011: 16).

The importance of relating, listening, or reading stories is not so much about the sharing of experiences as it is about the capacity it holds for helping us to understand ourselves in relation to those who shape our relationships. If we are prepared to listen to others' stories and to learn from others, we create opportunities to sensitise ourselves to 'issues of identity politics, to experiences shrouded in silence, and to forms of representation that deepen our capacity to empathize with people who are different from us' (Ellis et al., 2011: 274).

As a postcolonial pronouncement, it is possible to alter what it is like to be in this world, and to see one another as different, without a desire for an imposition of sameness. There are ways of being and acting in this world that, if acknowledged and recognised, can begin to undo the self-inflicted harm from being closed off to other forms of knowledge, especially as it pertains to the identities and life-worlds of others.

In sum, the book seeks to invite academics, university administrators, as well as students into an exploratory journey of what academic citizenship infers not only as a professional designation, but as a contractual, intellectual, emotional, and intuitive space. There are implications for academics when who they are and what they produce do not meet unquestioned prescriptions of Anglo-normative epistemologies. The experiences of academics cannot be segregated from that of the university; academic citizenship establishes and fosters the climate of the university. There are unending risks to understanding or approaching academic citizenship as a corpus in need of performative management. These risks are not limited to academic disengagement or apathy. There are also consequences for teaching, writing, supervising, and mentoring.

Perhaps more importantly, there are consequences for the purpose of the university, and whether it sees knowledge and its production as utterances of conformity and sameness, or as responsibilities towards innovation. In this regard, the book might also find appeal with a wider readership. It is not just that the public domain holds influence over universities. It is also that universities have responsibilities in relation to the public sphere and its citizenship. If universities are unwilling to do the hard work of recognising and assigning equal regard and trust for diverse representations of citizenship and knowledge, then can society really expect them to play any role in relation to undoing social harms and inequalities?

1.5 Organisation of the Book

The book is divided into three parts, taking careful note of the intersections between academic citizenship, identity, knowledge, and vulnerability, while simultaneously highlighting the signifying predominance of identity. Part one sketches the foundational concerns or problematique of the book. In this regard, chapter two commences with a focus on academic identities and citizenship. While academic citizenship is typically described as a list of key roles, this list does not only obscure the immense set of responsibilities, which accompanies academic work, but seemingly infers a homogeneous understanding of citizenship on all academics. There has yet to be a serious consideration of whether academic citizenship means the same to all academics. Here, the concern is not whether academics share the same understandings of their roles and responsibilities. Rather, whether all academics can participate in their citizenship.

Picking up on the underlying discord highlighted in chapter two, chapter three looks at academic citizenship as an agonistic space. While the extant literature shows an awareness of the challenges encountered by certain professional academic identities, there is limited consideration of academic citizenship as a contentious, belligerent, or agonistic space and experience. In maintaining that agonism is crucial for the accommodation and provision of competing truths and arguments, the chapter is interested in how universities might open themselves to difference and belligerence not as undesirable and avoidable expressions, but as central for democratic dissensus, and hence, advancement.

Following the concerns raised about the realities of differentiated forms of academic citizenship, the focus in chapter four is on the arising vulnerabilities. Not only are some academics more vulnerable than others, but some vulnerabilities are less visible than others—particularly when connected with certain identities. Notably, while some academics push through and find ways of coping without being too affected by estranging institutional contexts and cultures, others suffer tremendous harm, professionally and personally. And yet, vulnerability can be a source of strength. Being vulnerable is not only about stepping into one's own truth and being, but also about being willing to listen to other voices and perspectives and opening oneself to change. More importantly, I argue, that being vulnerable opens opportunities for the establishment of a new academic identities.

Chapter five provides an intensive look at diversity as vulnerability. In this chapter I argue that the very identification of diversity draws lines in the sand between those categorised as diverse, and those who are not. What this means is that even before stepping into a lecture theatre, or the first faculty board, the marker of diversity already says something about how academics are constructed and perceived, and hence, how they will be treated. Designated markers of diversity, therefore, hold implications for how certain academics are seen, and unseen. It also holds implications for the university in terms of who are seen, and hence who the university has been made for, and does not require management. Diversity, therefore, does not only direct attention to certain markers, but it also provokes an immediate vulnerability to being seen as different and in need of management. Of concern here is what these markers and vulnerability infer for the experiences of diverse academic citizenships.

Building on the concerns and questions raised in part one, part two attends to the need for renewed considerations of academic citizenship, as informed and influenced by knowledge and curiosity. Chapter 6, therefore, focuses on the idea that academics do not only produce knowledge, but they are also embodiments of knowledge. In this way, universities are not empty spaces, waiting to be filled with the voices, teaching and research of academics. Their establishment is already embedded in historical, political, social, and epistemological milieus, as well as certain forms and looks of academic citizenship. Academic citizenship, therefore, is not only cultivated through appointments, discipline specialisations, but also by knowledge economies which attach value to the citizenship of some academics, but not to others. As such, it is necessary for academics to consider what they know, as well as how they have come to know what they know. Specifically, I look at what academic citizenship might do in cultivating an openness to different and competing forms of knowledge, so that new ways of looking at the world might come into play, and so that we can all come into the presence of one another.

In line with my argument for an openness to different forms of knowledge and academic citizenship, chapter seven attends to the necessity of curiosity. It follows that unless academics recognise that they lack certain forms of knowledge, or that what they know might not be all there is to know on a particular subject, there can be no curiosity, and hence, no new forms of knowledge. Similarly, unless academics have a desire to engage with those with whom they are unfamiliar, there can be no awareness of different social realities and perspectives. The silo-effect of South Africa's apartheid, for example, continues to permeate the constructions of relationships among academics. There must, therefore, be a curiosity about who academics are, what they bring, and how they add to the epistemological foundations of the university, not only in terms of what they produce, but in what they contribute as embodiments of knowledge.

Arguments for the importance of curiosity necessarily takes us to scrutinising what we know, what we do not know, and whether what we know is useful, or harmful. If the knowledge we carry and propagate is misplaced, misguided, or prejudicial, then it becomes necessary to both unlearn and relearn. In chapter eight I consider whether it matters at all if academics produce new knowledge, or whether they learn anew, if there is no consideration of what this might mean for the necessity unlearning. While learning takes us towards the acquisition of knowledge, skills, values, as well as habits, unlearning, however, relies on a deeper interrogation of the very source of what we know, why we know it, how we have come to know it, followed by an openness to confront any inherent prejudices or biases. In deliberating on the worthwhileness of unlearning for academic citizenship, I look at the possibilities for universities in dismantling discursive norms which prevent endeavours towards new kinds of knowledge.

Now that I have provided insights into the importance of knowledge, curiosity, and unlearning to relearn, part three offers a more nuanced focus on identity and citizenship as transformation. In South Africa, for example, the transformation of higher education, has been dominated by the structural merging of historically advantaged and historically disadvantaged universities; employment equity policies, directed at the recruitment of historically disadvantaged academics and administrators, and of course, concerted efforts to increase student enrolment from historically marginalised communities. Central to chapter nine, however, is whether it is enough for academic citizenship to be representative of diversity for it (citizenship) to be transformed. Or does transformation demand something more in terms of delving beyond the shell of the external, and that which is immediately obvious, so that what is aspired towards are not only shifts in form and appearance, but in thinking and being? In response, I look at how academics might use their identities to assist processes of personal transformation, as well as institutional transformation.

In continuing with my focus on the valuable role of diverse academic identities, chapter ten turns directly to the voices and experiences of academics, situated in South Africa, the UK, USA, and Hong Kong. Their lived experiences offer profound insights into the nature of their academic citizenships, assigned to them by their identities. I contend that theory is often used to reify norms when what academics should be doing is to interrogate these norms. If academics conceive of themselves as citizens of the universities, then there are certain implications for citizenship itself, specifically, knowing who they *are* as citizens. Academic citizenship must start with academics wanting to know about one another, how they conceive of themselves, and how they conceive of themselves in relation to others. Stories provide us with knowledge, not only of experiences, but of emotions, intuitions, and vulnerabilities. As such, they offer platforms of engagement that hold potential for profound mutual sense-making, unlearning, and relearning.

Underlining this book is an emphatic recognition that academic citizenship cannot only be understood in terms of academic projects, or knowledge production. As highlighted in chapter eleven, there are privileged responsibilities, which accompany the production of knowledge, which demands that universities, and hence, its academic citizens, turn their gaze beyond the certainty of what is already known, and consider what might be other and otherwise. As social beings with stories, we are already entangled with others. We are always already in conversation with the world in which we find ourselves even when we are unconscious of those around us. It is up to academics to accept the responsibilities pertaining to that which is not 'purely academic' (Derrida, 2004) and to see the value of turning towards others, not only for the purposes of knowing about the other, but to become wiser about the worlds which constitute others. This turning, I argue, is necessary for the cultivation and support of new formations of academic citizenship—formations which are averse to othering and marginalisation.

The book concludes with my reflections on academic citizenship, collegiality, and especially, trust. I maintain that if academic citizenship does not provide a consistent frame of inclusion, recognition and belonging for all academic identities, then presumptions about presence or practices of collegiality are questionable. It also follows that if some academics experience vulnerability, which stem from marginalisation or suppression, there would be little motivation for co-operation, collaboration, or trust. The relationality of trust implies an immediate vulnerability: there is a risk that this trust could be betrayed. Yet, trust is critical, specifically in how it can be conceived and enacted as both a condition and consequence of academic citizenship. I consider, therefore, on how trust might be (re)prioritised as an institutional ethos and basis of academic citizenship. And I proffer that amid the complexities of diverse identities, knowledge, and knowledge production, as well as the embedded and unspoken vulnerabilities, we need a renewed ethos of trust in academic citizenship. This would mean cultivating an academic citizenship, which is open, curious, vulnerable, and trustworthy. More importantly, it would establish academic citizenship as a desirable space of belonging, opening possibilities for yet-to-be-considered intellectual and social contributions and thought.

References

Ahmed, S. (2006). The nonperformativity of antiracism. *Meridians, 7*(1), 104–126.
Alcalde, M.A., & Subramaniam, M. (2020). Women in leadership: Challenges and recommendations. www.insidehighered.com/views/2020/07/17/women-leadership-academe-still-face-challenges-structures-systems-and-mind-sets
Andreotti, V., Ahenakew, C., & Cooper, G. (2011). Epistemological pluralism: Ethical and pedagogical challenges in higher education. *AlterNative: An International Journal of Indigenous Peoples, 7*(1): 40–50.
Andreotti, V. (2010) Postcolonial and post- critical 'global citizenship education. In G. Elliot, C. Fourali & S. Issler, S. (Eds.), *Education and social change: Connecting local and global perspectives* (pp. 233–245). Continuum International Publishing Group.
Arendt, H. (1958). *The human condition* (2nd ed.). The University of Chicago Press.
Barnett, R. (2000). Supercomplexity and the curriculum. *Studies in Higher Education, 25*(3), 255–265.
Barnett, R., & Di Napoli, R. (Eds.). (2008). *Changing identities in higher education*. London: Routledge.
Beck, J., & Young, M. F. D. (2005). The assault on the professions and the restructuring of academic and professional identities: A Bernsteinian analysis. *British Journal of Sociology of Education, 26*(2), 183–197.
Bhabha, H. (1999). Staging the politics of difference: Homi Bhabha's critical literacy. In G. Olson & L. Worsham (Eds.), *Race, rhetoric and the postcolonial* (pp. 165–204). State University of New York Press.
Bhattacharya, K. (2016). The vulnerable academic: Personal narratives and strategic de/colonizing of academic structures. *Qualitative Inquiry, 22*(5), 309–321.
Bhopal, K., & Pitkin, C. (2020). 'Same old story, just a different policy': Race and policy making in higher education in the UK. *Race Ethnicity and Education, 23*(4), 530–547.
Bosniak, L. (2006). *The citizen and the alien: Dilemmas of contemporary membership*. Princeton University Press.
Butler, J. (2016). Rethinking vulnerability and resistance. In J. Butler, Z. Gambetti, & L. Sabsay (Eds.), *Vulnerability in resistance* (pp. 12–27). Duke University Press.
Castellacci, F., & Viñas-Bardolet, C. (2021). Permanent contracts and job satisfaction in academia: Evidence from European countries. *Studies in Higher Education, 46*(9), 1866–1880.
Clegg, S. (2008). Academic identities under threat? *British Educational Research Journal, 34*(3), 329–345.
Davids, N. (2022). Professing the vulnerabilities of academic citizenship. *Ethics and Education, 17*(1), 1–13.

References

Delanty, G. (2008). Academic identities and institutional change. In R. Barnett & R. Di Napoli (Eds.), *Changing identities in higher education* (pp. 124–133). Routledge.

Department of Education (DoE). (1997). *Education White Paper No. 3: A programme on the transformation of higher education transformation*. Government Printers.

Department of Higher Education and Training (DHET). (2019). *Employment equity policy*. Government Printers.

Derrida, J. (2004). *Eyes of the university: Right to philosophy 2* (J. Plug & Others, Trans.). Stanford University Press.

Doharty, N., Madriaga, M., & Joseph-Salisbury, R. (2021). The university went to 'decolonise' and all they brought back was lousy diversity double-speak! Critical race counter-stories from faculty of colour in 'decolonial' times. *Educational Philosophy and Theory, 53*(3), 233–244.

Ellis, C., Adams, T. E., & Bochner, A. P. (2011). Autoethnography: An overview. *Historical Social Research, 36*(4), 273–290.

Fitzmaurice, M. (2013). Constructing professional identity as a new academic: A moral endeavour. *Studies in Higher Education, 38*(4), 613–622.

Gilson, E. (2014). *The ethics of vulnerability: A feminist analysis of social life and practice*. Routledge.

Harris, S. (2005). Rethinking academic identities in neo-liberal times. *Teaching in Higher Education, 10*(4), 421–433.

Hartman, S. (2008). Venus in two acts. *Small Axe, 12*(2): 1–14.

Herman, N., Jose, M., Katiya, M., Kemp, M., Le Roux, N., Swart-Jansen van Vuuren, C., & Van der Merwe, C. (2021). 'Entering the world of academia is like starting a new life': A trio of reflections from Health Professionals joining academia as second career academics. *International Journal for Academic Development, 26*(1), 69–81.

Hornsby, D. J., & Osman, R. (2014). Massification in higher education: Large classes and student learning, *Higher Education, 67*(6), 711–719.

Jackson, L. (2018). Reconsidering vulnerability in higher education. *Tertiary Education and Management, 24*(3), 232–241.

Jones, C. (2006). Falling between the Cracks: What diversity means for black women in higher education. *Policy Futures in Education, 4*(2), 145–159.

Macfarlane, B. (2005). The disengaged academic: The retreat from citizenship. *Higher Education Quarterly, 59*(4), 296–312.

Macfarlane, B., & Burg, D. (2018). *Rewarding and recognising academic citizenship*. Leadership Foundation for Higher Education.

Marginson, S. (2016). The worldwide trend to high participation higher education: Dynamics of social stratification in inclusive systems. *Higher Education, 72*(4), 413–434.

Mendieta, E. (2008). Identities: Postcolonial and global. In L. Alcoff & E. Mendieta (Eds.), *Identities: Race, class, gender, and nationality* (pp. 407–416). Blackwell.

Merton, R. K. (1947a). Patterns of influence: Local and cosmopolitan influentials. In R. K. Merton (Ed.), *Social theory and social structure* (pp. 387–420). The Free Press.

Merton, R. K. (1947b). Patterns of influence: local and cosmopolitan influentials. In R. K. Merton (Ed.), *Social theory and social structure* (pp. 387–420). Free Press.

Mohanty, R., & Tandon, R. (2006). Identity, exclusion, inclusion: Issues in participatory citizenship. In R. Mohanty & R. Tandon (Eds.), *Participatory citizenship: Identity, exclusion, inclusion* (pp. 9–28). SAGE Publications.

Mouffe, C. (2014). By way of a postscript. *Parallax, 20*(2), 149–157.

Nixon, J. (2001). Not without dust and heat: The moral bases of the 'new' academic professionalism. *British Journal of Educational Studies, 49*(2), 173–186.

Nixon, J. (2008). *Towards the virtuous university: The moral bases of academic practice*. Routledge.

Nørgård, R. T., & Bengtsen, S. S. E. (2016). Academic citizenship beyond the campus: A call for the placeful university. *Higher Education Research & Development, 35*(1), 4–16.

Oforiwaa, O. A., & Afful-Broni, A. (2014). Gender and promotions in higher education: A case study of the University of Education, Winneba, Ghana. *International Journal of Education Learning and Development, 2*(1), 34–47.
Palmer, P.J. (2017). *The courage to teach: Exploring the inner landscape of the teacher's life*. San Francisco, CA: Jossey-Bass.
Peseta, T., Barrie, S., & McLean, J. (2017). Academic life in the measured university: Pleasures, paradoxes and politics. *Higher Education Research and Development, 36*(3), 453–457.
Peters, M. A. (2019). Manifesto for the postcolonial university. *Educational Philosophy and Theory, 51*(2), 142–148.
Sadiq, H., Barnes, K. I., Price, M., Gumedze, F., & Morrell, R. G. (2019). Academic promotions at a South African university: Questions of bias, politics and transformation. *Higher Education, 78*, 423–442.
Santos, B. S. (2014). *Epistemologies from the South*. Paradigm.
Santos, B. D. (2021). Postcolonialism, decoloniality, and epistemologies of the south. In *Oxford research encyclopedia of literature*.
Spivak, G. C., Bhatnagar, R., Chatterjee, L., & Sunder, R. (1990). The post-colonial critic. In S. Harasym (Ed.), *The post-colonial critic: Interviews, strategies, dialogues* (pp. 67–74). Routledge.
Spivak, G. C., & Grosz, E. (1990). Criticism, feminism, and the institution. In Harasym, S. (Ed.), *The post-colonial critic. Interviews, strategies, dialogues* (pp. 1–16). Routledge.
Sutherland, K. A. (2017). Constructions of success in academia: An early career perspective. *Studies in Higher Education, 42*(4), 743–759.
Taylor, C. (1994). *Multiculturalism: Examining the politics of recognition*. Princeton University Press.
Teichler. (2015). Academic mobility and migration: What we know and what we do not know. *European Review, 23*(1), 6–37.
Young, R. (2009). What is the postcolonial? *Ariel, 40*(1), 13–25.
Yuval-Davis, N. (2011). *The politics of belonging: Intersectional contestations*. Sage Publications.

Part I
Identity, Citizenship, and Vulnerability

Chapter 2
Academic Identities and Citizenship

Commonly, academic citizenship is framed and discussed in relation to a list of key roles and responsibilities. Describing and limiting academic citizenship to the core responsibilities of teaching, research, and administration, often belies the expanse of what each of these encompasses. Teaching does not simply mean presenting a lecture at a designated time. It is underscored by programme and module planning, assessments, and student evaluations, and of course moderation and review. So, too, the production of research is preceded by complex scaffoldings of reading, proposal writing, grant applications, ethical clearance applications, writing, and attending to reviews. Trajectories to promotions and academic growth are dependent not only on an ever-increasing list of commitments, but reviews and assessments by peers—providing yet another indicator of the endless stream of analyses academics accept as part of their citizenship.

While insightful and substantive, and with an increasing focus on the importance of engagement and collegiality, the existing literature has yet to pause on whether academic citizenship means the same to all academics. Here, the concern is not whether academics share the same understandings of their roles and responsibilities. But rather, whether all academics can access and participate in their citizenship. It is important, therefore, to ask how academics conceive of themselves in their citizenship? What does it mean *to be* and *become* an academic citizen? How much is really known about academic citizenship and how it is embodied? What are the understandings of and approaches to academic citizenship by universities? Do universities assign the same citizenship to all its academics? How prepared and responsive, if at all, are universities to diverse academic identities? What are the typical hindrances to becoming and being an academic, typically described in terms of disengagement and erosion?

2.1 Citizenship and Professionalism

Typically, we tend to associate notions of citizenship with access to a set of rights, whether legal, civil, political or social. The provision of a set of protective rights by the nation-state is implicitly understood and accepted by most citizens as a contractual obligation. It relies on a mutually contingent and beneficial arrangement, that for the state to provide these rights, citizens are required to act responsibly in respect of these rights. Implicit in the contractual framing of citizenship is that in surrendering some of their personal freedom to the nation-state, individuals can expect the civil freedom to think and act rationally and morally, while living in peace, free from harm and oppression (Locke, 2003; Rawls, 1971). This seems to suggest a workable arrangement, especially when citizens are assured by democratic apparatuses and discourses of equality, participation, autonomy, agency, and of course, freedom. Even when equipped with the knowledge, at times, that these apparatuses are, at best, normative ideals, rather than realisable practices, it is the idea of citizenship, which provides some measure of comfort, however uncertain. Armed with this same knowledge, the nation-state does not have to concern itself too much with who citizens are, or their possible struggles and tensions in finding social integration and inclusion, preferring instead to focus on propagating a collective (nationalist) identity.

Reasons for this approach are a lot more complex than a mere unwillingness to attend to the intricacies of citizenship. The subjectivities of citizens means that citizenship is never devoid of a psychological dimension, described by Carens (2000: 162) as 'one's sense of identification with the political community or communities to which one belongs'. Belonging to a citizenship is predominantly ascribed on legal grounds. But citizenship is not limited to political and legal criteria or descriptors. There are other ways of seeking or experiencing belonging, which, to Carens (2000), are based on emotional attachment, loyalty and identification. Of course, it is common for a natural connection to exist between the legal and psychological dimensions of citizenship. In the same breath, it is often not the case. For the overwhelming majority of 'black' (including those classified as 'coloured' and 'Indian') South Africans, for example, notions of citizenship were embedded in intricate structures of oppression and discrimination, ensuring not only a deeply stratified citizenry, but entrenching misconstrued lived experiences of citizenship. This resulted in a distorted psychological identification with what it meant to be a citizen; it is also meant differentiated race-based sets of membership.

Partisan experiences of citizenship are not always tied to oppressive regimes, like South Africa's apartheid. They are as prevalent in the socio-political conditions of immigrant communities whether in newly established democracies, such as South Africa or more established European democracies. All of these inevitable complexities notwithstanding, the significance of a psychological attachment—perhaps most sentimentally captured in Gertrude Stein's, 'America is my country, and Paris is my hometown'—resides in the extent to which citizens or individuals feel connected or find resonance with their citizenship. Attachment to one's citizenship might instil or stem from a sense of responsibility and loyalty. So, too, detachment might lead to apathy, disengagement, or even, misrecognition, resentment, and resistance.

Taking its cue from common associations of citizenship as members of a particular citizenry, professional citizenship, also sometimes referred to as citizen professionalism, refers to those who are members of a profession. Professional citizenship is predominantly an identity, defined by special kinds of expertise, skills, and qualifications. Professional citizens—such as, academics, teachers, researchers, doctors, engineers, or accountants—are understood to have a particular set of knowledge, which not only designates them as professionals, but presumably capacitates to participate and contribute to a field of expertise. Like citizens in the public sphere, however, professional citizens do not necessarily evolve just because they belong to a certain professional community.

For professional citizenship to thrive, it requires full participation from its members (Fulton, 2019). Unlike inhabitants, who are complacent and accept things as they are, or expect others to act on their behalf, citizens 'step up and create a preferred future' (Fulton, 2019: 153). The distinction between inhabitants and citizens might be explained in several ways. Certainly, it is common for professionals to provide the necessary knowledge and skills in relation to a specific profession without being inclined to consider let alone, create a preferred future.

For most, professions are seen as a means to an economic end. Echoing their experiences in the public sphere, professional citizens might be too preoccupied with other concerns—such as earning a living. Walzer (1990) explains that while economic activity belongs to the realm of necessity, politics belong to the realm of freedom. For professional citizens, this often implies a deeper commitment to the purpose of working, rather than doing something with the work—whether for the present or future. This is not to say that there is no collegiality or enjoyment within the fulfilment of professional responsibilities. In fact, certain professionals might consciously choose to disengage from the politics of their profession as a means of creating a less stressful environment, or they might just be disinterested.

But there might also be questions and hesitancy as to whether there are spaces and time to think about what it means to be a professional citizen. Fulton (2019), for example, points out that among the reasons for nurses' reluctance to engage in professional citizenship, are misalignment of personal values with organizational mission, fear of criticism or retribution by peers or employers, unfamiliarity with democratic principles and structures, limited understanding of the political process, and a sense of apathy and powerlessness. And although Fulton (2019) maintains that '[f]ear, ignorance, and apathy are not the attributes of a professional', one wonders, as is the focus of this book, what happens within the citizenship of academics.

2.2 Academic Citizenship

Academic citizenship pivots on a parallel commitment to an academic's institution and the wider mission of the university in relation to society (Macfarlane & Burg, 2018:3). While there is an array of shared practices, which constitute academic work, there is also differentiation based on appointment and institutional practices and cultures. Following a traditional Ph.D. trajectory, most newly appointed academics enter the profession as 'early career' or 'first career' academics (Simendinger et al., 2000). By this stage, most would have been initiated into a series of roles, including writing research proposals, academic papers, conference papers and presentations, as well as teaching.

Alongside 'early career' academics is the group referred to as 'second-career academics'. These are individuals with experience in their respective disciplines, and have established professional identities—such as engineers, health professionals, or bioinformatics specialists—and enter the academia later in their lives (Dash, 2018; Simendinger et al., 2000). They can offer immense knowledge and practical understandings of a particular discipline but transitioning into an academic space also relies on different kinds of knowledge and skills. Beyond teaching and research, this includes adapting to the spaces, cultures, practices and languages of the university (Trowler & Knight, 2000).

In their project report, 'Rewarding and recognising academic citizenship', Macfarlane and Burg (2018: 1) describe academic citizenship as a 'term widely used in higher education to refer to those activities distinct from research and teaching that support and offer services to both the university and wider society. It covers both academic and professional disciplines.' The wide use of academic citizenship could involve any number of responsibilities, including serving on university committees and panels, mentoring colleagues and students, assuming leadership and management roles within the university, acting as a peer reviewer for an academic journal or funding body, working as an external examiner, organising a conference for a professional or academic society, editing a journal, or serving on a public committee of enquiry (Macfarlane & Burg, 2018). The weighting of these roles might shift. Junior academics, for example, might find themselves with heavier teaching loads than the senior professoriate, who, in turn, might have to carry heavier research or supervision loads.

In turn, the promotion and advancement of some academics might see them adopt and fulfilling broader, more internationally recognisable responsibilities outside of their respective institutions. In this regard Merton (1947) distinguishes between 'local' and 'cosmopolitan' academics. 'Locals', explain Macfarlane and Burg (2018), tend to be loyal, long serving members of staff with high levels of tacit knowledge about how the organisation works and with a reference group largely consisting of colleagues working for the same organisation. By contrast, 'cosmopolitans', generally have higher levels of professional qualification, are more closely connected with members of an outer reference group, are likely to be more mobile, and tend to be more research oriented (Macfarlane & Burg, 2018).

Despite the increasing insights on offer on what academic citizenship involves, and its varying formations in relation to institutional cultures and expectations, there remains a worrying concern that very little is known about the experiences of academics—that is, *how* academics come into, and embody their citizenship, if at all. MacFarlane and Burg (2018) point out that given the increasing use of academic citizenship by institutions in rewarding and recognising academics, there is a need to understand better how academic citizenship is being defined in theory and how policies are operating in practice within the context of a rapidly changing higher education environment. It is a disturbingly common feature of universities for academics to be evaluated and rewarded based on their productivity only.

To Lyotard (1979: 53), the predominance of the performance criterion 'is sounding the knell of the Professor: a professor is no more competent than memory bank networks in transmitting established knowledge, no more competent than interdisciplinary teams in imagining new moves or new games.' Few would disagree with MacFarlane and Burg (2018) or Lyotard (1979). But the questions and concerns about academic citizenship, I believe, exceed that of the practical implementation of policy. There are embedded tensions within academic citizenship, that have little to do with theory, but with practices instead. It also exceeds the consideration of academic citizenship as mere performativity, especially when outputs are prioritised above the values sustaining professional work.

Of greater concern, is the deployment of academic citizenship as a unitary construct, with seemingly little consideration as to who occupies this citizenship, and whether those who occupy it do so in an equal fashion. On the one hand, there is a tacit acknowledgment and acceptance of the intricacies of universities' structures and cultures, which inevitably give shape to different constructions of 'academic' (Harris, 2005). Harris (2005: 422) explains that 'The hierarchical nature of the university traditionally has been mystified and underpinned by elitism, social and cultural hierarchies, in contrast to the highly formalized and transparent hierarchy of the civil service'. She contends that despite historical perceptions of the university representing a 'community of scholars', it remains a site of exclusion, elitism, and power (Harris, 2005). On the other hand, essentialist understandings about academic citizenship suggests indefensible presumptions about academic identities.

In South Africa, for example, notions of 'the academic' are male, 'white', and heterosexual. This, in part, explains, the barriers which 'black' academics encounter as they enter university spaces, which continue to see them as imposters. Barnett (2000) points out that across the disciplines, there are significant differences in the construction of the 'academic' as a particular form of identity, not only in terms of the relationships to the world of work, but also in terms of the relationships between research and teaching. The institutional cultures of universities necessarily play a powerful role in how academic citizenship is constituted, and hence, how certain academic identities are recognised and included, while others are not.

Like the nation-state, the university is constituted by hegemonic discourses, cultures, and tropes, which, while desirable as a realm of divergent and competing views, are not without risks of exclusion and alienation. Issues of social and emotional integration are as pertinent in academic citizenship as they are in the public square.

Considerations of citizenship are necessarily attached to the polis. One is not simply a citizen; one is always a citizen of this or that state. So, too, academic citizenship is unavoidably institutionally based. This is so regardless of whether academics are 'local', 'cosmopolitan', or 'migrant', considering the increasing drives towards internationalisation as a means of enhancing the diverse quality of education on offer (Teichler, 2015). And perhaps, because of the perceived public dimension—specifically, its perceived mandate of serving a public good—laying claim to an academic citizenship is as much about a legal appointment, as it is about an emotional attachment.

2.3 Identity, Recognition, and Participation

It is hard not to underestimate the immense the fluidity of the university. To many, this might constitute a desirable and necessary feature of the university, since fluidity can imply a flexibility and openness to change, and hence, an implicit responsiveness to society. But fluidity also implies an instability, often enforcing shifts and restructurings for which the university or more specifically, its academics, are unprepared or uninformed. The dissolution of the binary system between traditional, elite institutions, and the polytechnics in the UK (Barnett & Di Napoli), for example, has been equally prevalent in post-apartheid South African higher education system. In South Africa, this includes an additional undertaking of bringing up to par historically disadvantaged institutions with those advantaged and better resourced, which also included the merging of certain historically advantaged and disadvantaged institutions. As many academics and administrators will tell you, they had very little understandings or inputs into what the merging would entail or what it would mean for their academic careers (Mohuba & Govender, 2016).

Amid the contextual factors which necessarily influence and shape universities, there are the wider phenomena of massification, globalisation, audit and quality systems, accountability, managerialism, marketisation, as well as global pandemics, political upheavals, including wars (most recently between Russia and Ukraine). Adapting and responding to this plethora of phenomena can be beneficial to universities. Resorting to online teaching and learning during Covid-19, for example, allowed universities to sustain their educational imperative; it also opened them to the possibilities of new pedagogies, and reconfigured forms of student and staff engagement.

At play, is not only a re-imagination of the nature and scope of higher education, but the opening of spaces and opportunities for new and different academic identities. These spaces can take the form of local transitioning and re-positioning, as in the case of the appointments of 'black' academics at historically 'white' South African universities. They can also take the form of internationalisation—understood as a trend to increase border-crossing knowledge transfer and various related activities (Teichler, 2015). Teichler (2015) explains that since the 1990s, internationalisation 'mainstreamed' at higher education institutions, with substantial professional support and with most strategic key decisions reflecting what general policies mean for internationalisation and what internationalisation means for the general development of higher education. The intensification of internationalisation in Europe was seen as necessary for making the continent the 'most competitive economy', supported by a belief 'that academic progress depended on successful world-wide competition of the most excellent universities' (Teichler, 2015: 7).

Against a broader socio-political and economic context, however, academic mobility holds serious implications for certain countries. While some gain, others, and most commonly, poorer countries, suffer because of the 'brain drain' (Benedict & Ukpere, 2012). These socio-political concerns notwithstanding, the changing nature of universities provides a broader range of opportunities for the expression and recognition of diverse identities (Delanty, 2008), it also creates a need for a broader and more nuanced understanding of the diversity of identities which give or shape to academic citizenship.

Identity is probably best understood as a sense of self. Responding to the question of 'Who am I?' necessarily requires us to think about that which defines us and differentiates us from others. In this way, identity is a predicate which functions as an identifier (Sollberger, 2013) to know who I am and where I stand (Taylor, 1989). To Taylor (1989: 27), 'My identity is defined by the commitments and identifications which provide the frame or horizon within which I can try to determine from case to case what is good, or valuable, or what ought to be done, or what I endorse or oppose. In other words, it is the horizon within which I am capable of taking a stand.'

For some, this horizon or frame takes the shape of a particular nationality, ethnicity, culture, group, or religion. For others, this horizon might be more intimately tied to a family name or certain community. These frames do not only provide an indication of attachment, also provide the framework within which individuals determine where they stand on questions of what is good, or worthwhile, or admirable, or of value (Taylor, 1989).

By stating that one is a liberal, for example, implies both an attachment to those values, as well as its deployment as a frame of reference in exercising judgment. There is, therefore, an essential link between identity and a kind of orientation. For this reason, although the identity conferred on an individual by citizenship is seen mainly in formal, legal, juridical terms, 'the citizen must have a consciousness of him or herself as a member of a living community with a shared democratic culture involving obligations and responsibilities as well as rights, a sense of the common good, fraternity, and so on' (McLaughlin, 1992: 236). To know who one is, is to be oriented in moral space; 'What I am as a self, my identity, is essentially defined by the way things have significance for me' (Taylor, 1989: 34).

Concomitantly, when things have no significance for me, or when I am not attached to something (a family, a country, a profession), I do not define myself in relation to those things. However, neither identities, nor the horizons which frame them can tell us all what we need to know about another; they tell us something, but not everything. This is because identities can shift in relation to contexts and circumstances. They are always tied to historical, social, political, and cultural processes and events, or others.

For many historically categorised 'black', 'coloured', and 'Indian' academics, who succeed in being appointed at historically 'white' institutions in South Africa, the experience is often one of deep displacement and non-belonging. In many cases there are no historical ties with historically 'white' universities. In turn, given the inferior status assigned to historically 'black' universities by the apartheid regime, graduates and academics from these institutions are also perceived as having inferior qualifications, skills and competencies.

Identity, explains Clegg (2008: 329), is not a fixed property, but is 'part of the lived complexity of a person's project and their ways of being in those sites which are constituted as being part of the academic… the site of the academic may include relationships with other colleagues globally, be a particular fragment of a department, and may include a range of activities, some of which are experienced as being academic and others of which are not.' As a result, social locus, or how individuals define themselves, is always changing, constantly influenced by a 'social topography', rendering identities as 'fragile negotiations' (Mendieta, 2008: 412).

These 'fragile negotiations' are also at play in what it means to become an academic, which according to Fitzmaurice (2013: 621) involves 'a cognitive and emotive process, as well as a moral endeavour grounded in virtues of honesty, care and compassion' (Fitzmaurice, 2013: 613). The fluidity of the university—whether in terms of social crises, global pandemics, or new auditing regimes—ensures that there is an ongoing process of identity construction and deconstruction for academics in the negotiation of a professional identity regarding their various roles, and there is considerable (Fitzmaurice, 2013). The extent to which academics can navigate this fluidity depends on their understandings of the intricate workings and culture of the university. It also depends on their adeptness and attitude to change, both of which require intellectual as well as emotional work. For some, like younger or early career academics, the dynamic structures and discourses of the university might bode well for their nascent careers. They might see the changing terrain commensurate with their own struggles of settling into the university.

Interestingly, as Archer (2008) observes, younger academics are located at the nexus of competing discourses around what it means (or might mean) to be an academic. As new appointments, they have ostensibly not experienced the relations which characterised former eras and are therefore positioned differently to those already established within the field and may hold various competing interests and identity constructions (Archer, 2008). There might be a deeper acceptance that their identities 'will always be under construction in contexts that are characterised by indeterminacy, partiality and complexity' (Taylor, 2008: 35). But early career academics also identify key challenges in establishing their academic identities. These include heavy workloads, which impede their research performance; and a 'one size fits all' performance targets, especially in terms of research publications, which contribute towards stress and a lack of collegiality among academics (Pithouse-Morgan et al., 2016)—despite an awareness that in a context of diverse and changing identities, universities are not academically autonomous (Henkel, 2007).

2.4 Contestations

Few would disagree with Barnett's (2022: 156), opinion 'that the very idea of the university is in dispute.' Each era necessarily invites renewed considerations and interpretations of what the nature and purpose of the university should be. The traditional Humboldtian model, which constituted a union between teaching and research, evolved into three pillars: research, teaching, and service (internal and external). Yet, while clearly distinguishable, these three pillars can be come into a state of tension—both for individual academics and among academics. Reasons for these tensions are often bound by disciplines, departments, and faculties. Common to universities, however, is a struggle with priority-setting and resource allocation due to economic constraints, the imposition of quality audits, university rankings and the massification of tertiary education (Altbach et al., 2009). Today, 'the university is seen both as being too separate from its region and the wider society *and*, on the contrary, too much bound into the world. The shapes of the university's spaces are in motion, and with this movement flows the university's ephemeral qualities' (Barnett, 2022: 156).

This transiency and intangibility can, in part, be explained by the expectations and demands of what Derrida (2004: 148) describes as a preparedness by the university to find 'new ways of taking responsibility', constantly moving towards that which is yet to become. For Derrida (1992: 10–11), these new ways are not only a matter of simply asking questions for the sake of arriving at reasons, but also of 'preparing oneself thereby to transform the modes of writing, approaches to pedagogy, the procedures of academic exchange, the relation to languages, to other disciplines, to the institution in general, to its inside and its outside' (Derrida, 1983: 17). Fundamentally, therefore, the relevance and worth of the university, depends on its openness to the world in which it finds itself.

The ways in which academics respond to these new ways of taking responsibility depends as much on who they are personally, as it does on how they conceive themselves as professionals. Here, there are stark lines between academics who see their position as a professional occupation, and those who approach it as a calling. On the one side, being an academic is associated with a list of roles and responsibilities—generally performed within a structured timeframe. On the other side, is a commitment to what it means to be and act academically, instilled in notions of responsiveness and activeness. Even within this dichotomy, there might be tensions in how academics conceive of their responsibilities. For example, a performance driven reward system necessarily influences what academics do and prioritise. If research productivity is heavily weighted, academics might be less inclined to spend their time on reviews (Macfarlane & Burg, 2018). It might also influence certain academics to prioritise their own productivity and advancement above that of establishing and cultivating collegial relationships.

The inherent competitive character, exacerbated by an ever-intensifying performative ethos of the academy lends itself to multiple points of tension (Adcroft & Taylor, 2013), forcing academics into roles and positions, which they often do not fully comprehend. The hierarchical nature of the university often means that demands of teaching, tutoring, community engagement and administration are placed on early career academics. While valuable and necessary to forging an academic identity, overloaded teaching loads often means less time for forging a scholarly profile (Fitzmaurice, 2013). On the flipside, the embedded professional commitments within certain disciplines, such as nursing and teaching, often means that beyond teaching and administration, there is no time for research. Academics in these disciplines view the practical application of their teaching (linked by student practice in the field) as critical to the development of student efficacy (Billot, 2010).

In my own faculty, research production serves as a perennial source of contestation and discontent, especially when promotions are on offer. Several academics have high commitments in relation to managing and evaluating teaching practice in schools, some of which might not be located close to the university. These academic responsibilities are critical to teacher education programmes, and it is indisputable that undertaking these evaluations, which often involves 2–3 school visits per student is not only time consuming but emotionally taxing, considering that student evaluations necessarily involve navigating different school settings. Expectations of research outputs, therefore, is seen as an additional burden for which there simply is no time.

Moreover, it is seen as an unfair demand when considered against the fact that senior professors generally opt out of evaluating student practice. Adding to the tension, is the practice of sharing data on academics' research productivity with the entire faculty, at least once per semester. Inevitable comparisons are drawn not only between the three departments in the faculty, but between individuals, setting the scene for a deeply competitive, and at times, adversarial working environment.

Likewise, there are clear differences between those who abide by and assimilate to the historical and dominant traditions of a university, rather than those who might interpret the university as a space of resistance and critique. In South Africa, the onset of massification has spawned changes in organisational structures; the size and shape of systems; in curriculum (from particular canons of knowledge to curricula that are considered relevant and useful for economic purposes), in pedagogy (from knowledge transmission to competency-based approaches; generic skills transfer, and outcomes-based approaches); in modes of delivery (from pure classroom-based approaches to open learning or blended approaches); in research (from shifts in valuing pure research to so-called Mode 2 or applied research); and in the relationship of institutions with external communities (from town-and-gown approaches to community engagement) (Webbstock, 2016).

On the one hand, funding shortages due to massification, have meant that higher education systems and institutions are increasingly responsible for generating larger percentages of their own revenue (Altbach et al., 2009). And, '[i]ncreasingly, students are being asked to pay the cost of the regulation of higher education, rather than education itself' (Evans, 2004: x). A preoccupation with cost recovery in a climate of massification has meant a neglect of academic needs, and a distraction from the traditional social role and service function of higher education, which are central to contemporary society (Altbach et al., 2009; Ballim & Scott, 2016).

On the other hand, the paradox of contemporary universities, argues Evans (2004), is that as the world becomes larger, the academic head space becomes smaller and more narrowly defined, with little or no time for contemplation. The epistemological fragmentation that has resulted in a rapid expansion of subdisciplines (Macfarlane, 2005) has not translated into spaces and opportunities for 'head space'. There are worrying concerns, therefore, not only for thinking and critique, but also for the communality of participation and engagement. The risks to 'head space' are exacerbated by the implementation of a myriad managerial practices, such as audit regimes, quality assurance mechanisms, restructuring of academic departments, as well as budgetary devolutions and constraints (Anderson, 2008). Evans (2004: 63) argues that despite the 'various regulatory practices encourage mutual surveillance and informal discipline; what is never achieved through these practices is innovation, creativity or intellectual engagement.' Managerial practices can create both fear and demoralisation (Anderson et al., 2002), and lead to academic resistance.

That academics are trained in analytical thinking and critique, means, that (most) academics are unlikely to passively accept changes they regard as detrimental and are therefore likely to resist erosion of valued aspects of their work (Anderson, 2008). In a study, involving academics at ten Australian universities Anderson (2008) found that academics' capacity to assess, analyse and criticize commonly formed the basis of their resistance to managerialist practices. Many academics condemned managerial practices as inefficient, ineffective, and as compromising academic standards of quality and excellence, and refused to take up positions within a managerial discourse (Anderson, 2008).

Thus far, this chapter has focused extensively on what academic citizenship infers, and what it takes to 'become an academic'. By now, it should be clear that what this infers and how this takes formation, differs not only in terms of contexts, and appointments, but also among academics even when they are employed on the same rank and in the same department or faculty. Unmistakably, the possibility exists that certain academics might *not* 'become an academic'. Even when individuals occupy academic posts, they might not be seen as 'academics' by their colleagues, especially because of their poor research productivity. Sometimes, the decision by some academics to take on more administrative responsibilities, is seen by colleagues as a cop-out from academic responsibilities. Becoming and being an academic, are heavily laden actions.

The competing versions of how academic citizenship takes shape are influenced not only by individual career pathways, but also by encounters of conflict, inauthenticity, marginalisation, and exclusion (Colley et al., 2007). Professional identities can neither be separated from personal identities, nor the political climates which influence these identities. Colley et al. (2007: 174), therefore, question 'common-sense' understandings or implicit assumptions about the permanence of professional status once it has been attained. Instead, they contend that there is no unidirectional movement or pathway within a career pathway or a community of practice.

Hence, despite the seemingly theoretical agreement on academic citizenship as a virtuous undertaking, defined by engagement, care, loyalty, collegiality, and benevolence (Macfarlane, 2005; Nixon, 2008), because of who academics are, and how these identities are located in the university, academic citizenship takes on different orientations and navigations. These orientations are not limited to whether academics are 'locals' or 'cosmopolitans' (Merton, 1947), but includes whether academics see themselves as academics in the first place. This can result in resistance from some academics, and indifference from others. Academic resistance is not limited to managerial practices. Resistance can also manifest in response to the socio-political climate of a university, which plays a strong role in relationships, social interactions, and collegiality. At my university, for example, a few academics resist attending meetings when they are held in buildings, which continue to carry names in honour of apartheid proponents. In this way, their absence becomes a statement of their academic citizenship.

2.5 Erosion and Disengagement

Erosion, we know, takes time; it is a gradual process of breaking down, weathering away, even dissolving. For academics, erosion, 'academic disengagement' (Macfarlane & Burg, 2018), or 'professorial discontent' (Musgrave, 2022) can unfold for any number of reasons. For some, academic disengagement or disinterest might stem from growing concerns and resistance to the increased performativity of the university, and the effects thereof on the nature of modern academic life (Macfarlane, 2005). Of growing concern are not only the unending demands on what it means to 'become an academic', but the often-accompanying exclusionary structures, which prevent academics from directly participating in the conditions of their citizenship.

On the one hand, collegiality has given way to a bureaucratic and managerial culture, while, on the other hand, the exclusion of academics from practical roles in institutional governance has led to their political disenfranchisement (Macfarlane, 2005). In the absence of collegial support, and a general sense of academic displacement, despite intense expectations, as well as job insecurity, particularly at smaller, financially vulnerable institutions, the rising incidents of academic burnout are hardly surprising. Pope-Ruark (2022) laments that constantly trying to live up to the ideals of being an academic is exhausting, unrealistic, and potentially dangerous. She describes the academic job market as brutal, often leaving highly qualified colleagues on the outside struggling to maintain a life off the tenure track (Pope-Ruark, 2022). Of course, academics play a significant role in cultivating the professional climate and demands of the academy. Working late into the night, checking emails on weekends, and sacrificing family time to finish the latest manuscript, have all contributed to an academic culture, that in the end, comes at a price.

The lure of promotions means that whatever is published, produced, or rewarded, also means that it is never quite enough, there is always more to be done, with no clear idea of when enough is enough, or what it means to achieve professional satisfaction. While some academics are under pressure to attain tenured positions, others, as is the case in South Africa, are required to apply for research rating every five years. Overseen by the National Research Foundation (NRF), academics are expected to apply for a rating, which is viewed by the NRF as a valuable tool for benchmarking the quality of researchers against the best in the world (NRF, 2015).

2.5 Erosion and Disengagement

Typically, South African universities use the outcomes of the NRF evaluation and rating process to position themselves as research-intensive institutions. The pressure of rating is not only in attaining it, but in retaining it throughout one's career. The pressure is immense, with several academics either never attaining it, or others allowing it to lapse. The fact that it is used as a benchmarking tool, means that is also used as a distinguishing feature between academics, perpetuating, at times, an already competitive work environment and strained working relationships.

Less talked about, however, is academic disengagement due to factors which are not necessarily directly tied to professional roles, expectations and demands. Concerted drives to diversify higher education spaces—whether, in terms of race, gender, nationality or culture—do not always translate into comfortable and hospitable professional environments for diverse academic identities. Despite the 'all-consuming discourse' of diversity, says Mirza (2006: 101), 'that no right-minded university, old or new, would dare be without as an intrinsic part of its identity and image', this discourse often fails to recognise, understand and improve the lived experiences of academics from diverse identities and backgrounds (McClure & Fryar, 2022).

In South African universities, notions of transformation and democratised are subsumed into policy driven interventions and initiatives to diversify both student and staff demographics. One example is the 'Staffing South Africa's Universities Framework' (SSAUF) (DHET, 2015). Building on international experience, the SSAUF 'takes as a starting point the urgent and challenging imperative to recruit, support and retain black and female academic staff to address their very serious under-representation at all levels in the sector' (DHET, 2015). Notably, the framework recognises the need for explicit attention to be paid to setting out pathways through which new and existing staff through can be effectively developed, inducted, and supported.

The reality, however, is that academics, are frequently left with little, if any, support, and women, especially, remain marginalised within the higher education sector (Mahabeer et al., 2018). Different academics will necessarily respond in different ways to their contexts, and certainly, academic discontent, erosion, or disengagement does not necessarily manifest in academics existing the profession. While some might certainly opt to resign, others might choose to remain in positions, while actively choosing either not to participate or engage in certain activities, or to approach their responsibilities in different ways (McClure & Fryar, 2022). In this way, the disengagement, detachment, or 'quiet quitting' is more at an emotional level than a physical withdrawal—'[C]onnections to the institution have been frayed. The work is getting done, but there isn't much spark to it' (McClure & Fryar, 2022).

2.6 Key Considerations of Chapter

This chapter has served to provide an overview of conceptions, practices, and experiences of academic citizenship. While the concept of academic citizenship is widely used across universities as well as at times, used in relation to rewarding academics, there are overlooked or unexplored tensions between what it means to be, to become or not to become an academic citizen. Reasons for this neglect are as complex as the contextualisation of academic citizenship. One point of departure, however, is to discard notions of academic citizenship as a homogenous signifier or designation, because to assume is to believe that all academics come into and reside (if at all) in the academic citizenships in the same way.

In highlighting the increasingly diverse character of universities across various contexts—supported by drives to internationalise higher education—it is apparent that academic citizenship presents a contested field. Depending on who academics are, they embody academic citizenship in different ways. Unless, more is known about these formations take shape (or not), we can neither understand the vulnerabilities of academic citizenship, nor the reasons for discontent, disengagement and erosion.

References

Adcroft, A., & Taylor, D. (2013). Support for new career academics: An integrated model for research intensive university business and management schools. *Studies in Higher Education, 38*(6), 827–840.

Altbach, P. G., Reisberg, L., & Rumbley, L. E. (2009). *Trends in global higher education: Tracking an academic revolution. A report prepared for the UNESCO 2009 World Conference on Higher Education.* http://unesdoc.unesco.org/images/0018/001831/183168e.pdf

Anderson, G. (2008). Mapping academic resistance in the managerial university. *Organization, 15*(2), 251–270.

Anderson, D., Johnson, R., & Saha, L. (2002). *Changes in academic work—implications for universities of the changing age distribution and work roles of academic staff.* Department of Education, Science and Training.

Archer, L. (2008). Younger academics' construction of 'authenticity', 'success', and professional identity. *Studies in Higher Education, 33*(4), 385–403.

Ballim, Y., & Scott, I. (2016). *'Regulation' in South African higher education reviewed: Two decades of democracy.* Council on Higher Education.

Barnett, R. (2000). Supercomplexity and the curriculum. *Studies in Higher Education, 25*(3), 255–265.

Barnett, R. (2022). *The philosophy of higher education: A critical introduction.* Routledge.

Benedict, O. H., & Ukpere, W. I. (2012). Brain drain and African development: Any possible gain from the drain? *African Journal of Business Management, 6*(7), 2421–2428.

Billot, J. (2010). The imagined and the real: Identifying the tensions for academic identity. *Higher Education Research & Development, 29*(6), 709–721.

Carens, J. H. (2000). *Culture, citizenship, and community. A contextual exploration of justice as evenhandedness.* Oxford University Press.

Clegg, S. (2008). Academic identities under threat? *British Educational Research Journal, 34*(3), 329–345.

References

Colley, H., James, D., & Diment, K. (2007). Unbecoming teachers: Towards a more dynamic notion of professional participation. *Journal of Education Policy, 22*(2), 173–193.

Dash, D. P. (2018). Recruiting and developing second-career academics in universities. In R. Erwee, M. Harmes, M. Harmes, & P. A. Danaher (Eds.), *Postgraduate education in higher education* (pp. 1–16). Springer.

Department of Higher Education and Training. (2015). 'Staffing South Africa's Universities' framework. http://www.ssauf.dhet.gov.za/#:~:text=The%20Department%20of%20Higher%20Education,decisive%20response%20to%20these%20challenges

Delanty, G. (2008). Academic identities and institutional change. In R. Barnett & R. Di Napoli (Eds.), *Changing identities in higher education* (pp. 124–133). London: Routledge.

Derrida, J. (1983). The principle of reason: The university in the eyes of its pupils. *Diacritics, 13*(3), 2–20.

Derrida, J. (1992). Mochlos, or, the conflict of the faculties. In R. Rand (Ed.), *Logomachia: The conflict of the faculties* (pp. 1–34). The University of Nebraska Press.

Derrida, J. (2004). *Eyes of the university: Right to philosophy* 2 (J. Plug & Others, Trans.). Palo Alto: Stanford University Press.

Evans, M. (2004). *Killing thinking: The death of the universities*. Continuum.

Fitzmaurice, M. (2013). Constructing professional identity as a new academic: A moral endeavour. *Studies in Higher Education, 38*(4), 613–622.

Fulton, J. S. (2019). Professional citizenship. *Clinical Nurse Specialist, 33*(4), 153–154.

Harris, S. (2005). Rethinking academic identities in neo-liberal times. *Teaching in Higher Education, 10*(4), 421–433.

Henkel, M. (2007). Can academic autonomy survive in the knowledge society? A perspective from Britain. *Higher Education Research & Development, 26*(1), 87–99.

Locke, J. (2003). *Two treatises of government and a letter concerning toleration*. Yale University Press.

Lyotard, J. F. (1979). *The postmodern condition: A report on knowledge*, G. Bennington & B. Massumi (Trans.). Manchester University Press.

McLaughlin, T.H. (1992). Citizenship, diversity, and education: A philosophical perspective. *Journal of Moral Education, 21*(3), 235–250.

Macfarlane, B. (2005). The disengaged academic: The retreat from citizenship. *Higher Education Quarterly, 59*(4), 296–312.

Macfarlane, B., & Burg, D. (2018). *Rewarding and recognising academic citizenship*. University of Southampton.

Mahabeer, P., Nzimande, N., & Shoba, M. (2018). Academics of colour: Experiences of emerging Black women academics in curriculum studies at a university in South Africa. *Agenda, 32*(2), 28–42.

McClure, K. R., & Fryar, A. H. (2022). The great faculty disengagement. https://www.chronicle.com/article/the-great-faculty-disengagement

Merton, R. K. (1947). Patterns of influence: Local and cosmopolitan influentials. In R. K. Merton (Ed.), *Social theory and social structure* (pp. 387–420). The Free Press.

Mirza, H. S. (2006). Transcendence over diversity: Black women in the academy. *Policy Futures in Education, 4*(2), 101–113.

Mohuba, D. K., & Govender, K. (2016). The merger of historically disadvantaged tertiary institutions in South Africa: A case study of the University of Limpopo. *Cogent Business & Management, 3*(1258133), 1–12.

Musgrave, P. (2022). The season of our professorial discontent. https://www.chronicle.com/article/the-season-of-our-professorial-discontent

National Research Foundation (NRF) (2015). https://www.nrf.ac.za/

Nixon, J. (2008). *Towards the virtuous university: The moral bases of academic practice*. New York: Routledge.

Pithouse-Morgan, K., Naicker, I., Pillay, D., Masinga, L., & Hlao, T. (2016). 'Sink or swim?': Learning from stories of becoming academics within a transforming university terrain. *South African Journal of Higher Education, 30*(1), 224–244.

Pope-Ruark, R. (2022). *Unraveling faculty burnout: Pathways to reckoning and renewal.* Johns Hopkins University Press.

Rawls, J. (1971). *A theory of justice.* Harvard University Press.

Simendinger, E., Puia, G., Kraft, K., & Jasperson, M. (2000). The career transition from practitioner to academic. *Career Development International, 5*(2), 106–111.

Sollberger, D. (2013). On identity: From a philosophical point of view. *Child Adolescent Psychiatry Mental Health, 7*(1), 29.

Taylor, C. (1989). *Sources of the self: The making of the modern identity.* Cambridge University Press.

Taylor, P. (2008). Being an academic today. In R. Barnett & R. Di Napoli (Eds.), *Changing identities in higher education* (pp. 27–39). Routledge.

Teichler. (2015). Academic mobility and migration: What we know and what we do not know. *European Review, 23*(1), 6–37.

Trowler, P., & Knight, P. T. (2000). Coming to know in higher education: Theorising faculty entry to new work contexts. *Higher Education Research & Development, 19*(1), 27–42.

Walzer, M. (1990). *The civil society argument. Gunnar Myrdal Lecture.* University of Stockholm.

Webbstock, D. (2016). Overview. In *South African higher education reviewed: Two decades of democracy* (pp. 5–6). Council on Higher Education.

Chapter 3
Academic Citizenship as an Agonistic Space

We already know that although academic citizenship is often explained in terms of a performative list of responsibilities, how academics are situated, or how they embody their citizenship is less clear. The ways in which academics are appointed, whether their positions are permanent or contract, as well as the knowledge which they produce, are significant factors in relation to job security and experiences of comfortable belonging. That academics come into their citizenship along different pathways, and as different identities, means that the locus of their citizenship—the university—does not hold the same set of experiences for all academics. Who academics are, the knowledge they bring and produce, coupled with the institutional cultures and identities of universities, raise important questions about the reconcilability of universities with all forms of citizenship. Academics enter their citizenship with diverse identities, histories, stories, as well as vulnerabilities. They come to their respective disciplines and interests, driven by different imperatives, hopes, as well as hardships.

The emerging literature, which focuses on the challenges of professional academic identities, hints at these complexities. But there have been limited considerations of academic citizenship as a contentious, belligerent, or agonistic space and experience. If universities agree with agonism as critical for the accommodation and provision of competing truths and arguments, how might universities open themselves to difference and belligerence, seen as central for democratic dissensus, and hence, advancement? How might agonism be deployed and cultivated as useful to the production of knowledge, and hence, extended in a university's communal and societal responsibilities?

3.1 Agonism as Expressions of Pluralism and Disagreement

Diverse and pluralist groups, communities and societies imply an array of competing identities, and hence ideologies and perspectives. The more diverse a society is, the greater the potential engaging with difference and divergent views. Inevitably, differences of opinion lead to disagreement, and at times, to conflict. The prevalence and importance of this conflict should neither be undermined nor discouraged. Rather, it should be understood a healthy and desirable manifestation of democratic engagement of values—exemplified in Mouffe's (2000) conception of agonistic pluralism. For Mouffe (2000), agonistic pluralism presents a new way to think about democracy that is different from the traditional liberal conception of democracy as a negotiation among interests. A key feature of agonistic pluralism, firstly, is that it sees conflict as not an undesirable phenomenon to be overcome by democratic consensus, but rather as constitutive of politics.

Secondly, it recognizes the affective nature of political conflict, that is, the role of collective passions in politics (Des Roches & Ruitenberg, 2018). The central question for democratic politics, to Mouffe (2005: 14), is not about 'how to negotiate a compromise among competing interests, nor is it how to reach a 'rational,' i.e., fully inclusive, consensus, without any exclusion'. Instead, because it is impossible to eliminate conflict from the political arena, the central question is how we orientate ourselves to conflict that makes disagreement central for democratic possibility (Mouffe, 2005).

In many ways, the idea of the university as a 'disagreeable' space is intensified not only by its intellectual acknowledgement of competing truths and views, but also by its occupation of diverse identities (academics, students, and administrators). Yet, the diversification of universities only holds meaning when it is recognised, and individuals are afforded the freedom of articulation and expression. Unless individuals experience the freedom *to be* who they are, the democratic possibilities of diversity cannot yield. On the one hand, this means accepting the possibility of conflict. On the other hand, it also means creating and providing an arena where differences and disagreements can be confronted (Mouffe, 2005). At this point, it is important to clarify that when Mouffe (2000, 2005) refers to conflict, she does not have in mind violence: 'Precisely because adversaries share something in common, the 'grammar of democratic life', their struggle and confrontation does not take on an extreme, violent form. The very commonality they share serves as the limiting and moderating element in their confrontation' (Mouffe, 2013: 3).

By virtue of their shared identity as academic citizens or their shared location in the university, therefore, academics would be constrained in how they express their difference or conflict—often understood as professional regard or collegiality. In this way, there are limits to the extent academics might want to voice or show their disagreement. Their shared commonality with other academics frames them in being mindful not only of their own professional identities, but also of the rights of other academics to be safe from antagonism, and their own right to engage in agonistic contestation (Mouffe, 2005). Mouffe's (2013) argument for a 'grammar of democratic life', therefore, should not be interpreted as contradictory to being and acting freely. It is not the right to free speech which is constrained; it is *how* the speech is articulated, and *how* the engagement is approached, which needs to be moderated so that the encounter remains open to deliberation and debate, as opposed to being shut down.

At this juncture, it is useful to draw upon Rancière (2016), who holds that the right of individuals (academics) to assert their freedom, through free speech, reveals not only their capacity to disagree, but should also reveal them as being open to disagreement. It is not hard to think of examples of individuals, who instil fear and silence in others, not because of their convincing arguments, but because of the aggression in their speech. This often leads to some academics not participating or contributing anything in meetings, for example. Or worse, creating excuses not to attend at all. As such, academic citizenship also means 'opting out' of certain roles and responsibilities for the sake of 'being safe' as an academic.

The 'grammar of democratic life' also means making apparent one's argument or disagreement for the purposes of inviting in other points of view, rather than imposing a singular opinion or truth. Derived from the Greek *agon,* which commonly refers to a struggle or contest, for example, in sports or cultural and religious festivals, Mouffe (2005) clarifies that political agonists accept certain limits to the contest or struggle they engage in, such as a focus on the distribution of power that exists at a given time and about which disagreement is bound to persist. Notably, they do not deny each other the right to engage in the agonistic contestation, but they treat each other as (political) adversaries rather than (moral) enemies (Mouffe, 2005). Political agonists understand that political argument is at one and the same time 'the *demonstration* of a possible world where the argument could count as argument, addressed by a subject qualified to argue, upon an identified object, to an addressee who is required to see the object and to hear the argument that he or she 'normally' has no reason to either see or hear. It is the construction of a paradoxical world that relates two separate worlds' (Rancière, 2001: par. 24).

And, while consensus might be a desirable ideal, perhaps, insofar as it matters to collective departmental, faculty and university objectives, this ideal should not stifle pluralism and difference. It is inevitable, therefore, that a predominant agreement with one view, might signal the discarding of another view. By implication, this also means that democratic engagement or grammar is never rid of the possibility of exclusion, and hence, disagreement or dissensus, thereby sustaining democratic contestation. To Mouffe (2000: 99), however, any consensus is a temporary 'expression of a hegemony, of a specific pattern of power relation', which can be challenged. Agonistic pluralism makes room for disagreement, it also breaks down constructions of totality, particularly insofar as these subjugate minority identities and produce fictions of what it means to be a political subject (Des Roches & Ruitenberg, 2018). To Mouffe (2000: 2005), therefore, agonistic pluralism is critical for democratic vitality of institutions, including universities and academic citizenship.

3.2 Competing Truths and Academic Freedom

The idea of breaking down constructions of totality (Des Roches & Ruitenberg, 2018) implies that room has to be made for other considerations and voices. While one might assume that universities, populated by diverse academic identities would by implication be open and inclusive to this diversity, this is not necessarily the case. Diversity does not unfold in a linear or predictable fashion. The appointment of academics from minority groups does not provide a fair indicator of the degrees of participation, recognition, and inclusion of these identities. These appointments are also not a reflection of the willingness of departments, faculties, or universities to acknowledge the possibilities of multiple truths. In part, the neglect of a consideration of multiple truths resides in rigid constructions of collective identities.

On one level, this identity stems from the disciplinary specialisations of academics. When I took up my position in my current faculty, for example, there were clear delineations not only between departments, but between disciplines within departments. This spilled over into project collaborations, it also spilled over into how academics engaged with one another, as in co-authoring, project collaborations, or invitations for peer review, or examinations of theses.

On another level, collective identity is tied to designated faculties—at times symbolised through colour codes on academic regalia. Collective identity is also associated with the university, and here it is not only a matter of geographical location, or disciplinary focus, but also the ranking of institutions. In South Africa, university affiliation carries an additional signifier of either historically 'white' or historically 'black'. Despite nearly three decades of the dismantling of apartheid, these historical legacies continue to influence opinions, perceptions and expectations of universities.

At yet another level, an unwillingness to shy away from the possibilities of multiple truths resides in entrenched ideas about people and the world. It would not, therefore, be controversial, contends Ahmed (2003: 378), 'to say that truth is dependent on the norms that allow us to distinguish better and worse claims on the grounds of "how" they come to arrive at their judgments. Regardless, therefore, of the presence of diverse academic identities and evidence of difference in terms of religious or cultural beliefs, for example, these are not considered as holding any merit or value. The politics of the university, or faculty, is already always in place, with clear lines between those considered as being on the 'inside' own the mandate on truth, and hold power, and those who do not. At play are what Foucault (1997a, 1997b: 297) describes as the 'games of truth'—'a set of rules by which truth is produced'. Truth is not outside of power or deprived of power. Rather, argues Foucault (1988: 113–114), it 'is linked by a circular relation to systems of power which produce it and sustain it, and to effects of power which it induces, and which redirect it'.

Each university has its own 'regime of truth'—that is, 'the types of discourse which it accepts and makes function as true; the mechanisms and instances which enable one to distinguish true and false statements, the means by which each is sanctioned; the techniques and procedures accorded value in the acquisition of truth; the status of those who are charged with saying what counts as true' (Foucault, 1998:

3.2 Competing Truths and Academic Freedom

112–113). Hence, the more a university diversifies, the more what counts is true is brought into contestation. This presents a problem not only in relation to retaining what counts as true, but how to hold on to the power, which accompanies a 'regime of truth'.

'Regimes of truth' are intricate and are not easily disrupted. They are as embedded in how identities are constructed and enacted, as they are ensconced in a preservation of privilege, which will not easily be shared or relinquished. When new and diverse identities enter the university and disturb the status quo with their own truths and ways of seeing the world, the potential for disagreement, conflict, as well as fear, is apparent. But diversity, and multiple truths, are crucial to the development of a vibrant, curious university; it is also vibrant to cultivating inclusive and hospitable spaces for diverse student identities. In this regard, agonistic pluralism is helpful not only in propagating a questioning university community and environment, but also for the establishment of new 'institutions and configurations of power' (Mouffe, 2014: 153), while simultaneously recognising that these, too, will be contested. This is because universities are fluid spaces, shaped and influenced as much by political climates as they are new appointments of academics, and enrolments of students.

The South African case presents an interesting example of profound political shifts to a democracy, and hence the cultivation of a pluralist society, including the recognition of multiple truths. For universities, these truths manifest in immense policy reform, with an emphatic focus on the importance of an openness to different ways of thinking, being and acting. It has also meant a re-assessment of the 'regimes of truth', which sustained apartheid and its accompanying laws of race-based student segregation, and the exclusive appointment of 'white' academics at 'white institutions. This is not to say that the power struggle or 'games of truth' ceases.

The opening of university spaces to all identities means a reconfiguration of the power struggle, and a reconstruction of academics and their positions through hegemonic discourses and conflict. In sum, recognising and cultivating an ethos and environment, which are inclusive of multiple truths are crucial to the advancement of universities as curious, open, and reflective. In turn, the recognition of multiple truths means that agonistic pluralism is always in effect. For a diverse academic citizenship to find resonance with an institution, it is important acknowledge that the purpose of the university is not simply to produce graduates, or to be used as an instrument of state policy to deliver on the needs of society; rather, the purpose of the university is the pursuit of truth (Higgins, 2000).

This pursuit of truth, necessarily includes an acknowledged criticality of academic freedom, which, according to Burgess and Sedlacek (2015: 16), is associated with the free exchange of ideas and the development of an institutional culture, which tolerates those who hold diverse views. Unless a university is considered to be moving on a configuration of openness in which ideas are 'openly traded' and openness with society and the world for that matter widened, one would not remain hopeful of the new educational paths for such a university (Barnett, 2016, 47). Academic freedom is not undermined only from the inside, or from institutional directives, as might be encountered, for example, in the 'disinvitation' of speakers, curtailing dissenting views, regulating academic content, or controlling pedagogical practices. do not exclusively emanate from institutional directives of cultures.

Schrecker (2012) contends that whatever the content, attacks on academic freedom have almost always come from outside the academy. The corporate style restructuring of the academy has made the university vulnerable to proscriptions and constraints (Schrecker, 2012). Hence, the war being waged against the university is not simply against dissenting public intellectuals and academic freedom; this war is deeply implicated in questions of power across the university, specifically regarding who controls the hiring process, the organization of curricula, and the nature of pedagogy itself (Schrecker, 2012).

3.3 Research, Knowledge and Democratic Dissensus

Barnett (2022: 26) reminds us that 'although an association is often made between universities and research, in fact only a tiny proportion of the world's universities are research intensive (perhaps 2%), *teaching* being by far the dominant activity'. Regardless of the predominance of teaching, and the obvious importance thereof, research and knowledge are critical to the professional development of academic citizenship. While research is quite clearly determined by the specific disciplinary interests and locations of academics, it is also influenced by the interests and experiences of academics, and this includes how they wish to position themselves. As discussed in Chap. 2, some academics might opt to use their research to establish closer connections with members of their disciplinary community outside their institution, rather than dedicating their attention to their home-university. They do this through forging international collaborations on research projects, which includes co-authoring and co-presenting at conferences.

Motivations for these decisions vary among academics. Some might access existing collaborative networks, commonly found in specialist interest groups at conferences, with a clear intention of establishing a 'cosmopolitan' academic identity (Merton, 1947). Some might make conscious moves in working with certain scholars for the purposes of gaining, while also producing knowledge. It is common for academics to seek out the mentorship of others in relation to research topics or endeavours. Others, while affiliated with one university, might seek research ties with another university for the purposes of access to certain archives or other resources. And, again, others might find that their particular research interest will gain from engaging with scholars in other geopolitical or socio-economic contexts, with the possibility of seeking out greater political support for particular projects.

Apparent from these various pathways is an understanding that research is not necessarily detached from the researcher or academic. Of course, for many academics, conducting research, writing papers and proposals are tasks in fulfilment of their professional responsibilities. In the university where I am based, as I am sure is the case elsewhere, academics, based on their professional designation, are required to produce a certain number of accredited outputs annually. Alongside teaching, and community interaction and service, the performance of academics is evaluated based on their research. Some academics recognise this as a performative process and approach it as such by merely meeting the minimum requirements of their academic post. While the matter of how universities conceive of performance evaluation needs interrogation, the interest of the discussion here is how some academics approach their research. They do not necessarily see it as connected to who they are as academics, or in forging an academic identity.

To others, regardless of its implications for meeting performative criteria, research is critical to their teaching, their responsiveness to society, and to who they are as academics. There is an inherent curiosity not only about their research discipline, but what this research holds for their teaching, and society or a wider world. In this way, academics see their research and the knowledge that they produce as a manifestation of their citizenship. They seek to use their knowledge production as a reflection of who they are and how they see the world. They are intimately connected to their writing and recognise that the importance of research and knowledge is not only in the production, but in the potential for bringing about change, and for re-imagining new possibilities.

In turn, some academics also recognise that the production of knowledge is crucial to their own knowledge acquisition—that is, through writing and producing, they learn, realising that there is still more to question and know. The teaching and writing of some academics, who lived through apartheid South Africa, often reveal a strong interest in matters of equality, equity, and social justice. This is because they have had direct lived experiences of what it means to be oppressed and excluded. Their research, therefore, can become an extension of their identities and experiences, as well as a vehicle for drawing attention to issues and concerns.

The relationship between academics and their knowledge production is critical, and not only for the reasons already offered. Inasmuch as we understand the importance of knowledge in advancing new thinking, there are certain kinds of knowledge not necessarily embraced by certain departments, faculties, or universities. Knowledge, by virtue of who brings it and what it states, can create tensions within university structures. In this way, the perpetuation of a 'regime of truth' can be deployed against the facilitation of knowledge, deemed as unworthy, or illegitimate. One example resides in the advancement of postcolonial studies. Some academics and theorists see it as offering a language of and for those who have no place, who seem not to belong, of those whose knowledges and histories are not allowed to count (Young, 2009). Others, consider postcolonial studies as the intrusion of radically different perspectives into the academy (Young, 2009).

The importance about knowledge, as brought through and by academic identities is that it is always situated (Haraway, 1988). It is one thing, for example, to theorise about the effects and harm of racism; it's quite another to recount the lived the experiences thereof. There are those academics who can offer the direct experiences of 'subjugated knowledges' (Haraway, 1988: 584). And there are those, who either do not wish to know about it, or those, who believe that it is not worth knowing.

To extend the example: as 'black' academics began to take up positions in the historically 'white' faculty in which I am based, efforts to revise the content of certain modules, include historically (politically) dismissed texts or theorists, or to broaden teaching practice sites to include historically 'black' schools was met with strong resistance from some. There was an unspoken desire to keep things as they always were—in terms of content, pedagogy, as well as the kinds of schools pre-service teachers are placed at for their teaching practical. In this case, students were always assigned to historically 'white' schools, because the university exclusively served 'white' students. As efforts were made to broaden the variety of schools, which are more reflective of South African society, resistance came from all quarters: 'white' academics, 'white' students', as well as their parents, who expressed their fear about their children being sent to 'black' schools.

It is not only a matter of perceptions and myths about the competence and value of 'black' academics, but also the knowledge that they hold and wish to espouse is of no value. Knowledge, like language, or any other marker, is implicitly politicised and can be used as a means of exclusion. Attempts, therefore, to bring knowledges from 'below' or from the 'outside' can be met with disagreement and conflict. This is because knowledge is used and reproduced so that normative hegemonies remain in place to the extent that any difference is not seen as lived expressions of diversity but as irreconcilable and, hence, something to be suppressed and disregarded (Davids, 2022).

It is at this point that agonistic pluralism presents a new way of navigating faculty and university spaces, so that there is a negotiation of academics' identities and knowledge, while simultaneously recognising the arising dissensus as necessary for the cultivation of a vibrant and questioning democratic space. The objective, to reiterate Mouffe's (2005) argument, is not to attain an inclusive consensus, but rather to recognise that disagreement and dissent are inherent in any diverse setting, and inherent in the propagation of ideas and knowledge. And if the university is authentic about seeking truth, which, by implication, means being open to diverse forms and expressions of knowledge, then the emphasis must be on approaching dissensus with regard so that the possibilities for democratic engagement are maintained. The possibility that agonistic pluralism makes room for disagreement, and can break down hegemonic constructions, means that 'subjugated knowledges' (Haraway, 1988), and hence, identities, can come to the fore.

3.4 Criticality of Agonism for Academic Citizenship

Mouffe's (2000, 2005) theory of agonistic pluralism is the framed by clear parameters. Firstly, for the purposes of cultivating a space where individuals are free to be themselves and express their opinions, then we must allow for the possibility that conflict might occur and an arena must be provided where differences can be confronted. Secondly, that disagreement and conflict are not synonymous with violence or harmful speech. Instead, encounters of disagreement should be constrained by a 'grammar of democratic life', so that engagement might be opened and sustained, as opposed to being shut. Thirdly, when conflict arises, the involved

3.4 Criticality of Agonism for Academic Citizenship

parties should treat each other as (political) adversaries rather than (moral) enemies (Mouffe, 2005). As such, importantly, for Mouffe (2000, 2005), collective identity—as might be envisaged in ideas of academic citizenship—does not emerge from an essential homogeneity, rather, it is always already an effect in terms of political articulation in hegemonic struggle.

The importance of agonistic pluralism lies not only in its recognition of the rights of individuals to differ and disagree. The value of agonistic pluralism is also that it serves to create a robust environment of questioning, wondering, deliberation and debate—exactly the kinds of features and actions that should be cultivated and propagated in any university. The diversity of academic identities is immense, and extends from constructions of race, gender, nationality to disciplinary interests and capabilities. The pursuit of knowledge (as is the main imperative in educational institutions) must be underscored by a curiosity about the world around us, and this includes a curiosity about those we work. Too often, academics are appointed into departments and faculties, with very little attention devoted to who these academics are. Biographical data, even when it extends beyond qualifications and professional achievements, and includes personal details like family details, are insufficient in providing insights into *who* individuals are.

Questioning within the constraints of a 'grammar of democratic life' creates the opportunities for new identities to make themselves known, and in turn, for the existing structures and identities also to be laid bare. Every university is encased in its own institutional ethos and culture, most of which is not abundantly evident when applying to that university. Certainly, information gleaned from others and from websites provide some details, but until academics are on the 'inside', they will not fully grasp that being on the 'inside' of an appointment does not easily translate into a shredding of an 'outsider' status. There are many academics, who, after years in departments of faculties, still do not experience recognition, inclusion or belonging beyond a professional designation.

On the one hand, this can be because the 'regime of truth' which maintains the existing configurations of power are unacknowledged, unexplored and uninterrogated. On the other hand, even if there is a consciousness of the exclusionary nature or practices within departments or across faculties, and a willingness to engage on these practices, this does not imply a willingness to dismantle these practices. The mere presence of minority group academics is, at times seen, as a disruption of a hegemonic norm, or as a tolerant accommodation. To expect that minority groups are included in the discourse and culture of universities is a compromise beyond the realms of plausibility.

Resistance to newness and difference are often motivated by political desires to preserve the status quo. Tradition and existing institutional cultures are used as yardsticks and barriers to change. Any diverse appointments are accommodated on the basis that they fit into the existing culture and discourse. Most times, however, resistance to academics from different identities and backgrounds are driven by fear. Ahmed (2003) explains that to make truths is not only to make worlds, but also to make worlds in defence or fear that such worlds "could be" unmade. This means that when the demographics of a faculty or university changes, there are fears that the existing world and its accompanying truths will be discarded and replaced.

The fear is not only about losing the way the world (of the university) looks and functions, but the fear is also about the loss or displacement of the individual within that world. With the entry of diverse identities comes other truths and knowledge, which might bring into contestation the taken for granted norms of a department or university. And if the power dynamic shifts because of these new presences, existing power or privilege might dissipate. The deployment of fear as a response to the unknown or unfamiliar is counter-intuitive a 'grammar of democratic life' and democratic dissensus.

When fear becomes the dominant basis of a response, the inevitable outcome is to exclude, marginalise, and vilify. In South Africa, the rhetoric of segregated living was often fuelled through a discourse of fear constructed around 'black' people, especially 'black' men. The more fear enters the discourse, the greater the inclination to keep those who are unfamiliar at bay, and concomitantly, the easier it becomes to stoke the fear (Davids, 2015). Ahmed (2003: 377) shares that fear works 'to effect the very boundaries between subjects and others, partly through the feeling that such boundaries have already been threatened by the presence of others'; fear operates as 'an affective economy of truth: fear slides between signs and sticks to bodies by constituting them as its objects'.

The signs attached to certain bodies can stem from and be influenced by several factors, including, race, ethnicity, nationality, sexuality, religion, and culture. Certain competencies, capabilities, ideas and stereotypes are assigned to some bodies, while not to others, and this includes the right to be who one is. In a sense, as Butler (2016: 15) reminds us, 'we already know the idea that freedom can only be exercised if there is enough support for the exercise of freedom, a material condition that enters into the act that it makes possible'. In universities, this can create alienating and harmful professional environments, which in some cases, can spill over into strife, or disengagement between individuals or groups.

3.5 Key Considerations of Chapter

Whether in the context of existing strained and antagonistic relations among colleagues, or whether in a context of new and unexplored professional relationships, where silent nods and withdrawals often become an easier form of engagement, Mouffe's (2005) agonistic pluralism and contestation offer avenues out of unproductive identity politics. Mouffe (2013) stresses that the political in its antagonistic dimension cannot be made to disappear by simply denying it or wishing it away. This, state Des Roches and Ruitenberg (2018), is the typical liberal gesture, and such negation only leads to the impotence that characterises liberal thought when confronted with the emergence of antagonisms and forms of violence. And yet, as has been argued in this chapter, the diversity within universities implies the potential for binaries of inclusion/exclusion; we/they; and us/them.

Disagreement and conflict are, therefore, not only inevitable in a diverse, pluralist contexts, but are also constitutive of the political. But when conflict is understood as agonistic contestation, it opens new orientations towards democratic dissensus as necessary for the recognition of multiple identities, truths, and knowledges, and thereby cultivates a more inclusive and agential academic citizenship. The importance of recognising the role of agonistic contestation is not limited to the inclusion of minority group identities and knowledge. It also creates the space for existing hegemonies to reflect on normative constructions of power and discourses, with the possibility of interrogation and reimagined ways co-existence and engagement.

References

Ahmed, S. (2003). The politics of fear in the making of worlds. *International Journal of Qualitative Studies in Education, 16*(3), 377–398.

Barnett, R. (2016). *Understanding the university: Institution, idea, possibilities*. Routledge.

Barnett, R. (2022). *The philosophy of higher education: A critical reader*. Routledge.

Burgess, A. & Sedlacek, J. (2015). Academic freedom in christian church (Independent) institutions of higher education: Critical matters regarding academic freedom. *Stone-Campbell Journal 18*(1), 13–25.

Butler, J. (2016). Rethinking vulnerability and resistance. In J. Butler, Z. Gambetti, & L. Sabsay (Eds.), *Vulnerability in resistance* (pp. 12–27). Duke University Press.

Davids, N. (2015). Islam and multiculturalism in Europe: An exposition of a dialectical encounter. *American Journal of Islamic Social Sciences, 32*(2), 31–50.

Davids, N. (2022). *Out of place: An autoethnography of postcolonial citizenship*. African Minds.

Des Roches, S. J., & Ruitenberg, C. W. (2018). Mouffe. In P. Smeyers (Ed.), *International handbook of philosophy of education* (pp. 283–294). Dordrecht.

Foucault, M. (1997a). *Ethics: Subjectivity and truth*. Trans. R, Hurley and others. Allen Lane, The Penguin Press.

Foucault, M. (1997b). The ethics of the concern of the self as a practice of freedom. In P. Rabinow (Ed.), *Ethics, subjectivity and truth: The essential works of Foucault 1954–1984* (vol. 1, pp. 281-301). The New Press.

Foucault, M. (1988). *Politics, Philosophy, Culture: Interviews and Other Writings, 1977–1984*. (Trans. A. Sheridan & others). New York: London.

Haraway, D. (1988). Situated knowledges: The science question in feminism and the privilege of partial perspective. *Feminist Studies, 14*(3), 575–599.

Higgins, J. (2000). Academic freedom in the New South Africa. *Boundary, 27*(1), 97–119.

Merton, R. K. (1947). Patterns of influence: Local and cosmopolitan influentials. In R. K. Merton (Ed.), *Social theory and social structure* (pp. 387–420). The Free Press.

Mouffe, C. (2000). *The democratic paradox*. Verso.

Mouffe, C. (2005). *On the political*. Routledge.

Mouffe, C. (2013). *Agonistics: Thinking the world politically*. Verso.

Mouffe, C. (2014). By way of a postscript. *Parallax, 20*(2), 149–157.

Rancière, J. (2016). Critical questions on the theory of recognition. In K. G. Genel & J. P. Deranty (Eds.), *Recognition or disagreement: A critical encounter on the politics of freedom, equality, and identity* (pp. 83–95). Columbia University Press.

Rancière, J. (2001). Ten theses on politics. *Theory & Event, 5*(3). https://www.colorado.edu/hum anities/ferris/Courses/1968/Rancière/Ten%20Theses/Rancière_Ten%20Theses%20on%20Poli tics_Theory%20and%20Event5.3_2001.pdf

Schrecker, E. (2012). Academic freedom in the corporate university. *Radical Teacher, 93*(38), 45–60.

Young, R. (2009). What is the postcolonial? *Ariel, 40*(1), 13–25.

Chapter 4
Identities, Citizenships, and Vulnerabilities

Of course, there are overlaps and connections between formations of identities, knowledge, citizenship, and the arising of any vulnerabilities. The central argument of this book is that identity serves as the primary signifier and tone of the ensuing academic citizenship, as well as vulnerability. Not only are some academics more vulnerable than others, but some vulnerabilities are less visible than others. Vulnerability in the academy comes in numerous and intricate forms. It resides in contract and ad hoc posts; it resides in the nature of academic work, which demands a continuous subjection to scrutiny and review; it also resides in everyday experiences.

Much like the public square, which offers differentiated kinds of access, participation, and regard for different kinds of people, so, too, the university does not provide the same kinds of spaces for all academics (or students). Experiences of inclusion and recognition are not afforded to all academics in the same way. At times, these discrepancies stem from hegemonic structures—these are generally more clearly defined and understood. Less clear, and more complex are the kinds of vulnerabilities, which emerge from identity markers; experiences put into play through institutional cultures and discourses; and which are enacted through the epistemological functioning of the academy.

Conventionally, vulnerability has to do with letting go of our defences, opening ourselves to being hurt or harmed. There is much more to academic citizenship than simply meeting a prescribed list of roles and responsibilities. There are certain vulnerabilities, which underscore the performative measures of being an academic—as present in teaching and supervising, as it is in the production of knowledge. There are risks in exposing too much of ourselves, in sharing our insecurities or our fears. Notably, while some academics push through and find ways of coping without being too affected by estranging institutional contexts and cultures, others suffer tremendous harm, professionally and personally. And yet, vulnerability can be a source of strength. Being vulnerable is not only about stepping into one's own truth and being, but also about being willing to listen to other voices and perspectives and opening oneself to change. More importantly, being vulnerable opens the opportunity for the establishment of new academic identities.

4.1 Intersections Between Identity, Citizenship, and Vulnerability

As bodily, social, and affective beings, explain Koivunen et al. (2018), we all have the capacity to be vulnerable to one another and to conditions of inequality, discrimination, exploitation, or violence, as well to the natural environment. To them, mobilising the concept therefore entails challenging liberal notions of the individual subject as autonomous, independent, and self- sufficient, and somehow not touched by the capacity to be vulnerable. It also means critiquing the ways in which this notion of the individual subject has implicitly been male, white, Eurocentric, cisgendered, and able- bodied, allowing for 'vulnerable groups' to almost automatically signify those diverging from it (Koivunen et al., 2018).

Ideas about vulnerability are seemingly as unfixed as identity itself. Identity explains Mendieta (2008: 407), is constructed, invented, imagined, imposed, projected, and provides a 'social locus' of how individuals position themselves within a particular context. Depending on how individual negotiates the particular influences of their 'social locus'—whether imaginary or not—the social space is continually shifting and transforming. In this way, identities have to be understood as 'fragile negotiations' with their respective 'social topography' (Mendieta, 2008: 412). In turn, Spivak et al. (1990: 72) posit that the extent to which certain identities have to negotiate their social spaces and interactions, is linked to how vulnerable they are. While we might agree with both Mendieta (2008) and Spivak et al. (1990) on the interplay between individuals and their social topography, and the need for negotiations as the social space is traversed, it is important to recognise that the way in which vulnerability plays out in these instances is not contained on a continuous continuum.

Boldt (2019) explains that phenomenological and hermeneutic perspectives can help to delineate the various ways in which human existence is characterized by vulnerability. In the phenomenological traditions, vulnerability is closely tied to an analysis of the role of the body in perception and knowledge. The body is not perceived of as a mere tool for perception and knowledge acquisition. Instead, says Boldt (2019) the emphasis is on the ways in which the body constitutes how one relates to the world and acts in it, and on how this influence is experienced and shapes one's emotions, perceptions, and actions. 'The vulnerability of the body and its needs are thus considered to have an effect on emotion, perception and knowledge, and perception and knowledge are thought of as 'embodied' phenomena' (Boldt, 2019: 6).

Similarly, Butler (2016) avers that we cannot talk about a body without knowing what supports that body, and what its relation to that support—or lack of support—might be. To her, the body is less an entity than a relation, and it cannot be fully dissociated from the infrastructural and environmental conditions of its living. What this means, elaborates Butler (2016: 8), is that 'the dependency on human and other creatures on infrastructural support exposes a specific vulnerability that we have when we are unsupported, when those infrastructural conditions start to decompose, or when we find ourselves radically unsupported in conditions of precarity'.

Children, for example, might fail to flourish or develop a healthy self-esteem if subjected to parental neglect or abuse. Likewise, in the absence of articulated support and care, certain academic identities might find themselves at a loss in how to locate themselves within professional environments and communities. Here, it is not only a matter of race, culture, gender of sexuality, but also how the logic of these different markers intersects, and reproduce existing hegemonies (Mirza, 2013). Mirza (2006) highlights the paradoxical experiences of 'black' women in the academy.

On the one hand, 'black' women are seemingly highly 'visible' when their bodies help higher education institutions achieve their wider moral and ethical goals and help them appeal to a wider global market. This is often evident in the celebration of diverse images in brochures or on websites. One would be hard-pressed to find university websites which do not carry these kinds of images—where the importance of showcasing diversity far outweighs the reality of what happens beneath the representation. Typically, these same identities are called upon to serve and lead diversity and inclusion efforts.

On the other hand, however, states Mirza (2006), 'black' women slip into invisibility in the site that matters the most—how they are valued and embraced in everyday practice, and the transforming difference that they bring to higher education institutions. There is therefore, as Butler (2016: 11) alerts us, a 'certain kind of *dependency* on infrastructure, understood complexly as environment, social relations, and networks of support and sustenance the human itself proves to not to be divided from the animal or from the technical world, we foreground the ways in which we are vulnerable to decimated or disappearing infrastructures, economic supports and predictable and well compensated labor'.

In turn, says Boldt (2019), a hermeneutic account places emphasis on the limits of knowledge and knowledge acquisition—'Knowledge about how one is to understand oneself and normative knowledge, it is claimed, result from ongoing engagement in social relations. Claims to this kind of knowledge thus remain open to criticism and readjustment' (2019: 6). What, for example, does it mean for certain academic identities to be vulnerable? And if we agree that 'black' women are vulnerable by virtue of how gender and race intersect on their bodies and shape their citizenship, do we assume that the experiences for 'white' women are very or slightly different? In other words, which marker carries the heavier burden and tilts the experiences of women into a vulnerable zone: gender or race?

And to Butler's (2016) questions: if women or minorities seek to establish themselves as vulnerable, do they unwittingly or wittingly seek to establish a protected status subject to a paternalistic set of powers that must safeguard the vulnerable, those presumed to be weak and in need of protection? Does the discourse of vulnerability discount the political agency of the subjugated?

Many would agree that of course it is possible for individuals to overcome their vulnerability. The pursuit of higher education is often motivated by desires to overcome the vulnerabilities brought about by socio-economic deprivation, a lack of opportunities and social mobility, or poverty. In these instances, the promise held by education to undo these vulnerabilities instils a drive that probably would not have emerged in the absence of vulnerability. As such, vulnerability can translate into profound understandings and capacities to overcome and achieve. Porter (2020), for example, observes that despite a historical legacy of marginalisation, devaluation, and gendered-racist discrimination of 'black' women, they still find ways to thrive, progress, and attempt to change the very structure of academia piece by piece.

The problem, however, is that all vulnerable groups do not necessarily respond to a lack of infrastructural support or discrimination in the same way. It could be that what motivates one particular group to use their vulnerability as a form of resistance is the historical legacy of that experience. Racial discrimination has an uncomfortably strong foothold in professional settings, regardless of these seemingly being confronted and redressed in policies. It could be that the sheer number of 'black' women in Porter's (2020) study—she alludes to doctoral students, postdocs, academic administrators, and contingent and tenure-track/tenured faculty—presents a physical and quantitative support. To draw on Butler (2016: 19) again: 'And when this dismantling is undertaken by subjugated peoples, do they not establish themselves as something other than, or more than, vulnerable? Indeed, do we want to say that they overcome their vulnerability at such moments…? Or is vulnerability still there, now assuming a different form?'.

4.2 The (In)visibility of Vulnerability

It follows from the discussion, thus far, that notions and experiences of vulnerability are as distinctive to identities as they are to contexts. South Africa's history of colonialism (by the Dutch and British), followed by apartheid has ensured deeply entrenched constructions of the legitimacy of certain citizenship identities, as opposed to others. And although the country has rid itself of its apartheid structures and laws, the ideology of racism has not dissipated. Importantly, the scourge presented by racism is not unique to historical contexts of colonialism or apartheid. The potential for othering, marginalisation and oppression is implicit within any socio-politico-economic context. The greater the expanse of diversity—religion, culture, sexuality, class, ethnicity, nationality, ability, language—the wider the scope of and for discrimination.

In addition to the myriad shifts which accompanied South Africa's transition to a democracy, the desegregation of its educational sites has been especially volatile. At issue is not only the introduction of new diverse identities into historically racially

4.2 The (In)visibility of Vulnerability

homogenous environments, but how these race-based environments, including its historical hegemony open themselves to diverse identities.

On the one hand, there is an entry of new identities, as in 'black' students, followed by the appointments of 'black' academics and administrators at historically 'white' universities. These incoming groups deem themselves as vulnerable based on their historical marginalisation. They recognise that their insertion into historical 'white' spaces does not equate to inclusion. It is not simply a matter of the constructions of physically segregated buildings and architecture, and how some bodies were housed with dignity, while others were not. It is also a matter of what lives in the memories of these structures and systems—described by Rowlands (2008: 46) as 'the memory of a past that has written itself on you, in your character and in the life on which you bring that character to bear'. This, then, becomes the knowledge of self-understanding.

For some groups, historical memories might galvanise perceptions of superiority, while for others the trauma of oppression and exclusion might ensure internalised conceptions of inferiority. For some 'black' academics, the idea of teaching 'white' students can be an intimidating prospect. In my faculty, a few 'black' academics have shared their frustration about being undermined by 'white' students in class or being complained about to 'white' colleagues. Despite the faculty having clear guidelines for reporting any complaints, it is not unusual for a few students to bypass these protocols when they have a complaint about 'black' academics. Of greater concern, is that some of the 'white' academics being complained to, often do not re-direct students to the guidelines, and instead indulge the student and the complaint.

Confronting the real pain of what oppression and othering does, is harder than simply living with the effects thereof. As Ahmed (2018: 61) explains, 'Consciousness of racism becomes retrospective … To see racism, you have to unsee the world as you learnt to see it, the world that covers unhappiness, by covering over its cause. You have to be willing to venture into secret places of pain'. In turn, historically marginalised identities also recognise that the democratic oppositional discourse against racism—at least in terms of policy—simply makes way for other forms of exclusion and marginalisation. This is especially evident in dichotomous constructions of (white) competence and qualification, and competence as opposed to (black) incompetence and disqualification (Davids, 2019; Soudien & Sayed, 2004). In sum, there are far more questionable ways than racism to render certain identities as less than or not good enough.

On the other hand, there is the matter of the already-present identities. Their claim to certain spaces is of historical record, not only in terms of their own privileged right to live and function in race-based silos, but also in terms of who have they have the right to prevent from entry. It involves a dual process of preserving privilege by keeping other identities at bay—whether through exclusion or declarations of illegitimacy. For historically privileged identities, the dismantling of structural racism, means a sharing of space as well as privilege, with the chance of a loss of this privilege. In line with government strategies, employment equity initiatives in South Africa's higher education system, have given rise to a new vulnerability among 'white' academic identities.

The prioritisation of 'black' academics as a means of transformation through democratisation holds distinct implications for 'white' academics, who previously were not required to compete with racially constructed categories beyond their own. It also holds implications for 'black' academics in terms of how their appointments are perceived (I elaborate on this in Chap. 9). In this way the diversification and transformation of academic citizenship in South Africa have, at times, been interpreted as creating vulnerability among historically 'privileged' identities—even if the appointments of 'black' academics have yet to disturb the predominance of 'white' academic positions (Council on Higher Education, 2015; Streek, 2020).

These ambiguities notwithstanding, what we find is an unexpected turn in who self-describes as vulnerable. Butler (2016) explains this as the dual dimension of performativity—that is, we are invariably acted upon and acting. As such, 'the very meaning of vulnerability changes when it becomes understood as part of the very practice of political resistance' (Butler, 2016: 21). To Butler (2016), these kinds of 'self-interested appropriations' of 'vulnerability' by dominant groups' are problematic, because it effaces the condition of vulnerability in which precarious or marginalised communities live and constitutes an ideological seizure of the term to expand and rationalise inequalities.

Inasmuch as we might be inclined to agree with Butler's (2016) remark on the self-appropriations of vulnerability, it would be unwise to underestimate the influence and role of perception regarding vulnerability. Vulnerability, it seems, does not wait for permission (see Moriarty & Hayler, 2019). It has a way of sneaking up onto people, even as they try to dismiss or repress it. The more exposed or at risk someone feels, albeit momentarily, vulnerability waits to be embraced. Vulnerability is simultaneously shaped by its strength and fragility. On the one hand, there is a certain clarity of consciousness in being sensitised to one's vulnerability, in recognising the moment of capitulation so that certain buffers are no longer in place or reachable. There is a certain demarcation which happens when discerning between that which can be controlled and not.

Being vulnerable, says Gilson (2014), is defined by openness, and more specifically, to be vulnerable is to be open to being affected and affecting in ways that one cannot control. In this sense, being vulnerable can become the basis for learning and for empathy, connection, and community. Consider a senior academic sharing her experiences to an early career academic, revealing her struggles and disappointments in trying to get her work published. The early career academic might interpret this as a point of comfort. Both academics might perceive the exchange as a moment of authentic strength—one as being unafraid to share, and the other as learning, and together establishing a connection of empathy.

On the other hand, it seems not to matter whether being vulnerable is recognised or considered by others. In other words, the reality that certain academics feel vulnerable in their positions, or in departments, or whether they can indeed become academics, does not have to be acknowledged or shared by others. Vulnerability exists independently of the views and perceptions of others. The fact that male academics might not take the vulnerability of female academics at conferences seriously, for example, does not mean that they are not vulnerable (see Jackson, 2019). The pervasiveness of vulnerability (Gilson, 2014) means that it is both fluid and unpredictable.

4.3 Institutional Power and Vulnerability

The concept of vulnerability seems to occupy an ambiguous location between being open, whether in terms of articulating a harm, exclusion, or disadvantage; acknowledging shortcomings and being open to learning; showing strength by not shying away from pain and confrontation; and using vulnerability as a form of resistance against hegemonic structures and discourses. It also presents itself differently among identity groups, which, in some instances, can present more barriers and questions. On the one hand, the idea that all minority groups, or that all women are vulnerable by virtue of their social constructions, is simply not true; it is also risky. For feminist theory, the association between women or femininity and victimisation invokes a problematic imagery and presents vulnerability as a troubling concept (Koivunen et al., 2018). To Koivunen et al. (2018), making injustices visible may result in reinforcing gendered assumptions about vulnerability as non-agency. On the other hand, movements, such as #MeToo and #BlackLivesMatter have drawn global public attention and outrage to serious, pervasive issues.

Both movements, however, have also been criticised for claiming injury to a specific group, thereby dismissing the possibility of anyone's or everyone's vulnerability to that injury—that 'white' people can also be killed by the police, that men can also be sexually abused (Koivunen et al., 2018)—that 'All lives matter'. Here, explain Koivunen et al. (2018: 2), 'vulnerability is paradoxically equated with power: a voice, an experience, or a life that matters, that is worthy of attention and compassion'. In an interview with George Yancy and Butler (2015) contends when some people counter with 'All Lives Matter' they misunderstand the problem, but not because their message is untrue. 'It is true that all lives matter, but it is equally true that not all lives are understood to matter which is precisely why it is most important to name the lives that have not mattered and are struggling to matter in the way they deserve'.

Few would disagree that all lives matter and are open to potential harm or injustice. The arising problem, however, is that when vulnerability is understood in an ontological way (Butler, 2016), it is 'often mobilised to discredit and undermine the validity of movements focusing on the culturally and political produced vulnerability of specific groups (Koivunen et al., 2018: 2). In these cases, explain Koivunen et al. (2018: 2), the double edge of vulnerability concretises 'when the feeling of injury gathers affective charge around and for the privileged'—vulnerability is not only about weakness or immobilisation, but very concretely about agency.

Much of the discussion in this chapter, thus far, has centred on the inter-relatedness between vulnerability and identity, and hence, the type of citizens academics might or might not become. The influence of identity politics on the vulnerabilities of certain individuals or groups is immensely complex and at times, dismissed, in part because of the lack of attention afforded to academic citizenship and vulnerability. Before continuing with the latter focus, it is equally important to recognise the inherent vulnerabilities of academic citizenship by virtue of the expectations and demands of the profession itself.

Certainly, a case can be made for (romanticised) notions of working in the academy: teaching, engaging, supervising, mentoring, and deliberating with students, pursuing knowledge for the sake of epistemological advancement, and cultivating a more socially just society. This is indeed true for many academics, who succeed in finding a life-work balance, who foster deep collegial relationships, even lifelong friendships, and who, through their teaching and writing, continue to evoke appreciated scholarly and life contributions. Whether through concerted choices or disinterest, these academics are seemingly not too bothered by what is often experienced by others as an all-consuming neoliberalist knowledge factory.

Oleksiyenko (2018) reports that increasing numbers of universities in the east and west are adopting the industrial template of academic organization, which, under the pretext of enhanced productivity and corporate usefulness, the factory model stifles academic freedom, pollutes learning processes and corrupts community relations (see also Barrow, 2014). Moreover, according to Zabrodksa et al. (2011: 710), academic careers are increasingly characterized by 'an ever-intensifying workload, short term contracts, job insecurity, funding pressures, excessive competitiveness, the power imbalance between managers and academics, and weakened union power'.

Within the functioning of the neoliberalist knowledge factory, is the exposure to vulnerability as defined by what it means *to be* an academic. From the very outset of the academic journey, there are explicitly stated subjections to scrutiny. The attainment of a PhD—generally considered as a prerequisite to an academic career—involves not only a thesis examination by three or four examiners, but in several contexts, candidates are also required to subject themselves to a viva voce (oral examination) and ensure the publication of a journal article before the degree can be conferred. For most, this process can be daunting, sometimes even debilitating when confronted with harsh examination reports or interrogation.

It is not only that many students and aspirant academics experience intense levels of stress and anxiety as they try to meet deadlines, submit drafts of their work, and revise and revise—all while also trying to manage daily personal lives. It is also a matter of 'impostership'—'that at some deeply embedded level they possess neither the talent nor the right' (Brookfield, 1999: 11), which, of course, depending on specific identities and historical backgrounds, will play out differently. The more there is to navigate in terms of meeting academic demands, paying fees, attending to families, and responding to crises (like the recent global pandemic), the greater exposure to vulnerability.

While generally seen as the pinnacle of academic qualifications, the attainment of the PhD for those wishing to become an academic is just the beginning. Nearly every single aspect of being an academic involves a subjection to review and scrutiny. Every article, chapter or book must be peer reviewed. This practice can be valuable in improving arguments and texts, as well as the importance of subjecting academic work to scrutiny and different perspectives. Jackson et al. (2018) maintain that as a form of pedagogy, peer reviewing is both educational and instructive for both the reviewer and the author—that is, both are contributing to the process of shaping an article that opens the field to further conversation and thought while also playing the crucial roles of assessing quality of data and claims.

But peer review is also described as 'one of the most mysterious and contentious academic practices, causing anguish for many academics—both reviewers, and those whose work is reviewed—and sometimes more distress than is necessary' (Jackson et al., 2018: 95–96). Assigned anonymity can allow reviewers to neglect the importance of care and trust, thereby overlooking the duty to act in the best interests of an author and of the scholarly field. Responses from some reviewers can be excessive, harsh, and unhelpful, and can of course, be demotivating for some academics. They might interpret negative reviews as personal attacks or as refusals by some journals to consider certain bodies of work.

Similarly, applications for grants and projects often means competing with peers, sometimes within departments and faculties, other times across universities. The production of students relies on internal and external examiners. It is not only the student's thesis being examined, but the supervisor and the quality of supervision are also open to scrutiny. While teaching programmes must be moderated (internally and externally) by peers, the use of student feedback questionnaires to evaluate teaching performance and quality has become almost ubiquitous in higher education institutions.

Typically, evaluations are anonymous, to remove concerns of negative repercussions from academics if the student's feedback is not positive (Heffernan, 2023). This data provides the faculty and university with an idea of the academic's teaching performance, content preparation, student engagement, as well as the assessment practices, class content and an academic's teaching performance. These evaluations can be valuable in providing feedback to help academics in the improvement of courses, or investigating a known problem, such as high attrition rates, or poor academic performance, for example (Centoni & Maruotti, 2021).

Generally, universities are so confident of this system, that student evaluation reports are often used as a component of hiring and promotional decisions, but also in times of restructuring and ceasing an academic's employment (Heffernan, 2023). At my own institution, student evaluations and reviews are often used in assessing performance-based salary increases, as well as promotions. Evaluation reports are automatically sent to both the academic concerned and the relevant departmental chair, which can create immediate questions about the academic if these evaluations are negative.

As is the case with certain article or book reviews, students' evaluations of academics can be demoralising, and at times, abusive (Tucker, 2014; Heffernan, 2023). Students' evaluations can be influenced by their biases and prejudices. Heffernan (2023) reports that the largest group negatively impacted in student evaluations is almost universally accepted to be women. On the one hand, a female academic will receive lower scores than a male. On the other hand, a woman from a diverse background will receive lower scores than a white woman (Heffernan, 2023). Of the 674 academics, who participated in Heffernan's (2023) study, 59% indicated that they had received abusive comments in their student feedback. The study found that women and those from marginalised groups receive a higher number of abusive comments, and these attacks are also of a more personal and often sexual nature (Heffernan, 2023).

To Heffernan (2023), the study confirmed the abuse of academics, that the abuse affected their social and mental well-being, and impacted on their careers and career progression, particularly of women and marginalised academics. Universities, says Heffernan (2023), are aware of the inherent problems associated with anonymous student evaluations of academics, but prioritise the perceived value of data gained from these evaluations above their academics' wellbeing and their right to work in an abuse-free environment.

4.4 Academic Vulnerability as Openness

Apparent from the discussion in the previous section is that how vulnerability manifests is, at times, unpredictable and inconsistent. While some women, and some members from minority groups might be vulnerable in academic settings or be subjected to abuse or harmful comments in student evaluations, these experiences are not true for all women and all minority groups. In turn, the very design of the academy is framed by peer review processes and scrutiny, which extend beyond academic texts and into determinants of appointments and promotions.

Yet, peer review can be a powerful discourse of maintaining academic rigour and advancing scholarship. The point is, however, debilitating, at times, in the case of abusive student evaluations, or insensitive reviews, it seems impossible to eradicate the possibilities of and for vulnerabilities from the domain of academic citizenship. Much like the public sphere, where co-existence can lead to disagreement, friction, and protest, thereby creating vulnerabilities for certain citizens, so, too, academic citizenship is perpetually susceptible to vulnerabilities. It seems, therefore, that although there are certain vulnerabilities, directly tied to specific academic identities, which can lead to exclusion and othering, understanding the academy as an inherently vulnerable space is a necessary part of academic citizenship.

Consider, for example, the work that goes into teaching. Here, I am not only referring to the preparation and addressing the needs of many, diverse students. I am also referring to both the intellectual and emotional commitment, demanded by teaching. Research, including submitting for publication, says Mulgrave (2022) may be vulnerable but it is not intimate in the same way as teaching. For him, teaching involves one's personality more directly 'once I'm delivering that lecture, I'm putting my work out there in front of an audience whose acceptance, rejection, or crushing indifference gets delivered in real time'. The direct involvement of the teacher's personality extends into emotional responses of care and compassion.

Much has been written on the importance of care ethics, which relies on teachers' competence, attentiveness, listening, and responsiveness (Noddings, 2012). From the perspective of care ethics, explains Noddings (2012: 772) 'the teacher as carer is interested in the expressed needs of the cared-for, not simply the needs assumed by the school as an institution and the curriculum as a prescribed course of study'. The emotional labour is located in the teacher-student encounter, and the role of the teacher in providing a positive response that maintains the caring relation to the student's expressed need, even when she cannot respond positively to that need (Noddings, 2012). Hence, while it is clearly impossible to respond positively to every expressed needs of students (some of which can be wholly unreasonable, such as cancelling an assignment or test), the carer's objective is to maintain the caring relation (Noddings, 2012). By showing care through listening, being attentive or responding, the teacher makes herself vulnerable, because it is her responsibility to ensure that the lines of communication remain open.

Students, in turn, continues Noddings (2012), do not have to reciprocate by showing gratitude—thereby, possibility contributing to the teacher's vulnerability. As teachers, we have probably all experienced this scenario in one form or another, in which we avail ourselves to students, whether to listen to their stories, or to show compassion for whatever difficulty they might be facing.

There are numerous cases in which students claim illness or deaths of family members, which require academics to re-schedule tests, or accept late submissions. There are also endless cases of supervision sessions being used as counselling sessions—which, while necessary for the wellbeing of the student, can be emotionally taxing on academics, who might not be equipped to deal with certain matters. We have also probably held expectations of some kind of gratitude. Some academics might expect a simple thank-you from students after three to six, at times more, years of supervision. When this is not forthcoming, it can be discouraging and lead to academics being less inclined to give of their time and themselves to students.

Noddings (2012) reminds us that as teachers, we sometimes forget how dependent we are on the response of our students. Musgrave (2022) describes this as the emotional rewards for teachers—'It's one of the reasons why teachers love nodders—the people who nod along, even when they have no idea what's going on. Without human interaction, the whole relationship is lost'.

Despite the implicit vulnerability, showing care and compassion are critical to teaching, as well as supervision. Student supervision infers a one-to-one interaction and engagement, which is different to teaching. While some engagements and conversations with students might spill over into corridors and academics' offices, teaching is largely contextualised in the classroom or lecture theatre. Supervision invites a different set of expectations, some of which can extend into an even more intimate knowledge of students than teaching facilitates. It is not unusual for academics or supervisors to inquire about a student's background and commitments to gain some sense of how potential pitfalls and how best to supervise the student. In this way, supervision can involve a negotiated arrangement of expectations and due dates of drafts.

In my own faculty, students and academics are required to enter into a memorandum of understanding with regard to expectations and time-frames for the supervision process. Typically, these understandings and agreements vary among students, based on their own personal circumstances. This often means that academics become privy to the personal stories of students, not necessarily out of curiosity, but also because students often want their supervisors to be aware of their work or family commitments, as well as financial constraints. This also means that academics are alerted to the vulnerabilities of students, which can, in turn, result in the academic or supervisor responding with care or compassion.

Nussbaum (2001) clarifies that responding to others' situations of vulnerability involves making emotive judgements; that extending compassion relies on sharing an awareness of the same possibility vulnerability—that is, a willingness to place oneself in the same situation or emotion. Students can derive great support and benefit from a supervisor who shows a willingness to share in their vulnerability. On the other side of the coin, however, expressing vulnerability can be to detriment of some academics. Burbules (with Jackson et al., 2023: 5) points out the subtle workings of power between male professors and female students. He is 'very attuned to a context in which certain actions or comments toward students (including, but not only, female students) can lead to accusations that are personally and professionally damaging'.

While Burbules (with Jackson et al., 2023) acknowledges that his motivations are primarily about principled commitment to treating all his students with respect and care, and not just about 'avoiding trouble', his approach has led to a series of dilemmas and trade-offs in how he interacts with his students. This includes rarely talking with them about personal matters outside the academic and professional parameters of their work, leading him to questioning whether he has 'distorted or delimited' their pedagogical relationship, and what he has sacrificed 'in terms of a wholistic relationship with a student when you bracket certain topics of conversation and interaction as out of bounds' (Burbules with Jackson et al., 2023: 5).

Burbules (with Jackson et al., 2023) raises critical questions to which there are no easy or decontextualised responses. Notably, his questions suggest that even in the wake of trying to avoid talking with students about personal matters, there are concerns about the vulnerability of the pedagogical relationship. Jackson (2018) is of the opinion the vulnerability itself is not the problem. Rather, she argues, the problem is how vulnerability is experienced differently across individuals, across systems, universities, and disciplines. It would seem, therefore, as Jackson (2018: 233) observes, that vulnerability cannot simply be rid of or evaded, 'but as something which can be enhanced as circulating affect'. As such, vulnerability should be explored, because without acknowledging the inevitability of vulnerability, and its relational quality, it tends to be seen merely as a bad thing, faced by academics.

Jackson (2018: 234) proposes that normalising a place for vulnerability in higher education 'can be done to decrease rather than increase harm, but this would depend on *who* in the group is more and less vulnerable, and in what respects.' The appeal of accepting the university as a vulnerable space resides in how this normalisation might open the possibilities for new voices and identities to enter the dominant discourses. It also opens the questioning of hegemonic norms, and opportunities for those on the 'inside' of these hegemonies to question their own role in how they conceive themselves in relation to others.

4.5 Key Considerations of Chapter

Apparent from this chapter is that notions and experiences of vulnerability are both inconsistent and unpredictable. We might harbour certain preconceived notions of who constitutes vulnerable academic identities or groups, such as women or minority groups. But, this is not to say that this is true for all women or all minority groups, in the same way that it cannot be presumed that certain academic identities are exempt from vulnerability. Vulnerability manifests differently within individuals and might dissipate as easily as it takes root. That being said, there are persistent questions about minority groups in the academy—whether in terms of gender, ethnicity, culture, or sexuality, and these cannot be dismissed under a banner of normalisation.

This chapter has been clear in drawing a line between the systemic institutional vulnerability of academic systems—as made apparent in peer reviews—and the vulnerability, which stems from othering, exclusion, and misrecognition. The two sets of experiences are distinctive not only because of the origin of the experiences, but because of its effects on the personal lives and realities of academics. While the one set might be described as professionally based, the other, although located in a professional setting, departs from biases, stereotypes and prejudices, and, in fact, should have no place in any professional environment.

References

Ahmed, S. (2018). Feminist hurt/feminism hurts. In A. Koivunen, K. Kyrölä & I. Ryberg (Eds.), *The power of vulnerability. Mobilising affect in feminist, queer and anti-racist media cultures* (pp. 59–67). Manchester University Press.

Barrow, C. (2014). The coming of the corporate-fascist university? *New Political Science, 36*(4), 640–646.

Boldt, J. (2019). The concept of vulnerability in medical ethics and philosophy. *Philosophy, Ethics, and Humanities in Medicine, 14*(6), 1–8.

Brookfield, S. (1999). What is college really like for adult students? *About Campus, 3*(6), 10–15.

Butler, J. (2016). Rethinking vulnerability and resistance. In J. Butler, Z. Gambetti, & L. Sabsay (Eds.), *Vulnerability in resistance* (pp. 12–27). Duke University Press.

Centoni, M., & Maruotti, A. (2021). Students' evaluation of academic courses: An exploratory analysis to an Italian case study. *Studies in Educational Evaluation, 70*(101054), 1–14.

Council on Higher Education (2015). Vital stats public higher education 2013. Pretoria: Council on Higher Education. http://www.che.ac.za/sites/default/files/publications/Vital%20Stats%202013_web_0.pdf

Davids, N. (2019). You are not like us: On teacher exclusion, imagination, and disrupting perception. *Journal of Philosophy of Education, 53*(1), 165–179.

Gilson, E. (2014). *The ethics of vulnerability: A feminist analysis of social life and practice.* Routledge.

Heffernan, T. (2023). Abusive comments in student evaluations of courses and teaching: The attacks women and marginalised academics endure. *Higher Education, 85*, 225–239.

Jackson, L. (2018). Reconsidering vulnerability in higher education. *Tertiary Education and Management, 24*(3), 232–241.

Jackson, L. (2019). The smiling philosopher: Emotional labor, gender, and harassment in conference spaces. *Educational Philosophy and Theory., 51*(7), 693–701.

Jackson, L., Peters, M. A., Benade, L., Devine, N., Arndt, S., Forster, D., Gibbons, A., Grierson, E., Jandrić, P., Lazaroiu, G., Locke, K., Mihaila, R., Stewart, G., Tesar, M., Roberts, P., & Ozoliņš, J. (2018). Is peer review in academic publishing still working? *Open Review of Educational Research., 5*(1), 95–112.

Jackson, L., Davids, N., Thompson, W. C., Lussier, J., Burbules, N. C., Alston, K., Chatelier, S., Taganas, K. M. B., Mendoza, O. S., Cong, J. L., Frattura, A., & Taylor Webb, P. (2023). Feeling like a philosopher of education: A collective response to Jackson's 'The Smiling Philosopher.' *Educational Philosophy and Theory.* https://doi.org/10.1080/00131857.2022.2063719

Koivunen, A., Kyrölä, K., & Ryberg, I. (2018) Vulnerability as a political language. In A. Koivunen, K. Kyrölä & I. Ryberg (Eds.), *The power of vulnerability. Mobilising affect in feminist, queer and anti-racist media cultures* (pp. 59–67). Manchester University Press.

Mendieta, E. (2008). Identities: Postcolonial and global. In L. Alcoff & E. Mendieta (Eds.), *Identities: Race, class, gender, and nationality* (pp. 407–416). Blackwell.

Mirza, H. S. (2006). Transcendence over diversity: Black women in the academy. *Policy Futures in Education, 4*(2), 101–113.

Mirza, H. S. (2013). 'A second skin': Embodied intersectionality, transnationalism and narratives of identity and belonging among Muslim women in Britain. *Women's Studies International Forum, 36*, 5–15.

Moriarty, J., & Hayler, M. (2019). I found my mum in a box: Permission to be vulnerable in higher education. In J. Moriarty (Ed.), *Autoethnographies from the neoliberal academy: Rewilding, writing and resistance in higher education*. Routledge.

Musgrave, P. (2022). Emotional remuneration. https://musgrave.substack.com/p/emotional-remuneration

Noddings, N. (2012). The caring relation in teaching. *Oxford Review of Education, 38*(6), 771–781.

Nussbaum, M. (2001). *Upheavals of thought: The intelligence of emotions*. Cambridge University Press.

Oleksiyenko, A. (2018). Zones of alienation in global higher education: Corporate abuse and leadership failures. *Tertiary Education and Management, 24*(3), 193–205.

Porter, C. J. (2020). Black women as outsiders within the academy: A love letter. https://occrl.illinois.edu/our-products/voices-and-viewpoints-detail/current-topics/2020/12/12/black-women-as-outsiders-within-the-academy-a-love-letter

Rowlands, M. (2008). *The philosopher and the wolf*. Granta Publications.

Soudien, C., & Sayed, Y. (2004). A new racial state? Exclusion and Inclusion in Education: Policy and Practice in South Africa, *Perspectives in Education, 22*(4), 101–115.

Spivak, G. C., Bhatnagar, R., Chatterjee, L., & Sunder, R. (1990). In S. Harasym (Ed.), *The postcolonial critic: Interviews, strategies, dialogues* (pp. 67–74). New York: Routledge.

Streek, B. (2020). White academics dominate. https://mg.co.za/article/2000-02-25-white-academics-dominate/

Tucker, B. (2014). Student evaluation surveys: Anonymous comments that ofend or are unprofessional. *Higher Education, 68*(3), 347–358.

Yancy, G., & Butler, J. (2015). What's wrong with 'All Lives Matter'? https://archive.nytimes.com/opinionator.blogs.nytimes.com/2015/01/12/whats-wrong-with-all-lives-matter/

Zabrodska, K., Linnell, S., Laws, C., & Davies, B. (2011). Bullying as intra-active process in neoliberal universities. *Qualitative Inquiry, 17*(8), 709–719.

Chapter 5
Diversity as Vulnerability

Depending on contexts and conversations, diversity seems to be straddled with any number of connotations. On the one hand, it infers a representative inclusion of any number of markers, including gender, race, culture, nationality, class, ethnicity, and sexuality. On the other hand, the term seems to be used in an encompassing and interchangeable way, directed at addressing all manner of potential discriminations, such as inequality, unfairness, racism, sexism, and xenophobia. There are concerns when a term is meant to carry all burdens and all responsibilities. There is a certain reductionist employment of the term, especially when it is used in the form of diversity management. Not only are all differences condensed into a singular category of diversity, but the management thereof infers that diversity is something in need of control, and supervision.

The very identification of diversity draws lines in the sand between those categorised as diverse, and those who are not. What this means is that even before stepping into a lecture theatre, or the first faculty board, the marker of diversity already says something about how academics are constructed and perceived, and in some instances, how they will be treated. Designated markers of diversity, therefore, hold implications for how certain academics are seen, unseen, or misrecognised. It also holds implications for the university in terms of who are seen, and hence who the university has been made for, and unlike diversity, does not require management. Diversity, therefore, does not only direct attention to certain markers, but it also evokes an immediate vulnerability to being seen as different and in need of management. What do these markers and vulnerability infer for the experiences of diverse academic citizenships? How much negotiation is needed for diverse academics to be seen and included in their own citizenship?

5.1 (Mis)recognition

Typically, diversity evokes images of a kaleidoscopic canvas of differences, whether in terms of gender, race, ethnicity, culture, or sexuality, class, religion, language, nationality, and ability. The wide reach of diversity is reflected in its fluidity. The more differences are made apparent in terms of understandings and lived experiences, the more encompassing the concept of diversity. Diversity opens possibilities and opportunities for different perspectives, divergent arguments. If offers the potential for a reconsideration of views and ideas, for seeing ourselves from the perspectives of others, while also looking at others or situations in renewed and reimagined ways (Davids & Waghid, 2022).

For education, diverse classroom communities hold possibilities for engagement with an eclectic array of identities and accompanying viewpoints. If managed effectively, diverse classrooms hold the capacity for cultivating in students (and academics) capacities not only to learn from difference, but *how* to engage with difference and disagreement. In a world of increasing intolerance, disregard, and shutting down of dissension as opposed to engagement, the criticality of instilling regard for conflicting views cannot be emphasised enough.

For universities, diversity has become a non-negotiable aspect of how it defines and positions itself both locally and globally. Any permutations of citizenship in the sociopolitical arena will inevitably find their way into universities. Usually, these are more apparent in the inherent fluidity of student demographics, than academic citizenship. On the surface, one might argue that diversity is significantly less evident among academics because of the huge difference in numbers, and because the stringency of academic appointments far outweighs that of student enrolments. A closer analysis, however, as Mirza (2006) does, reveals that although ethnic minorities make up 6% of the working population in the UK, they make up 15% of all students. Young black people of African and Asian origin are nearly three times more likely to be at university than their white counterparts.

Moreover, in the band of young people under 21 on full-time undergraduate courses, black and minority ethnic women constitute the highest participants (Mirza, 2006). To Mirza (2006: 103) it is important to understand the significance of the 'invisibility/visibility split between staff and students' for 'black' women in higher education. More than a decade after Mirza's (2006) article, 'Advance HE' (2018) reported that 'Black and Minority Ethnic' (BME) groups continue to be marginalised in HEIs; they are underrepresented in the highest contract levels and overrepresented in the lowest, they are less likely to occupy senior managerial positions, less likely to be professors and less likely to be on the highest pay band compared to their White colleagues.

On the one hand, there is some realisation that a diverse university staff and student body speaks to an international allure, which, in turn, bodes well for the production and advancement of diverse forms of knowledge production. On the other hand, a potential acknowledgement of the value of diversity does not necessarily translate into assigning value to diverse identities. Their external inclusion brings value only insofar as it allows the university to identify itself as diverse, and not that this diversity is included in the internal discourses and ethos of the university (Ahmed & Swan, 2006; Mirza, 2006). Banks (2008) explains that the neglect to include diverse identities often stems from liberalist assimilationist notions of citizenship that assume that individuals from different groups have to give up their home and community cultures and languages to attain inclusion and to participate in a dominant culture.

The argument is that strong attachments to ethnic, racial, religious, and other identity groups lead to harmful divisions within society (Banks, 2008). The more citizens (academics or students) try to retain and foreground their respective identity groups, the less chance there is for integration.

These debates notwithstanding, there are complexities within a language of diversity, which, according to Ahmed (2012: 1) might make us cautious about 'the appealing nature of diversity and ask whether the ease of its incorporation by institutions is a sign of the loss of its critical edge'. She maintains that there is a particular kind of world (or university) that takes shape when diversity becomes part of its description. As such, it is important what to ask not only about the world or university, but about diversity. To me, one of the major impediments with a language of diversity is that it has become so encompassing, so fantastically embracing of every conceivable kind of difference, that we lose sight of the essence of diversity itself—that is, what it is meant to hold and infer.

To Ahmed (2012: 14), we need to ask what recedes or becomes obscured when diversity becomes a view—'If diversity is a way of viewing or even picturing an institution, then it might allow only some things to come into view'. Certainly, the impression one is left with when scrolling from one university website to another, is of happy, smiling students, accompanied by engaged academics. Diversity is not only made visible, but it is portrayed as happy, harmonious, and perhaps, most problematically, as equalising. The images lull one into a false narrative about what diversity holds, not in terms of its representation of difference—although this can also be misleading—but in terms of diversity being a tension free zone and experience. Hidden from the lenses of these images are individual identities, experiences, as well as realities of antagonism and struggle (Ahmed & Swan, 2006).

For example, Gouws (2007) explains that 'gender mainstreaming' in the academy is meant to institutionalise women's equality through standardised technocratic processes within institutions. Yet, according to her, it has resulted in the suppression of women's agency, while also giving policymakers the authority to control and monitor their development. Echoing this suppression, in their comparative study between the United States and South Africa, Johnson and Thomas (2012) found that black female academics in the academy continue to be seen as 'outsiders', 'invisible' and 'voiceless', and their experiences are ignored. Their 'outsider' status forces them to employ strategies that reflect constant negotiation to achieve power, identity, and voice (Johnson & Thomas, 2012).

So, too, Naicker (2013) highlights the pressures which accompany diversification as transformation in higher education in South Africa. She explains that since the country's transition to a democracy, the promotion and development of women and the advancement of black women in particular in higher education has been prioritised. Despite these objectives, 'black' women continue to experience prejudices, which according to Naicker (2013: 335):

> [L]ive in encoded speech about what is and what is not acceptable… A form of benevolent paternalism dictates, in veiled undertones, that women ought to remember their subservient position. As a result, they must still navigate the often hostile terrain of higher education because, irrespective of how hard they work, and how much they are able to prove their competence, theirs are regarded as token appointments, appointments based on race, class and gender.

It would seem, therefore, that for all the efforts towards diversification, diverse identities do not find inclusion or equality as diverse beings. Rather, the inclusion of their diversity is both framed and constrained to how diversity is approached and managed. Stated differently, inasmuch as diversity infers theoretical notions about an inclusive recognition of active representation and participation, this recognition is distorted by perceptions and preconceived ideas of who academics are, and who they are not. Here, the concerns are not only about associations and dichotomies of identity qualification and competence. Due consideration should also be given to the language of diversity, and specifically the blanketing of every potentially marginalised or excluded identity group. There are experiences which become lost and misrecognised when all diverse identities are placed into one basket, representative of the sum total of diversity. For this reason, Mohanty (1990) contends, that the central issue is not merely acknowledging differences, but rather how differences are acknowledged and engaged.

Benschop (2001) maintains that the challenge of diversity is much more than a change in terminology from categories like gender, ethnicity, age and class to the more encompassing and concealing term 'diversity', which also refers to dimensions like education, experience, jobs, opinions and ideas. Rather, asserts Benschop (2001: 1166), 'In contrast to gender and the other categories of identity, asserts which are often represented as sources of social inequality in organizations, 'diversity' does not so powerfully appeal to our sense of justice and equality'. Hence, Mohanty's (1990: 181), argument that to approach diversity as a 'benign variation… rather than as conflict, struggle, or the threat of disruption, bypasses power as well as history to suggest a harmonious, empty pluralism'. To Mohanty (1990), diversity is not just about accepting diversity, but diversity demands a discourse of difference.

5.2 Paradoxical Effects of *Doing* Diversity

Holoien (2012) explains that researchers have primarily studied three forms of diversity: structural, curricular, and interactional. Structural diversity refers to the proportion of diverse individuals in particular context, such as increasing the number of historically excluded groups of 'black' students at universities in South Africa. Curricular diversity continues Holoien (2012) refers to classes, workshops, seminars, and other programmatic efforts that expose individuals to diversity-related content.

5.2 Paradoxical Effects of *Doing* Diversity

In South Africa, this diversity is framed in larger discourses on postcolonialism and decolonisation, with an intention of reducing or erasing the predominance of western epistemologies and turning towards indigenous knowledges instead. In turn, interactional diversity refers to interpersonal contact with diverse individuals, whether horizontally via contact with peers and other equals or vertically via contact with diverse superiors or subordinates (Holoien, 2012).

Depending on the university (and typically the case at most South African universities), these policies might adopt a more structural approach at an executive or macro level, while faculties might be tasked with implementing curricular diversity. Regardless of how the broader category of diversity is dissected and delegated into sub-categories, as well as sub-committees, very few (if any) university human resource structures will not have a readily available policy on 'managing diversity' (Ahmed & Swan, 2006; Benschop, 2001). In their diversity statements or policies, most universities either frame the benefits of diversity from a moral perspective—that is, increasing fairness and justice—or from an instrumental perspective—that is, broadening horizons (Nunes, 2021).

Our faculty, for example, is yet again grappling with the establishment of faculty-based transformation committees, that would also be expected to ensure employment equity in the faculty. There is seemingly no interest from any academics to serve on this committee because they see it as yet another empty structure, that be expected to convene on a regular basis to 'discuss transformation'. By portraying or associating the university with the principles of diversity or 'managing diversity', explains Ahmed and Swan (2006: 114), 'the documents then become usable as they allow practitioners to make members of the university as well as the university itself as an imagined entity subject to those principles.' Benschop (2001: 1170) describes these documents or policies as the 'symbolic effects', which apparently facilitates the creation of a better public image and more legitimacy.

When we are confronted with happy diverse images, we are led to believe that the university is anti-racist and embraces diversity, but says Ahmed and Swan (2006), it also allows universities to conceal racism. In this way, the value of 'managing diversity' policies 'do something', even as 'they fail to describe what organisations do' (Ahmed & Swan, 2006: 114), or fail to recognise, understand and improve the lived experiences of academics from diverse identities and backgrounds (McClure & Fryar, 2022).

Instead, 'doing diversity' become forms of capital within organisations which circulate through the distribution of documents and 'good feelings' (Ahmed & Swan, 2006: 98). This is especially evident in the appointments of new academics at my university. The university's employment equity prioritises the appointment of South African 'black' academics, which, in line with national legislation, does not include the categories of 'coloureds' and 'Indians'—despite their similar historical realities of oppression during apartheid. Categories of potential applicants are excluded on the basis of race and nationality, which, unsurprisingly, raises questions about academic merit.

In a similar fashion, McKinley and Brayboy (2003) criticise universities which approach diversity as a free-standing policy, and as something that can be implemented without necessarily changing the underlying structure of the institution and its day-today operations. They explain that institutions think that they can merely offer new courses on diversity, hire diverse faculty members, assign these faculty to cover committee assignments, work with, and serve as role models for diverse students. But argue, McKinley and Brayboy (2003: 74) this is all 'window dressing', because the structure of the institution remains the same.

The deployment of diverse academics to visible spaces seems to be a common strategy in universities. Ahmed (2012: 2) draws our attention to the reality that 'some bodies become understood as the rightful occupants of certain spaces'. When it comes to matters of diversity, and transformation, or anything to do with departures from the 'way things have always been done', the bodies best suited for these tasks are almost always ones which represent diversity.

For example, in support of employment equity practices at my university, faculties are required to appoint designated 'employment equity', or diversity, equity, and inclusion (DEI) officers, as they might be known as elsewhere. Across the ten faculties at my university, the position of 'employment equity officer' is exclusively occupied by 'coloured', 'black', or 'Indian' academics. The implicit understanding is that the concern of ensuring equity is an issue of diversity, and hence, best overseen by an academic, who represents historical exclusion and marginalisation. The additional implication is that ensuring equity, is not the problem of 'white' academics.

Similar trends are found in higher education in the UK. Many respondents in a study conducted by Bhopal and Pitkin (2020) shared their concerns that the delivery of the Race Equality Charter (REC) would become the responsibility of BME staff, which was clearly reflected in the allocation of roles associated with applying for and gaining the REC.[1] If application for the REC was regarded as 'race work', according to Bhopal and Pitkin (2020), this could result in BME staff only being considered eligible to take this forward and later held accountable if the application for the REC was unsuccessful.

Following this logic, the responsibilities of diversity and employment equity are reduced to a racial audit—meaning, that as long as universities are seen to be changing in terms of representations of diversity, both diversity and transformation must be happening. So, too, the strategies employed in finding 'representations of diversity' can create problems, not only for universities, but for the individuals used in the function of diversity. Just having more diversity, argues Hansen (2022), is not enough to achieve either the moral or instrumental perspective for increasing diversity; the culture of the institution needs to change. To Hansen, this is evident in the fact that while universities are increasing recruitment of diverse students, they are less successful at recruiting and retaining diverse faculty. Diverse faculty, of course,

---

[1] In recognition of the vast inequalities experienced by BME academics in the UK, the Equality Challenge Unit (ECU) introduced the Race Equality Charter mark (REC) to address racial inequalities to improve the representation, progression and success of BME staff and students across the higher education sector (Bhopal & Pitkin, 2020).

is seen as critical to diverse students enjoying a sense of belonging and finding resonance with those who teach them (Davids & Waghid, 2022; Hansen, 2022).

According to Hansen (2022), although universities in the US say they want diversity in faculty and recruit for it, they frequently deny tenure to under-represented faculty, revealing that their real reason for diversity initiatives is for marketing to prospective students. Similar concerns are raised about higher education in the UK, where, according to Deem and Morley (2006), current 'equality policies appear to comprise both a weak redistributive concept of equality related almost entirely to occupational inequalities and a recognitional concept of equality based on the celebration of student and staff diversity without any reference to either social justice or the economic basis of sociocultural differences'. Hansen (2022) maintains that if universities truly embrace the idea as a moral obligation, and because it can improve learning, then they need to demonstrate this belief not just to recruit, but also retain diverse faculty.

It would seem, therefore, that efforts directed at diversity, might result in acquiring or appointing a representative look of diversity, which, might, in turn, be used in support of other diversity projects. These can include any number of 'diversity' responsibilities, which includes acting as DEI or equity employment officers, or serving on transformation and equality committees, or mentoring students or other colleagues. It also includes being assigned responsibilities for diversity management, or worse, diversity tensions and conflict, which might not be in the ambit of the socio-political understandings or interests of academics. Of course, there are some academics, like Ahmed (2012), who welcomed being involved in institutional work that was unrelated to her academic scholarship. For her, being part of the 'race equality group', allowed her to think more about her relationship to institutional worlds.

But a label of diversity does not translate into an interest or willingness to participate in matters concerning diversity, or a lack thereof. The view that any academic, labelled as marginalised or under-represented necessarily understands the lived experiences of other historically excluded groups or individuals is simply misplaced. And this is the risk of approaching diversity as if it means the same in all contexts or hold shared social realities for all individuals.

For universities to recognise differences within and beneath diversity requires another layer of unpeeling of presumptions, as well as stereotypes. The unfortunate reality is that in most cases this simply suggests too much hard work for those intent on maintaining the status quo at universities, made even harder by a sheer lack of interest or regard (Mirza, 2006). For many institutions, it is already too much to share the space of the university. To expect anything more, might eventually lead to a disruption of structural hegemonies, which, clearly will not serve those on the inside and centre. The whole purpose of 'doing' diversity, therefore, is precisely to manage it in such a way that margins remain intact by marginalised identities.

5.3 Negotiation, and Vulnerability

The idea that some bodies are understood as 'the rightful occupants of certain spaces' (Ahmed, 2012), implies that there are others which are not. Apparent from this position, is that the inclusion of some necessarily functions in a dyadic relationship to those, who are excluded. Rightful occupants, therefore, can only be rightful if there are those who are wrongful occupants. Who are the 'rightful occupants', and what makes them right and others wrong? Most of us have some sense of how the world has been made, how it exists and functions along intricate lines of binaries and hierarchies. We might also have a sense of the overwhelming predominance and presumption of forms of knowledge, which both relegate and rely on dichotomous constructions, which include, north/south; west/east; master/slave; black/white; man/woman; civilised/uncivilised; modern/primitive.

The decision to employ a postcolonial lens in this book is motivated to help us to critically look at the world in which in we find ourselves, and also to consider alternative ways of being in this world. Importantly, postcolonialism commences from its own counter-knowledges, and from the diversity of its cultural experiences. As such, it offers a language of and for those who have no place, who seem not to belong (Young, 2009)—those bodies, who are consigned as 'wrongful', not because of what they can and cannot do, but because of who they are.

The way in which the world is made is largely constructed and contained in transcendental norms, dictated to by 'whiteness' (Yancy, 2012). We are all inserted into an 'inherited vocabulary' of what constitutes these norms (Spivak with Hutnyk et al., 1990: 41). Unlike diverse bodies, which are marked and made visible by race, gender, ethnicity, culture, religion, language, and sexuality, 'whiteness', explains Ahmed (2004), is 'represented as invisible, as the unseen or the unmarked, as a non-colour, the absent presence or hidden referent, against which all other colours are measured as forms of deviance'. Social spaces (including universities) are not open for anybody to occupy (Puwar, 2004). Over time, explains Puwar (2004), through processes of historical sedimentation, certain types of bodies are designated as being the 'natural' occupants of specific spaces, they have the right to belong, while others are marked out as trespassers.

Diverse, 'wrongful' bodies are not only out of place, but their bodies are often used in the appropriation of enhancing the marketability of universities (Mirza, 2006). Sometimes, says, Mirza (2006: 103), 'black' women are highly 'visible' when their bodies help higher education institutions achieve their wider moral and ethical goals, and help them appeal to a wider global market. Other times, 'black' women in the academy are rendered as 'outsiders-within', invisible and voiceless (Johnson & Thomas, 2012; Mirza, 2006). If bodies are wrong and out of place, then they are 'different, deviant', and the antithesis to 'whiteness' (Peters, 2019: 663–664). 'Whiteness' only becomes visible when its effects become apparent on the experiences of diverse bodies.

For those rendered as 'wrongful occupants', 'whiteness' is not an abstract concept. Instead, states Yancy (2012), it is experienced as embodied forms of racism, othering

5.3 Negotiation, and Vulnerability

and marginalization. Hence, when we describe institutions as 'being white', contends Ahmed (2007: 157), then 'we are pointing to how institutional spaces are shaped by the proximity of some bodies and not others: white bodies gather and cohere to form the edges of such spaces.'

As a 'white' woman in the academy and the world, Clarence (2019) shares:

> I have learned over the years to take up just the right amount of space, or maybe a bit less than that. I have learned to be clever, but not so much so that the men in the room get uncomfortable (and some of the women too!); I have learned to be assertive, but not so much so that I am accused of being pushy and aggressive; I have learned to be ambitious, but not so much so that colleagues are threatened by me and don't want to work with me; I have learned to dress so that people take me seriously, but not too seriously because then I'm not feminine enough, or fun enough

Sometimes, it is an intersection of the politics of race and religion:

> I think I am probably treated…with a bit more hostility than if I was a young Muslim woman. Conversely, because I suspect if I was a young Muslim woman, I'd suffer greater disadvantages in society at large but not in an academic environment. Because White liberal academics like to champion certain people, they like to have pet projects, but I don't fall into that category. I fall into it because I am brown, but then I fall out if it because I am Muslim. My point is that White liberal academics can have the wrong prejudices; they want people to champion and promote but they prefer them to be non-threatening ('brown, male, Muslim, professor' in Bhopal, 2014: 10).

Or race and sexuality:

> Some people treat me with respect and dignity and others tolerate me as a person of colour who is queer and who is interested in social justice policies. I think it's been easier for people to say that my research is 'too political' or 'too subjective' or it is 'not really research' and you have to be careful about that. But I think those labels are based on particular types of prejudice. A Black male is threatening, but a Black queer male is even more threatening to what is considered the stereotype of what a Black male is and what he should look like ('black, male, gay, professor' in Bhopal, 2014: 11).

Some markers carry heavier burdens than others. Possibilities of shared experiences among certain racial groups can be interrupted by any number of additional signifiers. For example, Jones (2006) explains, that, collectively, 'black' and ethnic minority women academics have not attained the progressive benefits that have accrued to 'white' women in the wake of gender equality initiatives and directives. Moreover, the more the layers of diversity, the more there is to negotiate. For some it is not only a matter of racial and gender categorisation, but also a matter of how to negotiate their sexuality, religion, language, accent and ethnicity.

Diversity does not only arise internally within universities or within national boundaries of countries. It also flows academic mobility, or academic migration, which bodes well for international understandings and the internationalisation of universities (Teichler, 2015). The transnational movement of academics in recent years, explains Pherale (2012), is attributed to both the educational expansion of western universities internationally, as well as the appeal of universities that attract international staff to enhance their academic strengths. According to Pherale (2012), academics who migrate to English universities have to adopt and adapt to the teaching and learning culture in their new workplace, which can sometimes be stressful and contentious:

> I am concerned about the tone, language, and accuracy of what I write. I am always careful about not getting things wrong. I think when we operate in a second language in a different cultural context; we end up working much harder than the native users of the language. It is, I think, about the fear of making mistakes, and then the concerns about how people might perceive that mistake… (social work lecturer in Pherale, 2012: 324).

In South Africa, some 'black' academics from other African states, often complain about deliberate practices of discrimination and marginalisation:

> Ever since I came to this institution I have not taught a single course except to tutor in courses taught by others. In some instances I have to tutor courses taught by first degree holders, although I have experience in teaching courses to Masters Students elsewhere successfully… Despite a wide range of journal article publications, the institution still keeps me at the lowest rank of academic staff (computer science lecturer in Sehoole et al., 2019: 225)

Apparent from these experiences is the treatment of diversity as something that could be achieved by changing human resource practices, rather than something connected with tackling structural inequalities in society (Deem & Morley, 2006). Appointing academics from diverse local or international backgrounds, does not mean that diversity at universities is internalised. In several contexts, it only means that human resource efforts have been made to diversify the pool of academics. The experiences of academics in this regard are often a (stressful and uncomfortable) matter of negotiating how much of themselves they can bring into faculty lounges, their classrooms, departmental meetings, or social gatherings (Davids, 2022).

In a study consisting mostly of 'white' women, Fielding-Singh et al. (2018) found that they employed 'intentional invisibility' when they avoided conflict with colleagues, softened their assertiveness with niceness, and 'got stuff done' by quietly moving things forward without drawing attention to themselves. Spivak with Hutnyk et al. (1990: 40) maintain that certain groups or individuals always have 'to cathect the margins so others can be defined as central'.

Standing on the margins, however, provides vantage points, which the centre often obscures. Not being in the centre, allows for distance and fewer expectations of participation and engagement. Marginality or liminality can be reconceived as positions for negotiation. In an interview with Bhatnagar et al. (1990: 72), Spivak responds:

> If there is anything I have learnt in and through the last 23 years of teaching, it is that the more vulnerable your position, the more you have to negotiate. We are not talking about discursive negotiations, or negotiation between equals, not even a collective bargaining. It seems to me that if you are in a position where you are, as you have said, being constituted by western liberalism, you have to negotiate to see what positive role you can play from within the constraints of western liberalism (which is a very broad term) breaking it open… it seems to me that is the most negotiated position, because you must intervene even as you inhabit those structures.

Following Spivak (with Bhatnagar et al., 1990), diverse academics, or those categorised as minority group academics might not be able to change the space of the university. But, by virtue of their appointments and presence, they are in the space of the university, regardless of their positioning in that space. These academics are in fact, not working from the outside. Negotiation, as Spivak contends, means trying to change something that one is obliged to inhabit. And this includes using the existing structures not only for the purpose of bringing into question binaries, hierarchies, and hegemonies, but also for propagation of other kinds of academic citizenship. The issue argues Bhambra (2014: 116), 'is more about re-inscribing 'other' cultural traditions into narratives of modernity and thus transforming those narratives—both in historical terms and theoretical ones—rather than simply renaming or re-evaluating the content of these other 'inheritances''.

5.4 Diversity and Dialogue

So, what does negotiation entail? What does it mean for academics in vulnerable positions to negotiate? Is there a chance that negotiation might increase their vulnerability, and if so, then, what next? Are vulnerable academics the only ones expected to negotiate? When Spivak (with Bhatnagar et al., 1990) refers to a negotiated position or the necessity of negotiation, what she has in mind is articulated dialogue. To her dialogue cannot be neutral, it cannot deny history and structure, or the positioning of subjects (such as academics). Negotiation, therefore, is not about relinquishing one's identity, thinking or being. It is also not an adversarial or antagonistic encounter.

My own experiences in the academy have taught me how to 'read the room', to know when to remain on the side in silence and when to emerge. My experiences have also taught me the importance of how much of myself I bring into a room, and how much I should leave outside. This is in itself is a negotiation, a sort of pre-negotiation to the negotiation which invariably accompanies the dialogue. Negotiation involves a willingness to engage and deliberate on the basis that once the parties involved know and understand more than what they initially do, they would both be in a better position to arrive at a decision or choice.

Negotiation is not contingent on agreement or consensus, rather it signals an indication that those involved are interested in listening what the other has to say. By engaging in dialogue academics begin to make sense of others as well as of themselves in relation to others. Bhambra (2014: 116–117) proffers that 'by bearing witness to different pasts one is not a passive observer but is able to turn from interrogating the past to initiating new dialogues about that past and thus bringing into being new histories and from those new histories, new presents and new futures.' In a somewhat strange coincidence, this unpacking of dialogue resonates very strongly with a desire or purpose of diversity—that is, to enter new understandings and relationships, with possibilities of forging new ways of being in the world. It would seem, therefore, that part of the reason diversity stagnates against the barriers of hegemonies and binaries, is because of an absence of dialogue.

Plato, as we might know, used dialogues to expound a form of dualism, where there is a world of ideal forms separate from the world of perception. And we might also know that often the way we 'see' others, our academic colleagues, is informed not by who they are, but by preconceived ideas of who we think or presume they are. At a time, and in a world where our lives are hyper-visualised, and when the influence of the image is often greater than the written text, states Cooke (2001), the physical, cultural and visual baggage we bring to conversation with others carry heavy weight. This baggage has the potential to distort and misrecognise how we see others (Taylor, 1994). It also has the potential to pre-decide whether we will engage with certain individuals or groups in the first place.

Moving towards dialogue, therefore, is a moment of vulnerability within itself. Dialogue relies on a willingness and openness for engagement, with the possibility that the other party might not reciprocate at all or might not respond in an equally open way. It seems logical to assume that the more academic citizenship diversifies, the deeper the curiosity about this diversity, and hence, a desire to get to know and understand. But, as has become apparent in this chapter, diversity can lead to bracketed professional identities and treatment, as well as marginalisation and discrimination. Dialogue holds the potential not only for a disruption of hegemonies and hierarchies, but for new and renewed understandings about academics, their identities, their values, and views. In this way, dialogue can enrich academics' knowledge about others, and so, too, their own knowledge of themselves and in relation to others. It is in and through the dialogical encounter that meaning is made between varying perspectives, but also how this meaning and knowledge finds its place in a bigger world.

The challenges which academics experience in professional settings, for example, are not limited to these settings, or play out in isolation from societal norms. The types of biases and stereotypes about certain academic group identities, emanates from the way in which the world is made. Racism or sexism is not confined to universities. The racism, sexism, xenophobia, or homophobia which certain academics experience among colleagues are often an extension of what they encounter in the supermarket, or residential neighbourhoods. African nationals who succeed in being appointed in South African universities often experience the same kind of inhospitality within universities spaces as they do in societal settings. These hindering and, at times, harmful and debilitating experiences can only be disrupted and used for opportunities of renewal if there is a willingness to listen and engage with others.

In the end, if universities conceive of their function and responsibility as knowledge production, then the arising questions are what knowledge and whose knowledge? Are there some knowledges that have been silenced because of the marked bodies which produce them? Are them some knowledges, which are assigned value and accepted uncritically, because of who has produced them? Dialogue holds the potential not only to foreground and break open these debates, but argues Santos (2007: 74), can also allow all of us 'to confront the problems of incommensurability, incompatibility, or reciprocal unintelligibility'. To this end, dialogue can provide a means and space for mutual understanding, questioning, as well as to produce knowledge of greater value and deeper meaning for a broader scope of society.

5.5 Key Considerations of Chapter

A central focus of this chapter has been to contest monolithic and presumptive understandings of diversity, as if the concept can ever include all forms of differences and as if it holds the same meaning and experience for all identities, categorised as diverse. Universities might have understandings of the importance of diversity in terms of their marketability and positioning themselves as an international space. In most instances, however, universities adopt a surface and representative approach to diversity—that is, by strategically placing or making visible certain diverse images. Paradoxically, therefore, although diversity holds the potential for a broadening of perspectives and lived experiences, the fact that it is framed in an all-encompassing language, means that this diversity is not only muted but retained in the margins of universities.

There are consequences for individual academics as there are for their citizenship. If diverse academics are not provided environments, where they enjoy equal inclusion and recognition, they struggle to see themselves as belonging to a collective academic citizenship. Instead, the kinds of citizenship relegated to them, tells them that they are not seen as bringing the same value as academics, who occupy the hegemonic centres of the university. There are reasons certain academics or universities might not want to disturb these hegemonic structures.

When academics hold onto preconceived ideas and perceptions of others, it allows them to hold onto certain narratives and structures, which often also means retaining their own place and privilege in the university. As a response to interrupting the status quo which keeps minority groups or diverse identities at bay, I considered the critical role of dialogue as a means of bringing academics into each other's presence, of finding meaning through engagement and deliberation, with the hope of producing different and more encompassing forms of knowledge.

References

Advance, H. E. (2018). Equality in higher education: Statistical report. https://www.advance-he.ac.uk/knowledge-hub/equality-higher-education-statistical-report-2018

Ahmed, S. (2004). Declarations of whiteness: The non-performativity of anti-racism. *Borderlands, 3*(2), 104–126.

Ahmed, S. (2012). *On being included: Racism and diversity in institutional life.* Duke University Press.

Ahmed, S., & Swan, E. (2006). Doing diversity. *Policy Futures in Education, 4*(2), 96–100.

Ahmed, S. (2007). A phenomenology of whiteness. *Feminist Theory, 8*(2), 149–168.

Banks, J. A. (2008). Diversity, group identity, and citizenship education in a global age. *Educational Researcher, 37*(3), 129–139.

Benschop, Y. (2001). Pride, prejudice and performance: Relations between HRM, diversity and performance. *International Journal of Human Resource Management, 12*(7), 1166–1181.

Bhambra, G. K. (2014). Postcolonial and decolonial dialogues. *Postcolonial Studies, 17*(2), 115–121.

Bhatnagar, R., Chatterjee, L., & Sunder, R. (1990). The postcolonial critic. In S. Harasym (Ed.), *The post-colonial critic: Interviews, strategies, dialogues: Gayatri Chakravorty Spivak* (pp. 67–74). New York: Routledge.

Bhopal, K. (2014). *The experience of BME academics in higher education: Aspirations in the face of inequality.* Leadership Foundation for Higher Education.

Bhopal, K., & Pitkin, C. (2020). 'Same old story, just a different policy': Race and policy making in higher education in the UK. *Race Ethnicity and Education, 23*(4), 530–547.

Clarence, S. (2019). Creating bigger rooms for different bodies and beings in academia. https://phdinahundredsteps.com/2019/08/26/creating-bigger-rooms-for-different-bodies-and-beings-in-academia/

Cooke, M. (2001). *Women claim Islam: Creating Islamic feminism through literature.* Routledge.

Davids, N., & Waghid, Y. (2022). *Democratic education as inclusion.* Rowman & Littlefield – Lexington Series.

Davids, N. (2022). *Out of place: An autoethnography of postcolonial citizenship.* African Minds.

Deem, R., & Morley, L. (2006). Diversity in the academy? Staff perceptions of equality policies in six contemporary higher education institutions. *Policy Futures in Education, 4*(2), 185–202.

Fielding-Singh, P., Devon, M., & Swethaa, B. (2018). Why women stay out of the spotlight at work. *Harvard Business Review.* https://hbr.org/2018/08/sgc-8-28-why-women-stay-out-of-the-spotlight-at-work

Gouws, A. (2007). Ways of being: Feminist activism and theorizing at the Global Feminist Dialogues in Porte Alegre, Brazil, 2005. *Journal of International Women's Studies, 8*(3), 28–36.

Hansen, D. J. (2022). A disconnect in diversity recruitment in higher education. https://www.higheredjobs.com/articles/articleDisplay.cfm?ID=3230

Holoien, D. S. (2012). *Do differences make a difference? The effects of diversity on learning, intergroup outcomes, and civic engagement.* www.princeton.edu/reports/2013/diversity

Hutnyk, J., McQuire, S., & Papastergiadis, N. (1990). Strategy, identity, writing. In S. Harasym (Ed.), *The post-colonial critic: interviews, strategies, dialogues: Gayatri Chakravorty Spivak* (pp. 67–74). New York: Routledge.

Johnson, L. N., & Thomas, K. M. (2012). A similar, marginal place in the academy contextualizing the leadership strategies of Black women in the United States and South Africa'. *Advances in Developing Human Resources, 14*(2), 156–171.

Jones, C. (2006). Falling between the cracks: What diversity means for black women in higher education. *Policy Futures in Education, 4*(2), 145–159.

McClure, K. R., & Fryar, A. H. (2022). The great faculty disengagement. https://www.chronicle.com/article/the-great-faculty-disengagement

McKinley, B., & Brayboy, J. (2003). The implementation of diversity in predominantly white colleges and universities. *Journal of Black Studies, 34*(1), 72–86.

Mirza, H. S. (2006). Transcendence over diversity: Black women in the academy. *Policy Futures in Education, 4*(2), 101–113.

Mohanty, C. T. (1990). On race and voice: Challenges for liberal education in the 1990s. *Cultural Critique, 14*, 179–208.

Naicker, L. (2013). The journey of South African women academics with a particular focus on women academics in theological education. *Studia Historiae Ecclesiasticae, 39*, 325–336.

Nunes, L. (2021). New directions for diversity, equity, and inclusion in higher education. https://www.psychologicalscience.org/observer/words-to-action

Peters, M. A. (2019). Interview with George Yancy, African-American philosopher of critical philosophy of race. *Educational Philosophy and Theory, 51*(7), 663–669.

Pherale, T. J. (2012). Academic mobility, language, and cultural capital: The experience of transnational academics in British higher education institutions. *Journal of Studies in International Education, 16*(4), 313–333.

Puwar, N. (2004). Fish in or out of Water: A theoretical framework for race and the space of academia. In I. Law, D. Phillips, & L. Turney (Eds.), *Institutional racism in higher education* (pp. 49–58). Trentham Books.

References

Santos, B. D. (2007). Beyond abyssal thinking: From global lines to ecologies of knowledges. *Review, 30*(1), 45–89.

Sehoole, C., Adeyemo, K. S., Ojo, E., & Phatlane, R. (2019). Academic mobility and the experiences of foreign staff at South African higher education institutions. *South African Journal of Higher Education, 33*(2), 212–229.

Spivak, G. C., Bhatnagar, R., Chatterjee, L., & Sunder, R. (1990a). The postcolonial critic. In S. Harasym (Ed.), *The post-colonial critic: Interviews, strategies, dialogues: Gayatri Chakravorty Spivak* (pp. 67–74). Routledge.

Spivak, G. C., Hutnyk, J., McQuire, S., & Papastergiadis, N. (1990b). Strategy, identity, writing. In S. Harasym (Ed.), *The post-colonial critic: Interviews, strategies, dialogues: Gayatri Chakravorty Spivak* (pp. 35–49). Routledge.

Taylor, C. (1994). *Multiculturalism: Examining the politics of recognition*. Princeton University Press.

Teichler. (2015). Academic mobility and migration: What we know and what we do not know. *European Review, 23*(1), 6–37.

Yancy, G. (2012). *Look, a white! Philosophical essays on whiteness*. Temple University Press.

Young, R. (2009). What is the postcolonial? *Ariel, 40*(1), 13–25.

Part II
Academic Citizenship, Knowledge, and Curiosity

Chapter 6
Academics as Embodiments of Knowledge

Academics do not only produce knowledge; they are also embodiments of knowledge. Who they are, is defined by what they perceivably embody, and represent. While some are seen to exemplify unquestionable qualification and capability, others are seen as less so, evoking an immediate binary between those who carry value and those who do not. To this end, universities are not empty spaces, waiting to be filled with the voices, teaching and research of academics. Their establishment is already embedded in historical, political, social, and epistemological milieus, as well as certain forms and looks of academic citizenship. Academic citizenship, therefore, is not only cultivated through appointments, discipline specialisations, but by knowledge economies which attach value to the citizenship of some academics, but not to others.

As such, it is necessary for academics to consider what they know, as well as how they have come to know what they know. This view might be implicit within conceptions of epistemology—as more than just a way of knowing, but also systems and processes of knowing that are linked to worldviews based on the conditions under which people live and learn (Ladson-Billings, 2000). The problem, however, specifically in South Africa, remains a predominance of Anglo-normative epistemologies, which often overshadow, or worse, misrepresent, or erase, other forms of knowledge production. What might academic citizenship do in cultivating an openness to different and competing forms of knowledge, so that new ways of looking at the world might come into play, and so that we can all come into the presence of one another?

6.1 Othering and Erasure

Every time new academics step into a university, faculty, or classroom, they bring with them new kinds of knowledge. Here, I am not only referring to a specific discipline or disciplines, but more specifically to the knowledge which resides in their identities and backgrounds. Significantly, although it is possible, and necessary at times, to discern between what can be described as professional knowledge and knowledge of the self (however uncertain this might be in some cases), academics' identities are often used in the weighing of their professional knowledge. Academics, therefore, do not enter the academy only as bearers of specialised knowledge and skills. Whatever knowledge they have is implicitly influenced by their lived experiences of the world. The knowledge which they have acquired through an external process of studying and attaining a qualification becomes intertwined with an internal knowledge of who they are.

My own understandings of education, and more specifically, philosophy of education, are profoundly shaped by my experiences of apartheid schooling. In one reflective glance I am taken back into a juxtaposed Grand Narrative of 'liberation before education', or 'education before liberation'—a narrative which seeped into my entire schooling career and would, in the end, frame not only my relationship with education, but what I see its objectives as being. Whatever knowledge I have is inherently shaped or mis-shaped by my lived experiences, or at least, those I remember. For some, experiences of othering and exclusion might be buried beyond the retrieval of immediate memory, perhaps due to trauma, perhaps due to conscious choice, and hence my comment that sometimes there is uncertainty about what we know or what we desire to know.

Regardless, the point remains, knowledge in whatever form, is context bound, and such, is always inclined towards perspectives and perceptions. Or as Santos (2007: 77), details, 'All knowledges are testimonies since what they know of reality (their active dimension) is always reflected back in what they reveal about the subject of this knowledge (their subjective dimension.' On the one hand, the inclusion of the subjective dimension brings a rich dimension to knowledge, and in the context of universities, for the teaching of this knowledge. The more knowledge can be diversified in relation to contexts, experiences, and worldviews, the wider the scopes and possibilities of accessibility and resonance for students, as well as academics.

On the other hand, foregrounding the subjective dimension can, of course, skew, the active dimension of what is known and what is taught—giving rise to questions, such as 'Is this really what happened, or is this how you remember it'. What parts of history is taught, for example, is dependent on what political story needs to be propagated. The way certain academics might choose to draw attention to certain arguments can be measured against those they wish to push to the side or mute.

There is yet another layer to the subjective dimension of knowledge, and that is the subjects themselves. Who the owners of knowledge are, is often used as a predeterminant of whether their knowledge is of any valuable or stems from qualification and competence. In this regard, the knowledge that some academics might have of their peers or students cannot only be misinformed, but harmful as well. In a peculiar construction of knowledge and power, explains Maldonado-Torres (2016: 19), the world is divided into 'zones of being and not-being human', establishing clear lines between who knowledge matters and should be appropriated and whose should be violated and discarded (Santos, 2007).

6.1 Othering and Erasure

Typically, there are expectations of diverse or minority group identities to adopt the practices of the dominant group. For those who fall into the 'zones of being', these practices are often natural extensions of how who they are, instilling seamless enactments of their identities. For those relegated to 'zones of not-being human', expectations and demands of assimilation can occur at profoundly foundational levels, such as the dismissal of academics' native language or mother-tongue. Instead, they are required to adopt foreign languages, teach in it, write in it, and make sense of their academic citizenship through it.

Certain bodies, observes Das (2007), become repositories of knowledge, not quite theirs to possess. On the other side of the line, states Santos (2007: 47), 'there is no real knowledge; there are beliefs, opinions, intuitive or subjective understandings, which, at the most, may become objects or raw materials for scientific enquiry.' As a result, it is not only that some academics are seen as 'not-being' or without value, but also whatever knowledge they produce is considered as 'nonexistent' and 'radically excluded because it lies beyond the realm of what the accepted conception of inclusion considers to be its other' (Santos, 2007: 46).

Apparent from Das (2007) and Santos (2007) is that when bodies are consigned to 'not-being human', they are not perceived as carrying any knowledge, or any worthwhile knowledge. Rather, the emptiness and devaluing of their bodies mean that they should be provided *with* knowledge, as encountered in colonial impositions of language, traditions, dress codes, education, and architecture. As Maldonado-Torres (2016: 10) explains, the concepts of colonialism and decolonisation are considered as ontic concepts that refer to specific empirical episodes of socio-historical and geopolitical conditions, and usually depicted as 'historical episodes … locked in the past, located elsewhere, or confined to specific empirical dimensions.' Importantly, however, colonialism is not 'locked in the past'; the political end of colonialism does not equate with its ideological conclusion.

Instead, says Maldonado-Torres (2007: 243), coloniality which survives colonialism, persists in long-standing patterns of power, defines culture, labour, intersubjectivity relations, and knowledge production well beyond the strict limits of colonial administrations. It is maintained alive in books, in the criteria for academic performance, in cultural patterns, in common sense, in the self-image of peoples, in aspirations of self, and so many other aspects of our modern experience (Davids, 2019).

Consider, for example, the ongoing struggle reclaiming and restoring indigenous languages and knowledges in South Africa. Although the country's transition to a democracy has included an official recognition of eleven languages, this recognition continues to enjoy a very lukewarm reception politically and educationally. The unequal recognition of the eleven languages, coupled with a privileging of Afrikaans, and more so, English, as mediums of instructions in basic and higher education, hold serious often underexplored implications for those academics and students who are excluded on the basis of language proficiency. Tensions in this regard arise and intersect from multiple points and academic communities.

On the one hand, is a seemingly theoretical drive for a cultivation of multilingual universities, which is often reduced to a visual acknowledgment of two or three official languages. Like diverse imagery, multilingualism often adopts symbolic representations on signboards, letterheads, or greetings. On the other hand, pressures of internationalisation and establishing universities as international research hubs, involves an inevitable capitulation to English in South Africa. For academic communities, who enjoyed the historical privileging of Afrikaans as a medium of instruction, the prioritisation of English is seen as an infringement of their identities, their culture, and a way of life.

Darder (2012) reminds us that the complexity of language and how students and academics produce knowledge and how language shapes their world represents a major pedagogical concern for all educational settings. For her, the language question intersects other social phenomena such as the question of authority, reframing equality, and social and cognitive justice. And hence, the current debate and tension at my university is not only about the gradual displacement of a language (Afrikaans), but a dismissal of a source and framework of knowledge.

Unequal exchanges among cultures (as exemplified in South Africa's colonisation by the Dutch and British), contends Santos (2014: 92), 'have always implied the death of the knowledge [epistemicide] of the subordinated culture, hence the death of subordinated groups that possessed it'. And hence, continues Santos (2014: 153), epistemicide 'is not an epistemological artefact without consequences. ... it involves the destruction of social practices and the disqualification of social agents that operate according to such knowledges.' Notably, the destruction of social practices, ways of thinking and being do not only unfold in the face of colonialism or as a consequence of policy shifts.

For academics, this destruction and disqualification can happen amid 'transformed' and 'democratised' spaces. This is because the same markers used to differentiate them as 'diverse' are also used to measure whether the knowledge they embody is of value or not. The knowledge that certain academics have of their peers, or their students is often not informed by what they know, but rather by what they think they know, or what they prefer to know. As such, knowledge of others precedes knowing them, reifying presumptive and distorted understandings of others.

6.2 Knowledge and Academic Citizenship

One of the key considerations in Chap. 5 was that for all the hard work seemingly be done to afford equal recognition to academics (and students) from diverse identities and backgrounds, there continues to be glaring blind-spots between what this hard work seeks to do and what is experienced in practice. Bhopal and Pitkin (2020: 542), for instance, points out in the UK context, policy making such as the REC 'exists within a framework of White privilege and a normative culture of Whiteness, which does not specifically address structural frameworks which disadvantage BME groups at all levels in HEIs'. It also seems that unless the harder work required to bring into contestation structural and systemic norms and hegemonies, diversity will not extend beyond surface portrayals.

If there is a serious stocktaking of the tension and irreconcilability between diversity as policy and diversity as lived, then it becomes necessary to turn to the knowledge systems which sustain hegemonic thinking and practices through a persistence of marginalising discourse. Certain academics might be prepared to accept the appointments of diverse colleagues in their departments or faculties, they might even be prepared to engage with their ethnic, cultural, or religious diversity, but, maintains Santos (2007), this does not necessarily signify recognition of the epistemological diversity in the world.

In turn, amid shifting complexities, foregrounding diverse appointments via affirmative action and employment equity policies, because of certain histories (as is the case in South Africa) can lead to historically advantaged academics and students feeling marginalised. Several ethnographic studies show how the authority of 'white' experiences can shift the focus away from the experiences of the marginalized and how 'white' students re-centre attention back onto their own experiences and feelings (Applebaum, 2008).

Cross (2004: 402) holds the view that although affirmative remedies are introduced in some institutions 'to redress disrespect by re-valuing unjustly devalued group identities and the group differentiations that underlie them', these remedies represent surface reallocations of respect to existing identities or existing groups. The main failure of affirmative remedies, continues Cross (2004: 402), is their inability to promote equity and social justice effectively; they tend generally to promote group differentiation; and 'can stigmatise the disadvantaged, adding the insult of misrecognition to the injury of deprivation.

One way of beginning to address the inherent complexities of diverse, pluralist, and multicultural academic citizenships, is to consider whether knowledge about citizenship education might play a role. In other words, how might knowledge about what it means to be a citizen in a democratic, pluralist space, assist academics to step out of what they think they know about themselves and others and into reconsidered ways of thinking, being, and acting. One of the important considerations in this regard is how academics conceive democracy, democratic practices, and encounters. South Africa's transition to a democracy created expectations that its citizens would not only embrace democratic forms of engagement, but that they would know what that means.

But of course, even in far more established democracies, what it means to act as a democratic citizen is not synonymous with the ideals of a democracy. Firstly, most people have certain understandings and perceptions about what a democratic society might constitute, but these understandings seldom extend into the individual's role in relation to creating that society. So, too, academics might have ideas about the importance of participation, inclusion, consultation, and deliberation as core features of a democratic faculty. They might even call out when they experience a lack of any of these features. But this awareness does not equate with a self-conscious role of an academic's own actions or dispositions.

Secondly, while a department or faculty might function along democratic guidelines of ensuring participation, consultation and debates, these functions do not necessarily guarantee a climate of equal recognition, inclusion, or mutual regard. For example, as Jackson (2019) notes, women academics are more likely to be recognised by supervisors for achievements that are service-oriented, such as administrative work and teaching, rather than research, and often women are expected to do equal research to men while taking on more service and teaching. This is a notable trend in our faculty, where women academics generally assume the roles of committee chairs, and administrative loads. Thirdly, while some academics might experience their faculties or universities as upholding democratic principles, this experience is not necessarily the case for all academics. Those who are already in the centre, and for whom the structures and systems work, might be oblivious to what happens to and for academics, standing on the periphery.

In sum, a democratic university will not be experienced as such by all academics and given the often-invisible power dynamics within democratic practices, particularly regarding inclusion and recognition, might never be experienced by some academics at all. And yet, knowledge of what it means *to be* and *act* democratically at an individual level, can orientate academics towards questioning their own role in the cultivation (or not) of their democratic academic space. A good starting point would be to acknowledge that living in a democratic state, or working in a university which functions along democratic premises, neither infers an understanding of these principles, nor that academics would conduct themselves as democratic citizens.

Hence, if academics acknowledge that their citizenship, in fact, does not pivot around democratic principles and actions, that cultivating a democratic university space is always in potentiality, that they should always be questioning existing structures and discourses, and consider alternative possibilities of engagement and collegiality, then they will realise that the employment of diverse academics into a purported democratic university space is insufficient to cultivate, let alone sustain a democratic academic citizenship. In this way, having knowledge of these paradoxes and tensions can assist in reimagining what it means to be an academic citizen, as well as what it means in deploying that citizenship in relation to students. So, too, having knowledge of how the world works will also assist academics in understanding that the differentiated enactments and experiences cannot be separated from society.

To Biesta (2009: 42), it is important to have knowledge about how societies are organised and the historical experiences of societies of the past: 'Political knowledge and understanding (qualification) can be an important element for the development of political ways of being and doing (subjectification)....' Academics are not only responsible for producing knowledge in relation to teaching, supervision or research. Academic citizenship carries a direct inter-relationship with students (young citizens), and relationships with colleagues, however these are defined. Both these sets of relationships, contextualised on one level within university settings, and on another, within societies, and the world, require that academics know themselves, others and the world. To this end, academics' knowledge production cannot be limited to, or contained by disciplinary parameters. Being an academic is as shaped by the complexities of disciplinary knowledge as it is by a knowledge of the world. I am reminded of Derrida's very lengthy entitled chapter, 'The future of the profession or the university without condition (thanks to the "Humanities," what could take place tomorrow)' (Cohen, 2001: 25) in which he states.

> But whether these discussions are critical or deconstructive, everything that concerns the question and the history of truth, in its relation to the question of man, of what is proper to man, of human rights, of crimes against humanity, and so forth, all of this must in principle find its space of discussion without condition and without presupposition, its legitimate space of research and re-elaboration, in the University and, within the University, above all in the Humanities. Not so that it may enclose itself there, but on the contrary so as to find the best access to a new public space transformed by new techniques of communication, information, archivization, and knowledge production.

Following Derrida, academics should not only be producing knowledge for the sake of advancing their scholarship. Being an academic citizen includes actively advancing the unconditionality of the university—that is, 'an unconditional freedom to question and to assert, or even, going still further, the right to say publicly all that is required by research, knowledge, and thought concerning the truth' (Cohen, 2001: 24). In this way, academic citizenship extends beyond the confines of university walls and structures and recognises the critical role of knowledge in responding modern day controversies, injustices and dystopias. There are endless direct correlations between what happens behind university walls and what happens outside.

The rising incidents of xenophobia in South Africa, for example, holds implications for the appointments and experiences of specifically African foreign academics at South African universities (Obadire, 2018). On the one hand, having knowledge of how this plays out in civic society, and what this means for academics contributes to the knowledge of academic citizenship. On the other hand, if academics recognise their responsibilities in relation to the unconditionality of the university, then the knowledge which they produce should also be responsive in the face of any injustice.

6.3 Knowledge as Embodiment

How academics define themselves is influenced by the kinds of knowledge they produce and how they locate that knowledge. Some academics might prefer to focus their research production on local questions and concerns. They might also prioritise their responsibilities to their home-university, rather than seeking out international networks. Others, who Merton (1947) describes as 'cosmopolitans' are often more closely connected with members of their disciplinary community outside their institution and are more likely to prioritise research. Reasons for how and why different academics locate themselves on the local to international continuum vary. For some it is a conscious decision, or it can be matter of chance of working in collaborative projects, while for other academics it unfolds gradually as they migrate from one university to another.

Regardless of how academics define themselves, they share a common understanding of producing knowledge. The knowledge they produce holds particular meanings for them. Santos (2007) holds that there is no knowledge that is not known by someone for some purpose; all forms of knowledge uphold practices and constitute subjects.

Academics, as former students, would consciously have chosen disciplinary pathways, which they believe, would potentially define them as academics or professionals. For some this might happen serendipitously, as in being included in a particular project, or having an affinity with a supervisor. For others, it can be driven by a committed interest or passion, as in working with issues of social or gender justice because of specific experiences. Regardless of not having all the necessary knowledge or skills for particular subject areas or disciplines, whether it involves becoming a philosopher of education, a nephrologist or chemical engineer, the aspirant student or early career academic would already have some idea of what this entails, and initially, at least, says Dall 'Alba (2009), underpin their becoming.

Students seeking to become teachers, for example, often come into teacher education programmes with impressions of what kind of teacher they would like to become, based on their schooling experiences with certain teachers. They often also have a clear sense of what kind of teacher they would *not* like to become, based on these same experiences. As they are taken through various modules and encounter various lecturers or teachers, they not only witness different pedagogies, teaching styles and personalities, but they are provided with the knowledge of how to make sense of these differences. As some of them progress into postgraduate studies, they might begin to align themselves more strongly with some teaching styles and teacher identities than others, and as such begin to transition into becoming a teaching professional.

Importantly, however, learning to become a professional, explains, Dall'Alba (2009: 34), 'involves not only what we know and can do, but also who we are (becoming). It involves integration of knowing, acting, and being in the form of professional ways of being that unfold over time.' She elaborates that when aspirant professionals enter a profession, the practices they learn to embody have their own routines, histories, and traditions. For early career academics this might involve being initiated into communities of practice, attending, and presenting at specific conferences, joining societies, and publishing in key journals related to the discipline. There is an immersion that happens, which is separate to merely acquiring knowledge or skills within a specialisation. Something happens to some academics as they transition from student to early career and then senior academics in that they gradually adopt the language and thinking, so that they embody their specialisations.

To Dall 'Alba (2009), becoming a professional involves transformation of the self through embodying the routines and traditions of the profession in question, although this is not straightforward. At the same time, the traditions of which academics are a part tend to be taken for granted and are not always transparent to them (Dall 'Alba, 2009). Yet, as they move through the trajectory of becoming academics, they do not only produce knowledge, but they become embodiments of knowledge, and hence, are always situated within their professional identities (Davids, 2022).

Embodied knowledge, explains Ellingson (2008: 246):

6.3 Knowledge as Embodiment

> [S]ituates intellectual and theoretical insights within the realm of the material world. Embodied knowledge is sensory; it highlights smell, touch, and taste as well as more commonly noted sights and sounds. Knowledge grounded in bodily experience encompasses uncertainty, ambiguity, and messiness in everyday life, eschewing sanitized detached measurement of discrete variables. Such an epistemology, or way of knowing, resists the Cartesian mind–body split that underlies Enlightenment philosophy and its persistent remnants, including the scientific method and the glorification of objectivity. Embodied knowledge is inherently and unapologetically subjective, celebrating—rather than glossing over—the complexities of knowledge production. Fieldwork, interviewing, writing, and other qualitative methods involve embodied practices performed by actors occupying specific standpoints or positions within cultures. The researcher's body—where it is positioned, what it looks like, what social groups or classifications it is perceived as belonging to—matters deeply in knowledge formation.

Following Ellingson (2008), researchers or academics are always subjectively present in what they investigate, explore, teach, and write. This book, for example, is bring written because of my own experiences as an academic. I do not come to the topic of academic citizenship objectively or neutrally. Sometimes I see myself as comfortably located on the periphery of this citizenship. I recognise that a movement to the centre might never be possible, or if it is, I would need to lose too much of myself. Other times, the constant negotiation becomes exhausting, forcing me to detach myself entirely—even if it is possible only for a while in my head. So, I can try to make every effort to present nuanced arguments so that the book eventually reflects engagement with diverse opinions, but fundamentally, my embodied experiences and knowledge of being an academic steer the book and what I choose to critique. Embodied knowledge, therefore, is not only knowledge that resides in the body, but also knowledge that is gained through the body (Nagatomo, 1992).

Inevitably, different bodies gain and are subjected to different kinds of knowledge, with, as previously discussed in Chap. 5, 'some bodies become understood as the rightful occupants of certain spaces' Ahmed (2012: 2). And inevitably, the academic's body, what it looks like, the social groups it is perceived to belong, and this intersects with gender, sexuality, religion, and ethnicity, influences the kind of the knowledge produced. As such, intersectionality takes account of the converging ways in which the differentiated and variable organising logics of race, class and gender and other social divisions, structure the material conditions which produce economic, social, political inequality as well as academic inequality (Mirza, 2013).

Hence, on the one hand, research interests are often influenced by academics' interests and lived experiences, assigning often unexplored complexities to the subjectivity of knowledge production. giving knowledge an implicit subjective. On the other hand, knowledge is transferred onto academics' bodies, based on who they are and how they are classified. The interweaving of knowledge as embodied experiences can create both opportunities and barriers.

When academics experience marginalisation or unfair treatment based on their bodies, and not on the knowledge they have or skills they bring, they experience an imposition of unwelcome knowledge, which invariably alters the way they believe they should think and act. For example, highlighting the concern of gendered Islamophobia, Akel (2021) found that religious garments such as the niqab or hijab have been weaponised and politicised as tools. Her study revealed that 29% of Muslim students at the London Metropolitan University have had to defend their right to wear religious garments against those who harbour prejudicial views; 15.7% of Muslim women reported feeling unsafe wearing religious garments, some of whom have been physically or verbally assaulted:

> I took it [Hijab] off, and as horrible and disheartening as it is, I'm more comfortable and have had more pleasant interactions whilst [not] wearing a scarf... I would like to wear it again but for the time being, it's much safer without it. Especially with the media labelling Muslims as terrorists' (Akel, 2021: 40)

For academics, explains Akel (2021), exclusion based on their identity can have negative repercussions in terms of how this can become internalised—that is, how they act or present themselves. According to Akel, 23% of staff at the London Metropolitan University reported that they had modified or considered modifying their appearance in relation to their religious identity in order to avoid prejudicial treatment. In turn, another respondent described how they had witnessed Muslim staff members getting 'side-lined' due to 'not fitting in', which have consequences for their career progression and experiences of a demoralised academic citizenship, which can lead to their eventual departure from the institution (Akel, 2021).

Muslim students and academics are not unique in their experiences of ostracism. Marcus (2016: 348) notes that 'as Jews in North America enjoy unprecedented tolerance in most other institutions, the university has become, at best, a signal exception to benign social trends and at worst, the platform from which the forces of antisemitism are staging their return.' Abrams (2022), a Jewish professor at Linfield University in the USA, shares:

> Antisemitism on campus is not new or rare... As an outwardly observant Jew who celebrates Jewish festivals and traditions and also publicly supports Israel even when I deeply disagree with its government, I find faculty colleagues feel comfortable attacking Israel and me without worry. My professorial peers habitually make deeply insensitive and inappropriate remarks to me and regularly assert that Israel is an illegitimate, genocidal, and apartheid state. I have found Nazi imagery on my office door over the years and have been told to make no real issue of it.

As for the inter-relationship between academics and students, Akel (2021) reports that despite the existence of codes of conduct which govern academic settings, certain forms of discrimination have to an extent become normalised in academic spaces, as reported by 17% of academic staff who had been discriminated against or targeted by a student in relation to their religious identity.

Concomitantly, when certain bodies are perceived to be knowledgeable based on what their bodies present, there are also implications for how and what kinds of knowledge are produced. Associations of 'being right' with 'being white' (Friderer, 2015), suggest that whiteness is conflated with qualification and competence. It is also implies that 'white' academics are perceived as more competent and trustworthy than their colleagues of colour and receive better treatment and reviews from their learners (Jenkins, 2016). According to Jenkins (2016) because 'white' academics educators see themselves, their cultural values, and Eurocentric theoretical frameworks represented in their curriculum and do not have to consider or teach different cultural paradigms.

6.4 Academic Citizenship as Activism

Dall 'Alba and Barnacle (2007: 685) maintain that 'knowing is always situated within a personal, social, historical and cultural setting, and thus transforms from the merely intellectual to something inhabited and enacted: a way of thinking, making and acting. Indeed, a way of being'. Implicit within their argument is the idea that knowledge has to translate into action or activism—that is, that academics need to act in relation to what they know, they need to enact their responsibilities as academics by being responsive to dilemmas or crises both within and beyond the confines of the university. Having knowledge and being educated, says Mannheim (1991), enables intellectuals or academics to grasp the entirety of the social and political structure and adopt a broader point of view (Mannheim, 1991).

Academics are equipped to face the problems of the day in several perspectives and cannot or should not attempt to lay claim to neutrality in the face of being confronted by whatever dystopia. Being educated means being responsible and accountable. For Giroux (2019), a defence of neutrality 'hides its code for not allowing people to understand the role that education plays ideologically, in producing particular forms of knowledge, of power, of social values, of agency, of narratives about the world…' Teaching, that purports to be neutral, contends Hytten (2017), is teaching that supports the status quo; that reproduces the social order rather than seeking to challenge, disrupt, or transform it.

Academic activism involves a critical awareness of how the world functions, and the role that higher education can play in disrupting those functions, which propagate injustice. To Barnett (2021), academic work is not in itself a form of activism. Rather, 'the concept of activism gains traction where academic work is intentionally contending against an unfair or unjust situation. It has its place within a space that is contoured by what is seen as an illegitimate use of power of some kind. The activism has an *effect* of some kind in the public sphere' (Barnett, 2021: 522). In this way, academic activism 'is a form of rupturing that brings into play notions of dissent, scepticism and change agency' (Davids & Waghid, 2021: 12).

To have knowledge and to be educated, argues Giroux (2019), is about the production of agency, so that both academics and students can enlarge their perspectives, not only on the world but on their relationship to others and themselves. On the one hand, explain Flood et al. (2013), universities can be sites for activism to produce knowledge to inform progressive social change; as a means for conducting research, which involves social change; as a site for progressive strategies of teaching and learning; and as institutions whose power relations themselves may be challenged and reconstructed. Hence, the very idea, structure and system of the university lends itself to questioning, resisting countering, inventing, producing and reimagining without fear. Such an unconditional thesis, contends Derrida:

> [C]ould oppose the university to a great number of powers, for example to state powers (and thus to the power of the nation-state and to its phantasm of indivisible sovereignty, which indicates how the university might be in advance not just cosmopolitan, but universal, extending beyond worldwide citizenship and the nation-state in general), to economic powers (to corporations and to national and international capital), to the powers of the media, ideological, religious, and cultural powers, and so forth – in short, to all the powers that limit democracy to come. The university should thus also be the place in which nothing is beyond question, not even the current and determined figure of democracy, and not even the traditional idea of critique, meaning theoretical critique, and not even the authority of the "question" form, of thinking as "questioning." (Cohen, 2001: 26).

On the other hand, each time academics write a paper or step into a classroom to teach, they would have already adopted a particular ideological or political stance. Who they are, how they think, what they believe or devalue, is already implicit in their speech or text—whether they are conscious of this or not. When academics ask students to think critically about the world, to unpack their assumptions, to consider alternative viewpoints, to construct careful arguments, and to defend their perspectives, explains Hytten (2017: 387), this is a form of activism. To hooks (1994), teachers or academics are meant to serve as a catalyst that calls everyone to become more and more engaged and to become active participants in their learning. This is done not only through pedagogical choices and practices, but through the choices of texts, contents, and perhaps, most importantly, what academics see the purpose of education as being.

Now, of course, it might be the case, that for many academics, what, why and how they teach is not really a point of consideration. Teaching is just another responsibility, practised in designated time-table slots. But, of course, even this kind of passivity or disinterest embodies a subjective and political perspective on knowledge and education. In terms of research and writing, whether intentional or not, academics may produce knowledge that informs progressive social change (Flood et al., 2013). Academics may have an explicit social transformation agenda, engage in activities, and contribute to policy debates and political change. Others may use their research in support of community-based social or economic projects—at times, referred to as 'engaged scholarship' or 'research for social impact', as well as 'scholar activism'. Certain universities might acknowledge 'engaged scholarship' through their policies, or explicitly state that they value 'community activism' (June, 2015).

For academics to acknowledge the reproductive role of education in reproducing norms, which often perpetuate inequalities and othering, requires them to shift from merely *doing* academic work to being actively aware of what academic work *does* and can *do*. For some, there is no need to do this, especially when they conceive of academic citizenship as a set of roles and responsibilities, rather than a reflection of who they are. For others, the necessity and importance of academic activism is inherent to who they are, their values and what they stand for. This could be for any number of reasons centred on matters of justice, whether this involves social, gender, racial, health, or climate justice. Their academic activism is seen as a natural extension of their identities, histories, or positions in a community. They might even engage in activism not directly related to their paid work, outside working hours and off campus, which can provide an income and security that can help sustain activism (Flood et al., 2013).

This is not to say, however, that all academics, who might have been privy to some sort of injustice would necessarily embark on academic activism roles or see their work as embodying an activist agenda. For some, quiet diplomacy is a preferred form of academic citizenship, especially when there are risks tied to activism. On one level, this might involve concerns about securing tenure and professional security. Linked to this, is the additional concern of balancing academic responsibilities and expectations necessary for tenure or promotion with the commitment required by activism. Academics recognise that despite their apparent allegiances to academic freedom, most universities do not take kindly to criticism from their employees. There are repercussions in terms of promotions, opportunities, and rewards.

On another level, the risks are a lot more profound and far-reaching. Flood et al. (2013) explain that academics who engage in activism may face reprisals, both externally from political opponents and internally from those within the university who perceive their involvement as nonconformist. Internally, continue Flood et al. (2013), both academic peers and students may perceive activist academics as violating their appropriate roles, with students for example complaining that their lecturers teach 'propaganda' or that campus diversity initiatives are 'biased'. In certain contexts, academic freedom is not guaranteed. Universities, and by implication, academics, are subjected to regulatory interference in the governance of higher education institutions, retaliatory discharge of researchers or students, arrests of students or university personnel or more severe infringements of their physical integrity, as well as safety (Saliba, 2018).

In turn, state Flood et al. (2013), attacks by external opponents are often politically motivated, intended to silence academics and thwart their political impact. Attacks by outsiders can include sending hate mail, making threats of violence, sending complaints to employers seeking reprimands or dismissal and complaints to funding agencies seeking termination of funding, and vilification on websites and in e-newsletters (Flood et al., 2013).

In sum, academic activism is fluid not only in terms of how it is enacted in practice or policy, but it is also flexible in how academics adopt it, and indeed, whether at all. In some instances, academic identities play a significant role in an inseparability between academic citizenship and activism. In other cases, academic citizenship does not extend beyond a requisite set of performance criteria.

6.5 Key Considerations of Chapter

Most universities in the world position and market themselves as democratic spaces of inclusivity and equal recognition. Implicit within this language, readily available in policies, are presumptions about academic citizenship in relation to cultivating universities as democratic spaces. Quite simply: can we assume that all academics understand what it means to be and act democratically, and can we assume that they are all interested in wanting a democratic university. The answer, equally simply, is no. Not only are academics often unaware of what it means to engage democratically with colleagues and students, but their own worldviews and values might be decidedly undemocratic. The chapter, therefore, attends to the knowledge and responsibility of academic citizenship in advancing a democratic ethos, by arguing that it is not enough for academics to only have knowledge about the discipline.

Rather, because of the inherent social responsibility of universities, academic citizenship must reveal a consciousness of the world in which their teaching and research are located. Knowledge has to translate into action or activism—that is, that academics need to act in relation to what they know, they need to enact their responsibilities as academics by being responsive to dilemmas or crises both within and beyond the confines of the university. Academic citizenship involves a citizenship which extends beyond the walls of the university, and this responsibility must be made explicit in how academics teach, act, respond and prepare students for the world around them.

References

Abrams, S. J. (2022) Antisemitism is a problem in academia. Quitting is not the solution. https://www.aei.org/op-eds/antisemitism-is-a-problem-in-academia-quitting-is-not-the-solution/

Ahmed, S. (2012). *On being included: Racism and diversity in institutional life*. Duke University Press.

Akel, S. (2021). *Institutionalised: The rise of Islamophobia in higher education*. Project Report. London Metropolitan University.

Applebaum, B. (2008). 'Doesn't my experience count?' white students, the authority of experience and social justice pedagogy. *Race, Ethnicity and Education, 11*(4), 405–414.

Barnett, R. (2021). The activist university: Identities, profiles, conditions. *Policy Futures in Education, 19*(5), 513–526.

Bhopal, K., & Pitkin, C. (2020). 'Same old story, just a different policy': Race and policy making in higher education in the UK. *Race Ethnicity and Education, 23*(4), 530–547.

Biesta, G. (2009). Good education in an age of measurement: On the need to reconnect with the question of purpose in education. *Educational Assessment, Evaluation and Accountability, 21*(1), 33–46.

Cohen, T. (2001). *Jacques Derrida and the humanities: A critical reader*. Cambridge University Press.

Cross, M. (2004). Institutionalising campus diversity in South African higher education: Review of diversity scholarship and diversity education. *Higher Education, 47*, 387–410.

Dall'Alba, G., & Barnacle, R. (2007). An ontological turn for higher education. *Studies in Higher Education, 32*(6), 679–691.

Dall'Alba, G. (2009). Learning professional ways of being: Ambiguities of becoming. *Educational Philosophy and Theory, 41*(1), 34–45.

Darder, A. (2012). *Culture and power in the classrooms: Educational foundations for the schooling of bicultural studies*. Paradigm.

Das, V. (2007). *Life and words: Violence and the descent into the ordinary*. University of California Press.

References

Davids, N. (2019). Love in the time of decoloniality. *Alternation, 24*, 101–121.
Davids, N. (2022). Professing the vulnerabilities of academic citizenship. *Ethics and Education, 17*(1), 1–13.
Davids, N., & Waghid, Y. (2021). *Academic activism in higher education: A living philosophy for social justice*. Springer.
Ellingson, L. L. (2008). Embodied knowledge. In L. M. Given (Ed.), *The SAGE Encyclopedia of qualitative research methods* (pp. 245–247). SAGE Publications.
Flood, M., Martin, B., & Dreher, T. (2013). Combining academia and activism. *Australian Universities' Review, 55*(1), 17–26.
Frideres, J. (2015). Being white and being right. In D. E. Lund & P. R. Carr (Eds.), *The great white north?* (pp. 43–53). Sense Publishers.
Giroux, H. (2019). Those arguing that education should be neutral are really arguing for a version of education in which nobody is accountable. https://lab.cccb.org/en/henry-giroux-those-arguing-that-education-should-be-neutral-are-really-arguing-for-a-version-of-education-in-which-nobody-is-accountable/
Hooks, B. (1994). *Teaching to transgress*. Routledge.
Hytten, K. (2017). Teaching as and for activism: Challenges and possibilities. *Philosophy of Education, 2014*, 385–394.
Jackson, L. (2019). The smiling philosopher: Emotional labor, gender, and harassment in conference spaces. *Educational Philosophy and Theory, 51*(7), 693–701.
Jenkins, C. (2016). Addressing white privilege in higher education. *Academic Exchange Quarterly, 20*(4), 121–126.
June, A. W. (2015). When activism is worth the risk. https://www.chronicle.com/article/when-activism-is-worth-the-risk/?cid=gen_sign_in
Ladson-Billings, G. (2000). Racialized discourses and ethnic epistemologies. In N. K. Denzin & Y. S. Lincoln (Eds.), *Handbook of qualitative research* (pp. 257–277). Sage.
Maldonado-Torres, N. (2007). On coloniality of being. *Cultural Studies, 21*(2), 240–270.
Maldonado-Torres, N. (2016) Outline of ten theses on coloniality and decoloniality. Foundation Frantz Fanon. Available at: http://frantzfanonfoundation-fondationfrantzfanon.com/article2360.html
Mannheim, K. (1991). *Ideology and utopia*. London: Routledge.
Markus, K. L. (2016). Antisemitism in North American higher education. In S. K. Baum, N. J. Kressel, F. Cohen & S. L. Jacobs (Eds.), *Antisemitism in North America: New world, old hate* (pp. 348–373). Brill.
Merton, R. K. (1947). Patterns of influence: Local and cosmopolitan influentials. In R. K. Merton (Ed.), *Social theory and social structure* (pp. 387–420). The Free Press.
Mirza, H. S. (2013). 'A second skin': Embodied intersectionality, transnationalism and narratives of identity and belonging among Muslim women in Britain. *Women's Studies International Forum, 36*, 5–15.
Nagatomo, S. (1992). An Eastern concept of the body: Yuasa's body scheme. In M. Sheets-Johnstone (Ed.), *Giving the body its due* (pp. 11, 233). State University of New York Press.
Obadire, O. S. (2018). Towards a sustainable anti-xenophobic rural-based university campus in South Africa. *South African Journal of Higher Education, 32*(4), 186–198.
Saliba, I. (2018). Academic freedom in the MENA region: Universities under siege. In *IEMed mediterranean yearbook* (pp. 313–316).
Santos, B. D. (2007). Beyond abyssal thinking: From global lines to ecologies of knowledges. *Review, 30*(1), 45–89.
Santos, B. S. (2014). *Epistemologies from the South*. Paradigm.

Chapter 7
Academic Citizenship as Curiosity

Unless academics recognise that they lack certain forms of knowledge, or that what they know might not be all there is to know on a particular subject, there can be no curiosity, and hence, no new forms of knowledge. Similarly, unless academics have a desire to engage with those with whom they are unfamiliar, there can be no awareness of different social realities and perspectives. The silo-effect of South Africa's apartheid continues to permeate the constructions of relationships among academics. It is not uncommon for some academics only to interact in formal meeting settings, followed by mere nods in corridors. This is not argument for friendships which extend into social events outside of the academy. This is an argument for a citizenship, which recognises its historical distortions, and takes seriously the necessity to learn and to know about others.

There must be a curiosity about who academics are, what they bring, and how they add to the epistemological foundations of the university, not only in terms of what they produce, but in what they contribute as embodiments of knowledge. The stoic quality of the academy often unfolds in misplaced understandings of detachment from colleagues and collegiality. Academics lose sight of the possibility and necessity of learning *from* and *with* the other. What are the implications for academic citizenship when colleagues or co-workers remain unknowable? What might be gained from an academic citizenship, which recognises the embodied knowledges of academics, and is motivated by a curiosity of and for the other?

7.1 Why Curiosity Matters

One of the major criticisms levelled against schooling is that so much of it stifles young people's natural curiosity. So much time and energy are spent on enforcing regulated conduct and thinking, strict dress codes and classroom complacency, that any attempts at evoking curiosity by the few teachers who still try to do so, is rightfully met with learners' confusion as to what this actually means. Unsurprising, therefore, that by the time these same learners enter higher education institutions, they would have been so worn down by a system of uniformity that most of them would have lost any inclination towards curiosity, even when begged to awaken it by some academics. For reasons tied to schooling as an uncreative and unimaginative experience of compliance, directed at meeting sets of predetermined learning outcomes, curiosity seems to become a metaphorical soccer ball, kicked about when it is desired, and kicked away when not.

Universities often play the same game. Students are invited to think critically, ask questions, step out of boxes and into radical thinking, to be curious about the world, yet the teaching they typically encounter is devoid of any pedagogical openness to do so. Seemingly, inasmuch as curiosity is considered a desirable and valuable quality, not enough attention is devoted to nurture or enhance it. It helps, therefore, to commence this chapter to explore what curiosity is, why it exists, how it manifests and why, despite its compelling potentialities, it slips beneath the radar of academic citizenship.

> 'Helter skelter, hang sorrow, care'll kill a cat, up-tails all, and a louse for the hangman.'

This is a line from English playwright, Ben Jonson's comedy, 'Every man in his humour' (1598). The original 'care killed the cat' morphed into 'curiosity killed the cat'. The popular meaning of this idiomatic expression is that being curious or inquisitive can get one into trouble. Coincidentally, linguistically, curiosity is rooted in the other, regarding activities of 'care' and 'cure' (from the Latin cūrāre, to take care of) (Baumgarten, 2001). Although there can be a relationship between curiosity and care, this does not imply, however, that if individuals are curious about others, they also have to care about them (Baumgarten, 2001). I cannot be sure of the reach of the popularity of this idiom and the extent to which it might have impacted upon a general frowning on curiosity.

Certainly, however, it is evident across some cultures that being curious and asking questions about matters that perceivably does not concern one, is considered impolite and hence discouraged. We might agree that indeed in some settings asking certain questions, whether about private or political matters, might be considered as meddlesome or troublesome, or even a form of gossip mongering. This probably explains Foucault's (1988: 328) contention that 'curiosity is a vice that has been stigmatized in turn by Christianity, by philosophy, and even by a certain conception of science. Curiosity is seen as futility'. But this is not the curiosity I have in mind in this chapter. Instead, my interest is in a motivation of curiosity as a natural human disposition, that while we might be indifferent about some matters, we also have the capacity to wonder about the world around us. By seeking understanding on these matters, or on people, curiosity can be framed as an epistemic good.

Following Hume's (1986) expositions on curiosity as a 'love of truth', the concept of curiosity has undergone a metamorphosis from being considered a vice to something morally neutral, positive, a healthy passion, and most recently, an admirable character trait (Gelfert, 2013). At various points during this mutation, elaborates

7.1 Why Curiosity Matters

Gelfert (2013), it was suggested that the epistemic function of curiosity had been partially made redundant by science—that the growth of knowledge would be served best by the well-organized collective endeavour of science, as opposed to the curious whims of individuals.

For most, curiosity is aroused once there a desire to know—that is, once individuals realise either that they do not have any information or knowledge on a topic or someone else, or that that they have some knowledge or understanding but need to know more. Markey and Loewenstein (2014), explain that the gap between what is known and not known can be triggered by varieties of stimuli, such as hearing snippets of a conversation at an adjoining table in a restaurant, or, somewhat trivially, being asked a question to which one does not know the answer. In terms of the information gap account, continue Markey and Lowenstein (2014), curiosity arises when an individual's attention is drawn to a potential state of knowledge different from, and specifically greater than, their current state. The information gap, therefore, is the difference between an individual's current state of knowledge and a salient alternative state of knowledge (Markey & Loewenstein, 2014).

While Markey and Loewenstein (2014) offer us a psychological understanding as to why curiosity arises, Baumgarten (2001) draws our attention to the different formations, which curiosity might take, making it difficult to classify. As a character trait, says Baumgarten (2001), curiosity is a disposition to want to know or learn more about a wide variety of things. The more one has this character trait, the more often or the more intensely one will on particular occasions experience a desire or urge to investigate and learn more about something (Baumgarten, 2001). To this end, firstly, 'curiosity as a desire involves choice and judgment, the choice to select some things rather than others as objects for investigation and the judgment that something is worth investigating' (Baumgarten, 2001: 170).

Secondly, different people have varying capacities for curiosity. And thirdly, a person who experiences curiosity about something may or may not act on the desire which the curiosity arouses (Baumgarten, 2001). Baumgarten (2001) draws a distinction between curiosity and attentiveness or 'taking an interest'. To be interested is to care to know—that is, that it matters to individuals to know about something. For example, it matters to know if students have certain learning barriers, which might prevent from them actively completing certain tasks or assessments.

The virtuously curious individual, states Watson (2018: 295), 'is characteristically motivated to acquire worthwhile epistemic goods that she believes she lacks.' As such, firstly this individual is motivated to acquire epistemic goods, she values epistemic goods, and she demonstrates this by being motivated to acquire them (Watson, 2018). Secondly, she recognises that she lacks the epistemic goods about which she is curious (Watson, 2018). An academic, for example, might recognise that she struggles to connect with a doctoral student because of cultural differences. She recognises that this knowledge gap about the background of the student hampers the supervision process, and hence, has a desire to want to know more about the student's cultural identity and traditions so that she might cultivate an improved supervision process. And thirdly, the individual is motivated to acquire worthwhile epistemic goods, as opposed to trivial or insignificant goods (Watson, 2018).

Notably, explains Watson (2018), the latter condition does not demand that the virtuously curious person must acquire worthwhile epistemic goods, but rather, that the epistemic goods she is motivated to acquire must be worthwhile. In this way, 'It is the virtuously curious person's skilful identification of worthwhile epistemic goods that renders her curiosity virtuous. The virtuously curious person is characteristically motivated to acquire worthwhile epistemic goods that she lacks, or believes that she lacks' (Watson, 2018: 297).

For example, academics might be curious about the extent to which language proficiency impacts upon student's confidence to participate in class discussions. This curiosity might include trying to get an idea of students' mother tongue languages, and how certain concepts might differ in the academic space. As a pertinent example, a few years ago I was involved in running a Philosophy for Teachers (P4T) residential workshop in South Africa (Orchard & Davids, 2019). The workshop brought together twelve pre-service teachers from three higher education institutions in South Africa. The workshop generated and nurtured substantive dialogue around ethics and ethical conduct in teaching, but it also highlighted the necessity of clarifying the interpretation of concepts, such as ethics, ethical judgment, respect, care, and recognition, expressed in English (Orchard & Davids, 2019). In a country, which is home to eleven official languages, this is an especially pertinent issue.

In the workshop, participants offered different understandings of what it means to act ethically: some understood it as 'being good' and 'acting with integrity', while others tied the concept to 'religious beliefs', and 'childhood rearing'. In turn, certain participants disagreed about the interpretation of concepts, such as respect and compassion, revealing cultural beliefs and practices. Those who subscribe to the Xhosa and Afrikaner cultures, for example, interpreted notions of respect as being associated with patriarchy and age, and more specifically, with males and elder. Also, Xhosa students understood compassion as being synonymous with ubuntu—that is, recognising the humanity of the other (Orchard & Davids, 2019). These interpretations added a rich dimension to the workshop, but more importantly, it alerted the workshop facilitators and the participants to the importance of desiring to know about the social constructions and realities of others. This is why Baumgarten (2001) maintains that unlike attentiveness or 'taking an interest' curiosity involves a greater exercise of autonomy.

To Baumgarten (2001), what the attentive and interested person learns depends on what the world presents to her whereas the curious person raises questions that go beyond what it is possible to be attentive to. Although it does not always involve asking explicit questions, curiosity implies a questioning spirit of observation that goes beyond mere attentiveness. Unlike an attentive person, who might not experience an unfulfilled desire, explains Baumgarten (2001), a curious person will experience a lack before the desire for a particular kind of knowledge is satisfied. This is especially apparent in relationships, unless individuals actively enquire and show curiosity about another—whether in new or more established or intimate relationships—care and concern will not be apparent (Baumgarten, 2001). Showing curiosity in another, therefore has the capacity, on the one hand, to strengthen and deepen existing relationships, and on the other hand, to forge new relationships. Baumgarten

(2001: 74) contends that 'only curiosity will lead to going beyond the phenomena presented to asking "why," a form of engagement that may lead to both greater knowledge and caring.

7.2 Curiosity as Care

One of the appeals of curiosity is that it holds the potential to disturb how things are. By reflecting, wondering and questioning why things are the way they are, or why they are not different, there are possibilities for re-explanation, as well as reconsideration. There is often a kind of politeness when individuals become aware that their question might be out of place or create some awkwardness. These questions are, at times, preceded by 'forgive me for asking…', 'I hope you don't mind me asking…', so that politeness masks the curiosity. On the flipside, and as has already been touched on in this chapter, curiosity sits comfortably with expressions of care.

Simply asking whether a colleague is okay, how they are finding their new positions or new universities, or whether their expectations of the department or students match their experiences, reveals a desire to know, but can also be interpreted as a showing of care. In the absence of this curiosity, the new academic might think or state (eventually), that 'nobody even bothered to ask me if I was okay'. It speaks to the very basic human needs to be seen and acknowledged. In this sense, the potential contribution and importance of curiosity to citizenship becomes apparent.

Curiosity embodies certain processes which can potentially place academics in a state of reflection and wonder about the world and those around them. It relies on a recognition to want to know, for the sake of knowing as an epistemic good. Wanting to know can only unfold if academics acknowledge that they do not know. This is a lot harder than it sounds—especially for academics and teachers, who might define themselves as knowledge producers and teachers, rather than knowledge seekers. The authority that certain academics might enjoy in their designated positions and roles might make it hard for them to consider the possibility that they do not know, or that they do not know enough.

And yet, when the questioning curiosity reveals a desire to know and understand and moves academics into a dialogue with each other, it can be humbling both to the one asking and the one being asked—to the extent that both might feel for cared in that moment—the academic being asked responds, and by receiving a response, the questioner feels satisfied in her curiosity being fulfilled, as opposed to not knowing, or not receiving a response. And hence, Foucault's (1988: 328) assertion, that curiosity evokes 'care', 'it evokes the care one takes of what exists and what might exist'.

Curiosity holds the capacity to offer a certain kind of comfort to both the one who expresses curiosity and the one, who responds to that curiosity. While it can take the academic who enquires to a place of knowing, and hence some satisfaction and comfort in that knowledge, so, too, the one being asked can feel a sense of comfort not only by sharing, but also because being asked about. It is not only the act of enquiry that can potentially evoke care and comfort. It is what precedes the act of asking or dialogue—the very recognition that there was a desire to know, implying therefore that someone has been 'seen'.

Understanding dialogue as a process of learning and knowing, writes Freire (2000), establishes a previous requirement that always involves an epistemological curiosity about the very elements of the dialogue. To this end, 'dialogue must require an ever-present curiosity about the object of knowledge. Thus, dialogue is never an end in itself but a means to develop a better comprehension about the object of knowledge' (Freire, 2000: 18). In this regard, it is possible for both participants in the dialogue to develop a better comprehension, and not only the one, who might be perceived as the other, or in the out-group.

To develop a better comprehension about the object of knowledge, such as different academics in a university, or about academic citizenship itself, implies a desire to gain a better perspective and understanding. Curiosity, therefore, affirms, that something is missing in what is already known. In not knowing something or not knowing enough about something, suggests a deficient understanding of the object of knowledge. Generally, academics are not averse to acknowledging their lack of understanding in relation to a particular research area and might state that not enough is known about this or that, or more research is needed before conclusive findings might be made. This reluctance to make premature conclusions or judgments are considered indicators of sound research ethics and etiquette.

The same reluctance, however, is not always present in judgements and conclusions about academic colleagues. Judgements are often made before introductory meetings, let alone dialogues. Myths and stereotypes of who academics are thought to be, as well as what they are believed to be capable of, are pre-decided, rendering the need to know, superfluous. Even without preconceived ideas about others, some forms of academic citizenship exist neither with interest nor curiosity. As a result, departments or faculties can consist of multiple identities without any sense of, or attention to who these identities are—leading to a department of individuals, rather than a departmental team, who regularly converge for meetings. They are known only in terms of what they do. Expressing a desire to know, however, maintains Foucault (1988: 328), can evoke:

> [A] sharpened sense of reality, but one that is never immobilized before it; a readiness to find what surrounds us strange and odd; a certain determination to throw off familiar ways of thought and to look at the same things in a different way; a passion for seizing what is happening now and what is disappearing; a lack of respect for the traditional hierarchies of what is important and fundamental.

Foucault's (1988) encouragement to be ready to engage with the strangeness opens serious considerations for academics in terms of how they approach those who are new and strange. Does their newness equate to estrangement, as in there is no need to get to know those who are unfamiliar? Or does their newness create an opportunity for an expansion of knowledge and understanding? Importantly, Foucault (1988: 328) also sees curiosity as discarding 'familiar ways of thought and to look at the same things in a different way'. This can only occur if academics engage with one another, so that whatever preconceived ideas exist may either be confirmed or debunked. Either way, few would disagree that thinking and reflecting upon the world necessarily involves occasionally stepping away from that which is familiar, as in reconsidering certain viewpoints, or interactions with others. It is indeed possible, with enough openness, for academics not only to change their perspectives on ideas and arguments, but to approach diversity and what they perceive as otherness in different and more informed ways.

For Foucault (1988), the irony is that there is a plethora and an infinity of things to know, and the desire to know and to know it more deeply is already present, but there seems to be an inadequate means for thinking about everything that is happening. He suggests that perhaps there are 'channels of communication that are too narrow, almost monopolistic, inadequate' (Foucault, 1988: 328), that act as barriers and prevents individuals from exploring and asking about the world around them. Foucault (1988) cautions against adopting 'a protectionist attitude', to stop 'bad' information from invading and stifling the 'good'. Instead, he argues that individuals should rather increase the possibility for movement backwards and forwards—that is continuously consider and reconsider ideas and positions—'This would not lead, as people often fear, to uniformity and levelling down, but, on the contrary, to the simultaneous existence and differentiation of these various networks' (Foucault, 1988: 328).

Fear itself, says Nussbaum (2018), is usually born out of ignorance and prejudice, and often blocks rational deliberation and impedes constructive cooperation for a better future. Being curious, however, can allay both ignorance and prejudice, it can also open the way for a deeper awareness of why fear and its accompanying stereotypes exist in the first place. Asking colleagues, for example, about certain traditions and beliefs they might have, opens opportunities for new kinds of learning and understanding, as well as colleagues being seen and recognised.

7.3 Curiosity and 'Unfinishedness'

Human beings, states Freire (2000), are 'unfinished'.

> Whenever there is life, there is unfinishedness, though only among women and men is it possible to speak of an awareness of unfinishedness…I like being a human person because even though I know that the material, social, political, cultural, and ideological conditions in which we find ourselves almost always generate divisions that make difficult the construction of our ideals of change and transformation, I know also that the obstacles are not eternal (Freire, 2000: 151–152).

As 'unfinished', individuals (academics) are in a perpetual state of becoming, of not knowing and understanding, yet having the potential not only to know, but to grow and transform. Being in an 'unfinished' state, means that as human beings, we can never reach a state of completion of finality, because there will always be something about ourselves that has yet to reach fruition of full understanding. Lewis (2012) explains that the unfinished character of human beings and the transformational character of reality necessitate that education be an ongoing activity. If academics become conscious of their unfinishedness, then they will become aware of themselves in relation to those around them. Freire (2000) conceives of 'unfinishedness' as a critical motivation for curiosity.

To him, the whole purpose of teaching, learning, and pursuing knowledge is because of a recognition of the 'unfinishedness' of our lives; we do not know, and hence we pursue that which is yet to be known and experienced. Freire (2001: 101) holds that 'It would be impossible to know ourselves as unfinished and not to open ourselves to the world and to others in search of an explanation or a response to a multitude of questions'.

Freire's (2000) offering of 'unfinishedness' holds profound implications for what it means to be an academic citizen. On the one side, there are suggestions of incompleteness, of not fully understanding, and hence the constant potential to know more. On the other hand, is a recognition by academics to conceive of themselves as 'unfinished' in their place in the world. 'Unfinishedness' does not only pertain to what is yet to be known, but also refers to the state and condition of academics as 'unfinished' human beings—that, despite their knowledge and their positions of teachers and knowledge producers, they remain incomplete within themselves. A recognition of this incompleteness or 'unfinishedness' is crucial for academics' understanding that can never know or understand all there is to know, and that what they know remains open for questioning, revision and transformation.

Once academics acknowledge their 'unfinishedness', they release themselves to a curiosity about the world, thereby confirming their own 'educability' (Freire, 2001). He contends that the 'real roots of the political nature of education are to be found in the educability of the human person', which, in turn, 'is grounded in the radical unfinishedness of the human condition and in our consciousness of this unfinished state' (Freire, 2001: 80). Academics have the power and autonomy to decide whether to remain passive in their own knowledge, or whether to act in response to their educability so that they might open themselves to new possibilities, while also potentially questioning and subverting entrenched norms and hegemonies. The 'spontaneous curiosity' with which all human beings are born, according to Freire (2001), can either be transformed into 'epistemological curiosity' through critical pedagogy or 'anesthetized' by banking pedagogy.

'Banking education', as Freire (2001) explains, functions to conceal certain facts which explain the way human beings exist in the world, and as such, says Lewis (2012: 30), 'exchanges epistemological clarity for mythological common sense and an atrophied sense of "scientific" analysis'. Lewis (2012: 30) maintains that 'if banking education puts curiosity to sleep through mythological veiling of facts in relation to historical unfinishedness, then dialogic pedagogy reawakens our curiosity by directing it toward the world, by revealing the truth of our social relations, and by articulating theory and practice so as to transform the world'. The more spontaneous curiosity intensifies and becomes rigorous, the more epistemological it becomes (Freire, 2001). And hence, the greater the chance of peeling back the myths and the normalisation of hegemonic structures which draw clear lines between those are on the inside and those who are not.

7.3 Curiosity and 'Unfinishedness'

By foregrounding the link between curiosity as an individual desire to know with a curiosity about how various networks (such as the academy) functions, Freire (2000) alerts us to the political, as well as democratic potential of curiosity—that is, that with curiosity it is possible to bring into question structures and systems of dominance, which not only hampers curiosity but shuts down possibilities and freedom to consider of how things might be different. To Freire (2000), if individuals are not able 'to transform their lived experiences into knowledge and to use the already acquired knowledge as a process to unveil new knowledge, they will never be able to participate rigorously in a dialogue as a process of learning and knowing'. By virtue of already having knowledge, as well as producing it, academics occupy immensely privileged positions. In turn, by virtue of their teaching, supervision, and general engagement with students as well as an array of other knowledgeable academics, academics are privy to daily experiences not only with a diverse range of people, but with diversity itself.

Following Freire (2000), these daily interactions and experiences, must, at some point, translate into knowledge, which can be used to learn new forms of knowledge. In other words, through dialogue, listening and curiosity, knowledge can be gained for deeper understandings. In this way preconceived ideas about who certain academic identities are, can be disrupted through engagement, so that their lived experience of others brings into question what is perceivably known.

Sometimes certain characteristics as well as stigmas are associated with certain identities, based on stereotypes or structural notions of gender and competence, for example. Women are not only denied top leadership opportunities at the culmination of a long career, report Alcalde and Subramaniam (2020), but rather such opportunities seem to disappear at various points along their trajectories. As a global phenomenon, membership statistics of women in the academy do not correlate with leadership positions. The limited appointments of women into leadership positions place them under greater scrutiny and hence, visibility, typically not framed in positive evaluations (Alcalde & Subramaniam, 2020).

Women's under-representation in leadership positions is linked to several barriers. This includes a need to balance work and family roles, with women still being seen as the primary person responsible for child-rearing, cooking and cleaning. In some organisations, it also includes institutional cultures in which stereotypes and gender biases prevail (El-Tomany, 2022; Kuagbedzi, 2022). In recalling her experiences of working in the UK and the Gulf, an academic shares that she has observed 'different versions of the same reality—a reality where women have to constantly re-affirm their credibility, justifying their presence at meetings, conferences and leadership venues' (El-Tomay, 2022).

7.4 Curiosity for Liberatory Academic Citizenship

Much like university spaces are distorted by gendered ideas about women and the capacities, so, too, the world, is distorted through ideological mystification that suppresses curiosity (Freire, 2000). But social interactions can yield experiences quite different from expectations. By acting on the desire to know through questioning, or engaging in dialogue, there is an opportunity for both parties (the one asking and the other responding), to release themselves from preconceived ideas of each other, thereby creating a shared understanding. In this way direct social interactions and experiences of each other replace uninformed or generalised opinions and ideas, and perhaps more importantly, unveiling the world (Freire, 2000). It is reasonable to assume that among the numerous responsibilities of academics is that of knowledge production—whether in the form of writing, presenting or student supervision.

Most academics are intent upon building on and extending existing debates, as well as making meaningful and original scholarly contributions. As such, there is an implicit commitment to add something to the world, and hopefully, to make it a better place. It follows, therefore, to expect academics to engage with their citizenship in ways that open new understandings about others, and potentially question institutional norms and practices, are not too far-fetched.

At the fulcrum of seeking 'epistemological clarity' is a willingness to disrupt the imposition of norms, boundaries, binaries and hegemonies, to think more accurately not only about the world, but the role of academics in propping up this world. Consider for example that in the UK, the gender pay gap means that women in UK higher education will in effect work the rest of the year for free, with figures suggesting that they earn almost £4,000 less than men on average (Jack, 2022). According to Frank (2020), the gender pay gap in the UK has been persistent despite the Equal Pay Act 1970, and the fact that universities were given a duty to redress this in the Equality Act 2010. Some British universities, explains Frank (2020), introduced a system of 'professorial banding', which involved the re-grading of all professors from scratch. This, however, had no impact on the gender pay gap.

While the primary and immediate concern might be a gender pay gap, with an additional possibility that the situation might be 'even worse for women of colour' (Jack, 2022), there are social and political implications for how universities perceive and treat gender, and more specifically women. There are also ethical implications for how university practices feed into broader societal attitudes towards women. Quite frankly, if institutions of higher education, which pride themselves on pursuing knowledge, truth, and innovation, apparently see no problem in perpetuating gender injustice, what grounds do they have to speak out on any other form of injustice?

But, if academics are curious about why gender pay gaps exist, as one form of injustice, it opens the way to see its connection to other forms of injustice. In pondering upon this unfair and unequal practice by engaging with female colleagues, and gaining their perspective on the matter, allows academics to shift to an epistemological curiosity, which, in turn, holds the potential to transform the matter at hand as well as the relations between those engaging in dialogue. To Lewis (2012: 31), the interrogation and potential expulsion of imposed cultural myths (such as, men and women are unequal) 'enables the decodification of the world and in the process returns curiosity to its rightful place as *the* revolutionary cognitive faculty'. In this sense, curiosity is not only about filling an information gap, or about desiring to know. Rather, argues Freire (2001: 16), 'Curiosity as restless questioning, as movement toward the revelation of something hidden, as a question verbalized or not, as search for clarity, as a moment of attention, suggestion, and vigilance, constitutes. an integral part of the phenomenon of being alive'.

Pathak (2010), for example, recounts a conversation with a 'white' male colleague regarding their latest assigned group of advisees, which included a young African American male from an inner city who had been raised by a single mom. Her colleague stated: 'Of course you have way more in common with that student than I do'. Pathak (2010: 3), however, explains that she is 'a South Asian female raised in a two-parent, immigrant family that is firmly ensconced in the middle class, suburban US'. Unsure of how to respond, she realised that her colleague truly believed that their dark skin (hers and the student's) connected them, and enabled her to inherently engage with the student, his life and his needs. It did not occur to her 'white' male colleague, that the experiences of a young African American male from an inner city were vastly different from hers as a South Asian female. For her colleague, explains Pathak (2010:3), 'our skin color fixed us into the same reality'.

Although Pathak (2010) recognised that her lived experiences might indeed connected her with the student, she struggled with the vast chasm between her own reality of why she might be connected to the student and why her colleague believed she could best serve the student. Careful reflection on this conversation reveals embedded ideas about the homogeneous perceptions of race—that somehow a shared skin colour infers a common set of experiences. It also reveals as much of a gap of basic information about Pathak as a South Asian academic, and a new student. These kinds of conversations and encounters are fairly common in South African university settings. Decisions on who supervises and mentors postgraduate students are often based on race or ethnicity, even though the decisions are not explained as such. Instead, there is a resort to other kinds of markers, such as language and accent.

It is impossible to separate curiosity from what it means to *be* an academic. In the absence of curiosity, there can be no search for understanding, innovation, there can also be no imagination. Most importantly, however, as a moment of attention and vigilance, curiosity offers the capacity for liberation and transformation. To know, is to unshackle one from ignorance, and with knowledge comes a shift in thinking, with endless possibilities of transforming ideas, perspectives, as well as being and acting differently in this world. Hence, Freire's (2001: 17) contention, human curiosity is in a permanent process of social and historical construction and reconstruction.

7.5 Key Considerations of Chapter

Like citizens in the public sphere, academic citizens are inclined to gravitate towards that which is already known—both in terms of professional commonalities and personal identities. Unlike everyday citizens, however, being an academic necessarily centres on a curiosity about the world, its people, why things are they way they are, and what could be done to innovate and create so that humankind is in a perpetual state of change. Yet, this curiosity which drives professional agendas and research, is seldom evident towards the fostering of human relationships. On the one hand, the interest of this chapter, therefore, was to highlight the potential role, importance and contribution of curiosity in terms of seeking understanding among academics, and thereby cultivating a more open and mutually beneficial academic citizenship.

On the other hand, the chapter also explored the criticality of curiosity in relation to recognising the 'unfinishedness' or incompleteness of all human beings, which, if reflected upon, holds the potential for academics to step out of their zones of familiarity or fear. By acting on the desire to know through dialogue, academics have an opportunity to release themselves from preconceived ideas or ignorance about each other, and enter a space of mutual understanding, as well as care. By stepping out and crossing over into the other life-worlds (if only temporarily), academics can act upon their responsibility to add to the world in ways that exceed their professional roles.

References

Alcalde, M. A., & Subramaniam, M. (2020). Women in leadership: Challenges and recommendations. www.insidehighered.com/views/2020/07/17/women-leadership-academe-still-face-challenges-structures-systems-and-mind-sets

Baumgarten, E. (2001). Curiosity as a moral virtue. *International Journal of Applied Philosophy, 15*(2), 169–184.

El-Tohamy, A. (2022). Female university chief explores barriers for women in academic leadership. https://www.al-fanarmedia.org/2022/11/barriers-for-women-inacademicleadership/#:~:text=%E2%80%9CWomen's%20underrepresentation%20in%20leadership%20positions,stereotypes%20and%20gender%20biases%20prevail.%E2%80%9D

Foucault, M. (1988). *Politics, philosophy, culture: Interviews and other writings, 1977–1984* (Trans. A. Sheridan & others). London.

Frank, J. (2020). The persistence of the gender pay gap in British universities. *Fiscal Studies, 41*(4), 883–903.

Freire, P. (2000). *Pedagogy of the oppressed*. Continuum.

Freire, P. (2001). *Pedagogy of freedom: Ethics, democracy, and civic courage*. Rowman & Littlefield.

Gelfert, A. (2013). Hume on curiosity. *British Journal for the History of Philosophy, 21*(4), 711–732.

Hume, D. (1986). *Treatise of human nature*. Penguin Classics.

Jack, P. (2022). Equal pay day 2022: What is the gender pay gap at my university? https://www.timeshighereducation.com/news/equal-pay-day-2022-what-gender-pay-gap-my-university

Kuagbedzi, F. N., Dhlamini, N., & Njenga, B. K. (2022). The struggle of women for power and leadership in universities. https://www.universityworldnews.com/post.php?story=20220426094831132

References

Lewis, T. E. (2012). Teaching with pensive images: Rethinking curiosity in Paulo Freire's pedagogy of the oppressed. *Journal of Aesthetic Education, 46*(1), 27–45.

Markey, A., & Loewenstein, G. (2014). Curiosity. In R. Pekrun & L. Linnenbrink-Garcia (Eds.), *International handbook of emotions in education* (pp. 228–245). Routledge.

Nussbaum, M. (2018). *The monarchy of fear*. Oxford University Press.

Orchard, J., & Davids, N. (2019). Philosophy for teachers (P4T) in South Africa—re-imagining provision to support new teachers' applied ethical decision-making. *Ethics and Education, 14*(3), 333–350.

Pathak, A. A. (2010). Opening my voice, claiming my space: Theorizing the possibilities of postcolonial approaches to autoethnography. *Journal of Research Practice, 6*(1), 1–12.

Watson, L. (2018). Educating for curiosity. In I. Inan, L. Watson, D. Whitcomb & S. Yigit (Eds.), *The moral psychology of curiosity* (pp. 293–310). Rowman & Littlefield International.

Chapter 8
The Vulnerability of Unlearning

Universities, and by implication, academic citizenship, are driven by unending imperatives of studying, learning, and knowing. There is a driving emphasis on a pursuit of knowledge and knowledge production, which while considered as an implicit condition for the university, demands careful thought and interrogation. On the one hand, we are taken back to the unending debates on the purpose of knowledge, what it seeks to do, why, and perhaps, less commonly up for discussion, whose knowledge matters, and whose does not. On the other hand, as is the primary interest of this chapter, is whether it matters at all if academics produce new knowledge, or whether they learn anew, if there is no consideration of what this might mean for the necessity of unlearning.

Unlearning infers a somewhat different, and perhaps more complex undertaking than learning. Learning takes us towards the acquisition of knowledge, skills, values, as well as habits. Unlearning, however, relies on a deeper interrogation of the very source of what we know, why we know it, how we have come to know it, followed by an openness to confront any inherent prejudices or biases. Learning is dependent not only on acquiring knowledge, but on a reflective contemplation on what is already known, and the accompanying possibility that what is known might in fact be preconceived or misinformed. And hence, the necessity of unlearning to relearn, without preconception and presumption. What is the value of unlearning to academic citizenship? How might unlearning assist academics, and by implication, universities, in dismantling discursive norms which prevent endeavours towards new kinds of knowledge?

8.1 Experience and Learning

All of us, regardless of our disciplines or our interests, whether we are reading this book with a specialist interest, or not, come to these words shrouded in our own experiences and vantages points. It is impossible to fully comprehend and to peel back just how much of who we are comes into our reading and writing—much in the same way that the decision to write this book in the first-place stems from my own lived realities, encounters, and perspectives. Academics, as researchers and authors, recognise, or should recognise, just how much of who they are influences and steers the kinds of research they choose to pursue. In the end, there's very little in the humanities which can line up as being objective or neutral. Our entrapment in particular histories, identities, cultures and languages mean that we always already skewed in our judgement, how we live in the world, and how we live with others. Alcoff (2006: 5) explains as follows:

> The reality of identities often comes from the fact that they are visibly marked on the body itself, guiding if not determining the way we perceive and judge others and are perceived and judged by them. The road to freedom from the capriciousness of arbitrary identity designations lies not, as some class reductionists and postmodernists argue, in the attempt at a speedy dissolution of identity—a proposal that all too often conceals a willful ignorance about the real-world effects of identity—but through a careful exploration of identity, which can reveal its influence on what we can see and know, as well as its context dependence and its complex and fluid nature.

Exploring our identity has to do with going back into how we have come to be who we are, and how we come to know what we know. It requires considered reflection on our initiations into the world, our primary role-models, what we have been socialised into and how to be with others. We might, for example, as Taylor (1989) explains, describe ourselves in relation to our specific contexts, or specific individuals and communities, so that we begin to recognise how what and who we are, is defined by that which has significance for us. For some of us who grew up in family units, there might be strong memories and emulation of familial, even patriarchal traditions, which we have unquestioningly accepted as 'just the way things are'.

For others, experiences and memories might be more jagged, painful, even traumatic, often signalling a harsher socialisation into the world, perhaps also coupled with mistrust and suspicion of others. The point is, as Mendieta (2008) makes us aware, our identity is always constructed as well as imagined as a 'social topography'. It is not captured in a convergence of one moment of time, geography, nationality, or language. Identity stretches across experiences, influence as well as disruptions by people and events, leading to reconstructions of who we are and who we might become. All the while we are learning about others and orientating ourselves to the world, regardless of whether we have come into this learning with love and care, or with displacement and pain.

Some academics teach on these very topics of identity formation and politics, and fostering social justice through inclusion, recognition, and mutual regard. Curricular and pedagogical initiatives, explains Todd (2001), frequently focus on learning about those who have been Othered, their untold histories, their narratives of self-identification; and their demands for recognition, in order to disassemble the structures of power that distort, or destroy, certain individuals and their communities. Even within these educational attempts to make sense of others, we often come to these explorations and conversations with only our own learning and perspectives on the world, not considering the possibility that what we already know and how we have come to know might already taint what we seek to know next.

It is not only that we might look at the world in a biased or skewed way, but also that, we, too, have been changed or damaged by the way in which the world looks upon us. Merleau-Ponty (2002) tells us that the world is a field for and of perception, which is assigned meaning through human consciousness and imagination. Unless we become aware of how perception informs our knowledge of others and ourselves, we cannot achieve consciousness of the world (Merleau-Ponty, 2002).

For example, if we spent our childhood being reared by a family to believe that some people are better and smarter than others, because of race or ethnicity, we have to question what the origin of this knowledge actually is. Apartheid South Africa thrived on ensuring its citizens' beliefs in racial hierarchy and supremacy. The distorted outcome is not only that certain 'whites' bought into their own supremacy and the oppression 'black' people, but also that certain 'black' people subscribed to 'white' hegemony and their own inferiority and subjugation. Hence, three decades into South Africa's democracy, while there are still a few 'white' individuals, who resort to racist rants and treatments, it is also not unusual to encounter 'black' people who continue to adopt subservient dispositions in the presence of 'white' people.

Here, I am reminded of how some 'black' students and academics change their demeanour when in the presence of 'white' academics. They become conciliatory, and agreeable. Other times, 'black' people succumb to a desire to become 'white' – described by Fanon (2008) as the 'epidermalization of inferiority', also referred to in South Africa as a 'verblankingsproses' or a 'whitening process', which allowed individuals to apply for a reclassification of their racial category, under the Population Registration Act of 1950. Nathane (2019: 188) writes:

> I have always strongly felt that one unforgivable atrocity perpetrated against black South Africans was in masterminding an education system that made black people think less of themselves, and instilled a persistent sense of inferiority. This is an education system, in some corners, ['black'] people still think was better than the current education system – possibly further evidence of the negative effects it had on black people's minds.

Perceptions and experiences of and by individuals are, of course, not misplaced and extend into (mis)constructions of 'epistemic inferiority' (Grosfuguel, 2013: 74) Standing in diametric opposition to 'epistemic privilege', explains Grosfuguel (2013: 75), 'epistemic inferiority', the knowledge produced by other epistemologies, cosmologies, and world views arising from other world-regions, characterized by different geopolitics and body-politics of knowledge are considered 'inferior' in relation to the 'superiority' of western knowledge. Hence, in South Africa, 'black' academics are not seen as having 'the kind of habitus ... that is, the values, attributes, gazes, and dispositions that are valued and legitimated ...' (Hlatshwayo & Alexander, 2021: 51).

Who they are and what they bring in terms of knowledges and values are not considered to be of any value by those who occupy constructions of 'epistemic privilege'. This is evident in how they are addressed or spoken over during meetings. Their opinions are heard, but not listened to or taken seriously. It is odd, therefore, to find that when 'black' academics remain quiet and retreat from any deliberations or debates, they are confronted with accusations and complaints that they do not participate or contribute.

Apparent from these understandings is the implicit dyadic relationship between privilege and inferiority or subjugation—that is, in order for privilege to exist and flourish, it requires the perpetuation of inferiority. Inasmuch as marginalised and privileged academic identities have experiences of their respective categories, it is also apparent that these experiences are constructed through social, political and economic ideas of who should not carry value so that others might lay claim to having more value. The point is the way individuals and groups of people are socialised into pre-existing ideas and frameworks of being is through learnt behaviour and observation. This is why when some individuals are confronted about particular ideas or traditions, the response quite simply is, 'but this is what I learnt' or 'this is how I grew up'. Hence, one finds not only the perpetuation of beliefs, for example, that men are natural leaders and women are not, but also certain practices related to the treatment of women, based on a patriarchal lens,

Academics occupy and fulfil especially powerful roles in their teaching and supervision, because it places them into direct relationships with their students. Their knowledge of their specialisations and why they teach, matter as much as how they teach, how they draw students into their teaching and the kinds of teacher-student relationships they establish. It follows, therefore, that how academics are socialised or initiated into their knowledge, both of their discipline and the world around them need to be questioned and reflected upon. Both are equally important because sometimes it is not only the home or personal backgrounds of academics which have cultivated questionable ideas and perspectives on the world. Other times it is also schooling, the type of education, and teachers and their teaching which have shaped the dispositions of academics.

For example, in a recent class discussion with my PGCE students, about a third of the 160 students shared that they were not averse to practising corporal punishment in their classrooms. They justified this on the basis that their respective schools had implemented corporal punishment (despite it being illegal in South Africa since 1994), and that it instilled a stronger school discipline. A few also shared that it made them 'stronger and resilient', and they did not see corporal punishment as inflicting violence but a necessary resort when learners commit serious offences, and most importantly, they did not experience corporal punishment as harmful.

In another example, academics often adopt the supervision methodology they experienced with their own supervisors. According to Vilkinas (2002), good supervisors ought to have professional knowledge and interpersonal skills, which include being innovative, problem solvers, resource orientated, decisive, dependable, as well as capable of exhibiting care and concern for the personal well-being of students. As such, the supervisor-student relationship involves both a professional and personal

8.1 Experience and Learning

dimension (Vilkinas, 2002). While students are assumed to be 'always/already' autonomous scholars at the beginning of their candidature, postgraduate supervisors are assumed to be 'always/already' effective at supervising once they had endured the process themselves (Manathunga & Goozée, 2007).

Although this relationship appears straightforward and reliant on a set of academic criteria which would have allowed the student onto a particular postgraduate programme, the supervision process often starts without any clarity or understanding as to the assumptions about the student or the supervisor. And often the set of assumptions on which supervision unfolds is based on the supervisor's own experiences of being supervised (Stephens, 2014). In turn, Blose et al (2021) found that their relationships with their supervisors constituted a basic supervision experience that formed the basis of their learning and the construction of a supervisor identity. In some cases, this can be a positive learning experience, as Moriarty (Moriarty et al, 2019) shares:

> From the outset of my own PhD, I got a strong sense from my supervisor that he had faith in my abilities as an academic – he wanted me to succeed, and he never stopped telling me that he believed I could succeed… Lastly, he instilled in me a passion for networking and collaboration, both of which have proved invaluable throughout my academic career… Over the past few years, as I have taken up the mantle of PhD supervision, the lessons I learned from my supervisor have stayed with me. As well as guiding my students' research and writing, I always take time to share some of the transferable skills that I acquired … Following the example of my own supervisor, I want my students to know that I will do my best to nurture their abilities and support their endeavours as much as I can.

On the flipside, however, academics might avoid emulating the way that they were supervised themselves (Lee, 2007). According to Bitzer (2011), poor supervision could be due to any number of factors: from inexperienced or overburdened supervisors, inadequate preparation of candidates, poor planning and management, methodological difficulties, to personal problems outside research, insufficient financial support for students, poor relationship between student and supervisor, and overall ineffective infrastructural support for postgraduate studies.

Scott (1991: 777) explains that when the 'evidence offered is the evidence of 'experience', the claim for referentiality is further buttressed-what could be truer, after all, than a subject's own account of what he or she has lived through?' Scott (1991) posits that when experience is taken as the origin of knowledge, the vision of the individual subject becomes the foundation of evidence on which explanation is built. As such, 'the evidence of experience 'becomes evidence for the fact of difference, rather than a way of exploring how difference is established, how it operates, how and in what ways it constitutes subjects who see and act in the world' (Scott, 1991: 777). Consequently, to Scott (1991), the evidence of experience reproduces, rather than contests given ideological systems, as found in students who would reproduce the practise of corporal punishment, because their own experiences of it did not raise any questions, discomfort or concerns for them.

There are several reasons for this reproduction. It might be that the experiences of gender-based roles, for example, are so entrenched that it becomes impossible for individuals detach themselves from these frameworks and consider the possibility of other ways of being and acting. It might also be that a reluctance to consider new possibilities or other perspectives is based on a fear of disrupting what has 'always been the case'. The fear itself might stem from several reasons, including the possibility of a loss of privilege as well as a realisation that what individuals have been socialise into and learnt might in fact been incorrect or based on discriminatory thinking. In this sense, following Scott (1991), experience is not the origin of our explanations, but rather that which we seek to explain, that about which knowledge is produced.

8.2 Learning to Unlearn

Part of the challenge in peeling back what academics know about the world and those in it, is a willingness to confront inherent taken-for-granted assumptions and stereotypes. Constructing certain academic identities as othered, whether because of their gender, religion, race, sexuality, or culture, presents a barrier to new learning and thinking. When otherness is framed as being wrought by oppressive or at least exclusionary social circumstances, contends Todd (2001), they (others) become undesirable. Teaching about marginalised groups, states Todd (2001), often falls into a form of rhetoric to get students to learn about how people came to be designated as Other and what needs to be done in order to change this.

The problem with this rhetorical dimension of education is that it calls into question the ethical benefits in learning *about* Others (Todd, 2001). In other words, the orientation or preconceived understanding adopted by academics or students play a role in whether new learning can unfold. If, for example, academics already believe that immigrant academics are incapable of research excellence, then it becomes impossible for new knowledge about or from immigrant academics to be received or valued. In this way, explains Todd (2001) the Other remains 'an object of *my* comprehension, *my* world, *my* narrative, reducing the Other to me.'

For Todd (2001: 68), in the first place, knowledge requires an openness to something new, something foreign, something totally other beyond the self—'The *approach* to knowledge implies first and foremost an ethical relation to difference; that is, what we learn is conditioned upon an initial susceptibility to what is outside of and exterior to us.' This involves an appreciation of 'the infinite unknowability of the Other—her fantasies, desires, life problems, creativity, passions, emotions remain hers and hers alone, and how an individual makes cultural meaning for herself is always an indeterminate process of translation' (Todd, 2001: 72–73). This understanding demands that academics discard what they think they already about other academics or their students, not only because preconceived ideas distort how others are seen, but also because it prevents academics from seeking knowledge in the first place.

An ethical dialogue explains Ahmed (1997) can only occur by assuming that the dialogue or conversation itself does not lead to 'grasping' the truth of an other but allows a movement in between. She posits that 'Such a movement can only take place by respecting the alterity of who may be speaking: that one does not and cannot know what she will say' (Ahmed, 1997: 33). The reality, however, is that not only are certain academics treated differently and unfairly because of their identities, but presumptions are made about their competence, their knowledge, values and beliefs.

In most South African universities, the challenges are not only that 'black' academics, and 'black' female academics more commonly, might encounter discrimination and exclusion (see Khunou et al., 2019). Whether because of knowing about the discrimination against 'black' academics or whether because of direct experiences, at times, there are also preconceived ideas about 'whiteness' and its uncritical association with exclusionary practices. For example, a 'black' academic might think that the reason for his non-promotion is because of the racist attitudes of his 'white' colleagues. This, however, might not be the case. And the real reason might be that the 'black' academic needs to improve on his research or postgraduate production. But because the 'black' academic believes that he already knows 'white' academics, how they think and act, he cannot bring himself to consider the possibility that his non-promotion is not due to his race. And because of a distorted understanding that all 'white' academics must be racist, the 'black' academic cannot bring himself to enter a conversation with them, and instead, can only hold onto the limited knowledge he already has.

How can academics unlearn or abandon certain knowledge, values and beliefs which produce rigidity in thinking and acting, thereby limiting their potential to be open to others and their ways? To Matsuo (2018) unlearning is a process by which individuals consciously choose to give up, abandon, or stop using knowledge, values, or behaviours to acquire new ones. This definition, according to Matsuo (2018), involves three assumptions. Firstly, that individual unlearning is a conscious process of giving up knowledge, values, or behaviours. Secondly, that what is unlearned is not permanently lost, but it is not used by an individual. And thirdly, that the abandoning of existing knowledge, skills, and behaviours often occurs simultaneously while acquiring new ones. This understanding is shared by Baldacchino (2013), who maintains that unlearning is not a simple act of rejecting bad habits to learn new virtues, which, when turned once more into bad habits, would need to be replaced by something else.

Importantly, continues Matsuo (2018), learning and unlearning are not identical; instead, unlearning is a key step within learning. Learning involves the acquisition or addition of knowledge and skills without abandoning old ones. By contrast, when an individual acquires knowledge and skills by transforming, updating, and refining the old ones, this type of learning involves unlearning, and can be associated with exploratory activities, including experimenting with new approaches and reconsidering existing beliefs (Matsuo, 2018).

Some theorists, like Tsang and Zahra (2008), distinguish between forgetfulness as an unintentional or involuntary loss of memory, and unlearning as a conscious and intentional process. Others, like Baldacchino (2013: 424) refers to 'willed forgetfulness and unlearning', while also discerning between 'unlearning oneself and unlearning what one expects to learn from an object or something' (2013: 425), like a presumed depository of knowledge, or presumably also from someone. To

Baldacchino (2013: 422), unlearning is a willed act, and not simply a case of getting into a place where one cannot progress anymore. It is a process which recognises the need 'to extend our horizon beyond what our habits of learning have been trained to expect. To this end, the importance of unlearning is not limited to an individual academic's openness, growth, and transformation. The necessity of unlearning extends into unlearning the often-unquestioned dominant norms of universities, which might perpetuate experiences of marginalisation for some academics.

The value of unlearning, therefore, starts with individuals, but can take effect institutionally, and as such, it is not only tied to individuals or relationships, but to knowledge production. According to Hedberg (1981: 3), knowledge grows, and simultaneously it becomes obsolete as reality changes—'Understanding involves both learning new knowledge and discarding obsolete and misleading knowledge. The discarding activity—unlearning—is as important a part of understanding as is adding new knowledge'.

By all accounts, unlearning is not only a never-ending process, but also a very challenging one, 'where we continuously unlearn what we have naturalized in different (colonial) guises' (Capan et al., 2020)—such as presuming superiority and authority or adopting personas and accents more palatable to the dominant cultures in which academics might find themselves. Vasic (2021), for example, notes that one of the biggest obstacles to an inclusive academic culture is the disparity in opportunities between men and women because of these ingrained rules that favour what are traditionally considered masculine working styles. These rules also include dress codes, with 'norms' dictating that unless female academics dress modestly and conservatively, they look out of place in academia, because fundamentally, they don't have the right bodies to be academic authorities' (Stavrakopoulou, 2014).

In turn, reports Vasic (2021), while most men are aware of their position in the hierarchy and the influence it affords them, they often fail to understand their advantage over women, who are often lower in the hierarchy than men in similar professional standing. Moreover, women are often either unable or unwilling to compete in the hierarchy. Consequently, more women than men often accept bigger responsibilities without appropriate promotions or financial compensations, which contributes to the gender pay gap (Vasic, 2021).

The necessity for unlearning expands into understandings and calls for decolonisation. In his critique of an African Studies programme at a historically 'white' university in South Africa, Mamdani (1998) questions a curriculum which seemingly re-enacts a version of Bantu education and presumes that Africa has no intelligentsia worth reading. He contends: 'The idea that natives can only be informants, and not intellectuals, is part of an old imperial tradition. It is part of the imperial conviction that natives cannot think for themselves; they need tutelage' (Mamdani, 1998: 71).

To undo and unlearn this, requires recognizing, questioning, and finding ways to change these unwritten rules (Vasic, 2021). It requires a preparedness to disrupt the status quo, to bring into disrepute a complacent willingness to accept things as they are for fear of change or transformation. In the end, unlearning fulfils an emancipatory role not only for individual academics, and universities, but as a critical pedagogy, geared towards ensuring that students question the world in which they find themselves. Ultimately, writes Chokr (2009: 6), unlearning is about 'unshackling oneself'; it is about 'emancipating' or 'liberating' oneself from variously entrenched and often unquestioned ways of thinking, doing and living by radically questioning, criticizing and rejecting the assumptions and premises of much of what one has learned as part of the 'dominant and established system(s) of knowledge'.

8.3 Learning *from*

Being willing to unlearn what we know requires academics to step back and establish a vantage point that removes them from any attachment to that knowledge. It requires considerations of other perspectives, knowledge, values, beliefs and arguments, which are inevitably connected to diverse identities. It also requires an acknowledgement that whatever is already known might possibly be incorrect or insufficient. Part of the complexity of this process resides in the fact that much about it centres on the beliefs and viewpoints of individual academics. It is possible and easy for academics to articulate their support of policies of diversification and democratisation, to commit themselves to policy directives. But this hardly translates to an internal recognition of the need for diversification.

I would describe my own faculty as relatively diverse in comparison with other faculties at my university. On the surface, there are some motions of respectable collegiality among certain groups, with several individuals functioning on the periphery. Once or twice a year we might socialise and exchange polite small talk. Even under these social circumstances, pre-existing groups naturally gravitate together, negating possibilities of forging new relationships or new understandings. Despite our faculty's collegiality (mostly), I would not say that we all know each about each other, which, according to Lugones and Spelman (1983), means that we are not fully of each other's worlds, and hence our intimacy is incomplete. Here, it is useful to consider Ahmed's (1997) elucidation of intimacy as providing protection to individuals from both loneliness and coldness. To Ahmed (1997: 32):

> [A] politics of becoming-more-intimate is a politics bound up with responsibility - with recognising that relations between others are always constitutive of the possibility of either speaking or not speaking… We are, so to speak, right in it. Beginning from this 'in-it-ness', a politics of more intimate engagements, gets closer in order to allow the difference between us, as a difference which involves power and antagonism, to make a difference to the very dialogue between self and other. Here, the difference between us, necessitates the dialogue, rather than disallows it - a dialogue must take place, precisely because we don't speak the same language.

Ahmed's (1997) argument offers a compelling reconsideration. Typically, academics, like most other professional communities, connect with those with whom they enjoy a shared language, whether in terms of a language of communication or a disciplinary language. A familiarity and affinity exist because of a commonality. Yet, Ahmed (1997) proposes that a dialogue between individuals or academics becomes necessary because they speak different languages. Difference, therefore, becomes a motivation for engagement and learning. The logic is clear: dialogue is less important with those already known to us, but incumbent with those unknown to us.

Significantly, she sees this 'politics of becoming-more-intimate' not as a voluntary act, but as a responsibility, because the dialogue itself will make a difference to how difference is conceived and judged. Stated differently, by engaging in dialogue, opportunities are opened for mutual understanding. It seems fair to expect academics to make an effort to either initiate or respond to colleagues, whether new or longstanding. But the realities of academic spaces can be isolating and lonely, especially for early career academics or new appointments.

Reasons for this differ in some respects between faculties and universities, but in most cases, it comes down to a shared reluctance to engage with difference and newness. Other times it might also have to do with disapproval of a particular appointment, or fear that a new academic might present competition to the existing hierarchical structures. Many academics simply 'go with the flow'—they come to work, move between their office and lecture theatres or seminar rooms, as is required, and leave for home. They only engage with their immediate circle, sometimes determined by disciplinary interests, other times by external or historical connections. Whatever contrary views they might have often remain contained with those with whom they already share relationships.

When all the layers are peeled back, and if unlearning for the purpose of emancipation and transformation is to evolve, then there must be an uncompromising openness to diversity in all its forms and expressions. And with such an understanding is an unmistakable vulnerability. If one is exposed to the Other, explains Todd (2001: 73), one can listen, attend, and be surprised; one can be affected by the Other—'And insofar as I can be receptive and susceptible, I can learn *from* the Other as one who is absolutely different from myself.'

Of course, when academics willingly share their stories, and perhaps also their insecurities and concerns about being an academic or being in the university, they also make themselves vulnerable. But the vulnerability being foregrounded in this discussion is that which is revealed when academics are either curious or recognise deficiencies or distortions in what they already know. It is a matter and a process of acknowledging that if one part or some aspects of the knowledge of others are misplaced or biased, the possibility exists that more about what is known could also be wrong or in need of clarification. Once academics open themselves to desiring to know and make it known to others, this, act offers opens the possibilities for working across and through differences (Todd, 2001).

[L]earning *from* as opposed to *about* allows us an engagement with difference across.

> space and time, it focuses on the here and now of communication while gesturing toward the future, it allows for attentiveness to singularity and specificity within the plurality that is our social life. It is only when we learn *from* the stories that Others have to tell that we can respond with humility and assume responsibility (Todd, 2001: 73).

Thus far, I have drawn attention to why some academics might not want to learn about, let alone from others. Preconceived ideas about others makes it easier to shut

8.3 Learning *from*

down the necessity and possibility of dialogue and intimacy, it also makes it easier to retain the status quo. Once the stories of others reveal a contrary understanding to what has been presumed, there is a strong chance of disruption, and for some academics, this is not a desired outcome. This brings me to another reason why academics might not want to unlearn for the sake of relearning, and it has to do with what it means to be a *thinking* academic. In an interview with Danius and Jonsson (1993), Spivak explains that when she initially spoke and wrote about 'unlearning one's learning', she had in mind how to behave as a subject of knowledge within the institution of neocolonial learning.

More recently, however, she understands all her work 'as being a sort of stream of learning how to unlearn and what to unlearn, because my positions are growing and changing so much...' (Danius & Jonsson, 1993: 24). Here again, is the idea of unlearning as a process, but what Spivak provides is a positioning of unlearning as implicit to what it means to being an academic, and more specifically, to being an academic, who is conscious and critical about what she reads, writes, says and teaches, so that she does not stagnate, but is constantly changing in her thinking and the way she sees the world.

Most times when academics think about what it means to having their work subjected to critique, they have in mind reviews from other academics. But to Spivak (Danius & Jonsson, 1993) unlearning to learn and relearn also involves that academics critically engage and revisit their own scholarship. Apparent from her own reflection is the vulnerability of ideas and arguments, that they are always open to interrogation and re-interpretation. To this end, she alerts academics to the fleeting nature of their own thinking, writing and theory. No matter how compelling an idea or argument might be, unlearning demands the possibility that the idea can and should be revisited. It places academics in a liminal space of on the one hand, writing and arguing with conviction, while on the other hand, recognising the fragility of that conviction.

At the same time, unlearning also involves a release of power and privilege. If academics believe in the concreteness of their arguments and perspectives, and in their ownership of ideas, they become rigid in their thinking and in their responses. By contrast, in letting go by recognising that there is more to know and learn, academics end up releasing themselves from being trapped in their own thinking. And while this release of power over ideas and thinking might be considered as a loss of privilege, it stands to open profound new ways of relearning. Unlearning one's privilege by considering it as one's loss, says Spivak (Landry & MacLean, 1996) constitutes a double recognition. She holds that:

> Our privileges, whatever they may be in terms of race, class, nationality, gender and the like, may have prevented us from gaining a certain kind of Other knowledge: not simply information that we have not received, but the knowledge that we are not equipped to understand by reason of our social positions. To unlearn our privileges means, on the one hand, to do our homework, to work hard at gaining some knowledge of the others who occupy those spaces most closed to our privileged view. On the other hand, it means attempting to speak to those others in such a way that they might take us seriously and, most important of all, be able to answer back (Landry & MacLean, 1996: 4–5).

8.4 Key Considerations of Chapter

The central concern of this chapter is to draw attention to the fact that how academics come to know what they know, or why they hold the values and beliefs which they do, is often not reflected upon. There are certain assumptions and presumptions about the world and people, sometimes based on experiences and other times not, that are accepted and lived by uncritically. Being an academic, however, requires a critical consciousness of how the world is constructed as socio-political space, which puts into play inherent structures of centres and margins, and hence, privilege and subjugation. Like in other settings, there are academics, who stand in the centre and enjoy full academic citizenship, and there are those who do not.

Becoming aware of how certain identities, knowledge and values are used to sustain this imbalance of power, depends on being open to a process of unlearning. Unlearning involves a never-ending and conscious process of questioning, and discarding certain knowledge values, or behaviours, if these create barriers to understanding and growth, and if they cast others as 'Othered'. By radically questioning assumptions and criticising entrenched norms, unlearning holds the potential for relearning which can liberate academics not only from their own rigid thinking but from distorted perspectives and engagements with others.

Unlearning is not without its own experiences of vulnerability. Recognising the limits of one's knowledge and beliefs and being willing to change these, is an act of vulnerability. Acknowledging a willingness to want to learn from others so that opportunities for dialogue and intimacy might unfold, is an act of vulnerability. Understanding that being an academic necessarily involves self-critique of ideas and values, is an act of vulnerability. But of course, as has been argued for in this book, while vulnerability exposes and makes apparent the 'weakness' or 'un-knowing' of academics, by revealing this un-knowingness, coupled with a desire, is a manifestation of vulnerability as strength.

References

Ahmed, S. (1997). Intimate touches: Proximity and distance in international feminist dialogues. *Oxford Literary Review, 19*(1/2), 19–46.
Alcoff, L. M. (2006). *Visible identities: Race, gender, and the self*. Oxford University Press.
Baldacchino, J. (2013). Willed forgetfulness: The arts, education and the case for unlearning. *Studies in Philosophy and Education, 32*, 415–430.
Bitzer, E. M. (2011). Doctoral success as ongoing quality business: A possible conceptual framework. *South African Journal of Higher Education, 25*(3), 425–443.
Blose, S., Msiza, V., & Chiororo, F. (2021). Developing a supervisor identity through experiential learning: Narratives of three novice academics working in a South African University. *Journal of Education, 82*, 28–43.
Capan, Z., Garbe, S., & Zöhrer, M. (2020). How do we teach the world? *Acta Academica, 52*(1), 76–88.
Chokr, N. N. (2009). *Unlearning: Or 'How NOT To Be Governed?'* Societas Imprint Academic.

References

Danius, S., & Jonsson, S. (1993). An interview with Gayatri Chakravorty Spivak. *Boundary, 20*(2), 24–50.

Davenport, T. R. H., & Saunders, C. (2000). *South Africa: A modern history.* Macmillan.

Fanon, F. (2008). *Black skin, white masks.* Grove Press.

Grosfuguel, R. (2013). The structure of knowledge in westernized universities epistemic racism/sexism and the four genocides/epistemicides of the long 16th century. *Human Architecture: Journal of the Sociology of Self-Knowledge, 11*(1), 73–90.

Hedberg, B. (1981). How organizations learn and unlearn. In P. C. Nystrom & W. H. Starbuck (Eds.), *Handbook of organizational design* (pp. 3–27). Oxford University Press.

Hlatshwayo, N., & Alexander, I. (2021). "We've been taught to understand that we don't have anything to contribute towards knowledge": Exploring academics' understanding of decolonising curricula in higher education. *Journal of Education, 82,* 44–59.

Khunou, G., Phaswana, E.D., Khoza-Shangase, K., & Canham, H (Eds.). (2019). *Black academic voices: The South African experience.* Cape Town: HSRC Press.

Landry, D., & MacLean, G. (Eds.). (1996). *The Spivak reader.* Routledge.

Lee, A. M. (2007). Developing effective supervisors: Concepts of research supervision. *South African Journal of Higher Education, 21*(4), 680–693.

Lugones, M., & Spelman, E. V. (1983). Have we got a theory for you! Feminist theory, cultural imperialism and the demand for 'The Woman's Voice.' *Women's Studies International Forum, 6*(6), 573–581.

Mamdani, M. (1998). Is African studies to be turned into a new home for Bantu education at UCT? *Social Dynamics, 24*(2), 63–75.

Manathunga, C., & Goozée, J. (2007). Challenging the dual assumption of the 'always/already' autonomous student and effective supervisor. *Teaching in Higher Education, 12*(3), 309–322.

Matsuo, M. (2018). Goal orientation, critical reflection, and unlearning: An individual-level study. *Human Resource Development Quarterly, 29,* 49–66.

Mendieta, E. (2008). Identities: Postcolonial and global. In L. Alcoff & E. Mendieta (Eds.), *Identities: Race, class, gender, and nationality* (pp. 407– 416). Oxford: Blackwell.

Merleau-Ponty, M. (2002). *Phenomenology of perception.* Routledge.

Moriarty, P., Schnellman, J., Jack, Z. M., Blyth, C., & Majumdar, S. (2019). How to be a PhD supervisor. https://www.timeshighereducation.com/features/how-be-phd-supervisor

Nathane, M. (2019). Sitting on one bum: The struggle of survival and belonging for a black African woman in the academy. In G. Khunou, E. D. Phaswana, K. Khoza-Shangase & H. Canham (Eds.), *Black academic voices: The South African experience* (pp. 178–194). HSRC Press.

Scott, J. W. (1991). The evidence of experience. *Critical Inquiry, 17,* 773–797.

Stavrakopoulou, F. (2014) Female academic: don't power dress, forget heels—and no flowing hair allowed. https://www.theguardian.com/higher-education-network/blog/2014/oct/26/-sp-female-academics-dont-power-dress-forget-heels-and-no-flowing-hair-allowed

Stephens, S. (2014). The supervised as the supervisor. *Education & Training, 56*(6), 537–550.

Taylor, C. (1989). *Sources of the self: The making of the modern Iientity.* Cambridge: Cambridge University Press.

Todd, S. (2001) On not knowing the other, or learning *from* Levinas. *Philosophy of Education,* 67–74.

Tsang, E. (2008). Transferring knowledge to acquisition joint ventures: An organizational unlearning perspective. *Management Learning, 39*(1), 5–20.

Vasic, M. (2021). Do women have to be masculine to succeed in academia? https://hbsp.harvard.edu/inspiring-minds/do-women-have-to-be-masculine-to-succeed-in-academia

Vilkinas, T. (2002). The PhD process: The supervisor as manager. *Education & Training, 44*(3), 129–137.

Part III
Identity and Citizenship as Transformation

Chapter 9
Identity and Transformation

Like my concerns about the expanded-use and over-employment of diversity, I wonder about this term transformation. On the surface, it suggest change or modification, whether in form or appearance. In South Africa, for example, the transformation of higher education, has been dominated by the structural merging of historically advantaged and historically disadvantaged universities; employment equity policies, directed at the recruitment of historically disadvantaged academics and administrators, and of course, concerted efforts to increase student enrolment from historically marginalised communities. In this instance, transformation is achieved by how a university appears or presents itself.

But what does it mean in terms of re-thinking, re-conceiving and re-imagining universities? What is transformation meant to achieve? Is it enough for an academic citizenship to be representative of diversity for it (citizenship) to be transformed? Or does transformation demand something more in terms of delving beyond the shell of the external, and that which is immediately obvious, so that what is aspired towards are not only shifts in form and appearance, but in thinking and being? What might it mean for academic citizenship to embody the kinds of transformation it seemingly endeavours towards not only in policy, but in pedagogical practices and knowledge production? How might academics use their identities to assist processes of personal transformation, as well as institutional transformation?

9.1 Transformation as (Mis)representation

According Cross and Motala (2020), epistemologically, conceptually and in the context of the nation-state, 'transition', 'reform' and 'transformation' can be placed within two distinct analytical domains. The first is the consensus or national equilibrium model, which is premised on the assumption that society is fundamentally consensual and that its functions are based on almost static logic. A consensus model through which most reform strategies can be understood, presupposes harmony, stability, and a context where members of society agree with the objectives of the change project. It also assumes a smooth interaction of society and higher education institutions in the context of a social pact between them around an agreed need in society, whereby higher education institutions are tasked to meet this need (Cross & Motala, 2020).

The second, based on Marxism, is known as the conflict model, explain Cross and Motala (2020), and maintains that the timing and focus of transformation take place in the context of class relations and class struggles waged by the working class under the capitalist mode of production. In this context, the state and its institutions are constantly called upon to mediate the contradictions determined by conflict (Cross & Motala, 2020).

To Cross and Motala (2020), the South African case, for example, can best be understood within the conflict paradigm, which emphasises and points to degrees of social instability in the change process in respect of values, resources and power. They argue that the radical, democratising reform could hardly be achieved within the framework of compromises and concessions determined by transition politics. Hence, within this paradigm, 'higher education change can be viewed as part of an ongoing struggle between social groups that have fundamentally different interests and negotiate change in the context of inherently contradictory relations, different values, and conflicting perspectives over the redistribution of resources and power (Cross & Motala, 2020: 4–5).

Following an emphasis on radical change as a marker of reform, transformation in higher education immediately became subsumed with a language of de-racialisation, with, says Badat (2018), a focus on achieving a quantitative shift in the participation levels of 'black' students and 'black' academic staff. Badat (2018) shares that racism and patriarchy profoundly shaped the social composition of academic staff. In 1994—just as the country transitioned to a democracy—academics at South African universities were overwhelmingly white (83%) and male (68%). Consequently, explains Rensburg (2020), 'black' academics were recruited into universities with principally 'white' academic staff.

However, often, these 'black' academics were neither embraced nor were conditions created for the deliberate establishment of diverse yet inclusive academic cultures (Rensburg, 2020). This is not surprising, since the recruitment of 'black' academics cannot be separated from the problems of institutional racism and 'whiteness', and the question of institutional culture, which includes the experience of historically white universities as discomforting and disempowering cultural environments that exact a considerable personal, psychological, and academic toll (Badat, 2018).

In South Africa, the narrative of transformation in entrenched in a severing from its colonialist and apartheid past, which has meant a dual break from eurocentrism and 'white' Christian, Afrikaner nationalism, and stark moves toward decolonisation. Decolonisation has taken centre stage in debates on curriculum renewal in higher education (see Du Plessis, 2021; Le Grange, 2016). This is a reasonable and logical response when one considers that historically, higher education institutions were

9.1 Transformation as (Mis)representation

shaped by apartheid ideology and planning, they were reserved for different 'race' groups and also allocated different ideological, economic and social functions in relation to the reproduction of the apartheid social order (Badat, 2008). Similar motivations are implicit in the renaming of university buildings. In this thinking, a university's institutional culture is seen to be held up, and adorned by the sight, feel and sound produced by its architecture, spatial layout and visual representations on the streets, buildings, lecture halls, and residences (Fataar & Fish, 2022). While the authors acknowledge that visual redress is merely symbolic, they nevertheless see it as stimulating changes in the university's aesthetical domains—that is, from replacing its apartheid association with an institutional ethos and culture based on norms of inclusiveness, restitution, and redress.

And of course, as has already been mentioned, is the issue of affirmative action as a means of undoing historical inequality and inequity, which in South Africa, often translates into a physical and representative placement of 'black' academics without recognising the more critical need of addressing the institutional ethos and culture. The hope that the transition to democracy would result in a shift to nonracialism, has not been realised, not only because the government has failed to provide a coherent strategy for dealing with race in a post-apartheid milieu, but because race and ethnicity are being reinscribed as central to debates about citizenship, rights, diversity and claims to marginalisation in the new socio-political context (Adhikari, 2004; Battersby, 2005).

In this way, transformation is being propagated without creating conditions necessary for sustaining transformation. And hence, Hlatshwayo's (2020) view that the plethora of post-apartheid policies, directed at the prioritisation of transformation and social justice, have 'substantively failed to sufficiently dismantle the underlying epistemic logic of apartheid in South African higher education'.

Moreover, states Badat (2010), while higher education holds the promise of contributing to social justice, development and democratic citizenship, this promise often remains unrealised and instead universities frequently continue to be powerful mechanisms of social exclusion and injustice, through both their own internal thinking, structures, cultures and practices and their external conditioning by the wider society, for both students and academics. To Badat (2010), this regime of social exclusion extends well beyond issues of access and admissions to universities. For him, it includes the questions of the opportunities for intellectual, social and (academic) citizenship development, it also extends to the issues of institutional and academic cultures, and largely ignored epistemological and ontological issues associated with learning and teaching, curriculum development and pedagogical practice.

While the discussed examples speak to a South African context, there is a high probability that similar experiences are encountered elsewhere, irrespective of different geopolitical backgrounds. More importantly, it raises critical questions about what transformation is. What is transformation meant to do? What does it look like? How do we know when transformation has happened? And what happens thereafter? As inferred by the term, transformation has in mind processes of change and transition, and the important word in this description, really is 'processes'. This is because transformation, as I understand it, suggests a perpetual state of flux.

It might be possible to transform a dilapidated building into a fresh, modern one, so that it reaches a fully transformed state (but of course, it will still need maintenance). But when it comes to universities, the topic of transformation is not only seen from myriad perspectives. Because the university has so many moving parts, transformation can never just respond to one part. Within the discourses of neoliberalism, managerialism, globalisation, internationalisation, universities, writes Henkel (2002), have adopted new roles in local and regional economies, developed strategic connections with large firms, and encouraged individuals, research groups and departments to make new and multiple forms of relationships with businesses, government bodies and other educational institutions, largely in the name of income generation. All of this, and perhaps most importantly, continually changing student and academic demographics.

Moreover, the university's response is always up for debate and scrutiny, because its purported public good always involves students, academics, and a broader society, and how well the university prepares its students for an ever-changing world. Implicit in this understanding is that while a university exists in the now, its preparation is for the future. Hence, Waghid's (2002: 459) contention, 'Transformation in higher education involves a process of new knowledge production, reflexive action, which means seeing new problems and imagining new ways of approaching old problems and, deconstruction and reconstruction or constant exploring beneath surface appearances'.

Transformation in higher education necessarily involves knowledge or knowledges, which according to Lange (2020) are usually neither explicit nor systematically examined by institutions. She, therefore, distinguishes between 'knowledge *for* transformation (the kind that must be produced in order to make change possible) and knowledge *of* transformation (the kind we generate about transformation itself) (Lange, 2020: 41).

Failure to examine these kinds of knowledge systematically, maintains Lange (2020: 42) has four unfortunate consequences for theorising and implementing transformation: 'it reduces transformation to the manipulation of quantifiable evidence; it disregards history and context, and creates orthodox versions of the 'right' kind of transformation based on generic performance indicators; it keeps politics out of the life of people and institutions by preventing engagement and deliberation over what constitutes transformation, and consensus for action and implementation; and it isolates South Africa [or any other context] from broader debates about knowledge and social justice that challenge accepted orthodoxies'. Lange (2020) argues that 'the knowledges *for* and *of* transformation' operate in a dialectical relationship that itself needs to be examined if we are to improve our understanding of the tensions, contradictions, and risks institutional transformation.

9.2 The Risks for Academic Citizenship

Previously, in Chap. 5, I discussed that for universities, diversity has become a non-negotiable aspect of how it defines and positions itself both locally and globally. This means deliberate policies and strategies that will ensure the marketing of the university as an open and diverse environment. The concern, however, with transformative strategies, such as employment equity or affirmative action, is that in its efforts to undo historical discrimination, it not only continues to deploy racial categorisation as a 'legitimate' marker, but it also reduces individuals into representatives of transformation. Consider the following excerpt from the South African Department of Higher Education and Training (DHET):

> The Employer [DHET] fully embraces the provisions of the EE [Employment Equity] Act and affirms its commitment to government's socio-economic transformation policy. Employment Equity initiatives interlink and require complementary processes to be active and in place in the DHET, such as Change Management, effective management of diversity in the workplace and an Organisational Culture mind shift to accommodate previously disadvantaged groups namely black people, women and people with disabilities (DHET, 2019: 6).

As a long-term end, the Employment Equity Act, has in mind the appointment of people in proportion to the country's racial demographic profile. As such, says Soudien (2010), representivity as a racial-numbers proposition, informs its approach, in higher education as well. For Soudien (2010), there are two discourses, which inform transformation through race-based representivity. The first is that the university as a social site is located in and takes its politics from the broader society in which it finds itself, a kind of 'from the outside in' view of how higher education works. This discourse, elaborates Soudien (2010), has regularly been invoked by both those in power and those outside of it. While those in power want the university to reflect their interests and to be made in their image, those who feel marginalised decry its antagonism towards them and want the university to change to reflect their own interests.

This discourse provides an adequate description of the higher education system in South Africa during apartheid, and specifically the Extension of Universities Act of 1959, which instituted racialised universities, as a reflection of the segregated character of apartheid society (Soudien, 2010). In the post-apartheid era, therefore, a similar consideration arises insofar that universities should reflect a democratic and pluralist society. A key consideration in the idea of the transformation of the university is that it does not reflect the new South Africa. Importantly, whether it is expressed from a position of power or powerlessness, is that the university should take its character from the society in which it is located—'The 'outside' should be *in* the university' (Soudien, 2010: 228).

Although the second discourse is in opposition to the first, it co-exists with it and has to do with the emplacement of the South African university in a globalised setting, making it a global and therefore decontextualised enterprise with little obligation to the local context (Soudien, 2010). Soudien (2010) explains that this is a move that takes its integrity from the supposedly intrinsic character of the university and shapes up as a 'from the inside-outwards' discourse. In this regard, the university is not a proper university until it is recognized as such through the processes and rituals put in place to measure and understand excellence by the global community (Soudien, 2010). Similarly, the academic only has status and standing when recognition is conferred upon him or her through an internationally recognized process (Soudien, 2010).

In adopting an 'outside should be in' discourse, transformation in South Africa has remained fixated on ensuring a representative body of academics in universities. In the context of the Employment Equity Act (Department of Labour, 1998), the term 'black' is inclusive of 'African', 'coloured' and 'Indian' academics. In reality, however, preference is given to 'black' academics above 'coloured' and 'Indian', purportedly because 'blacks' were subjected to a more extreme form of oppression than the other two groups. Universities are required to design a plan that is based on an organisational analysis of barriers and contains affirmative action measures to work towards employment equity.

Moreover, the Employment Equity Act (Department of Labour, 1998) requires that if academics from one of these three groups ('African', 'coloured' or 'Indian') meet the minimum qualifications of the job or has the capacity to acquire the skills to do the job, they must be considered to be qualified for the job. In addition, the designated employer or university must provide training and skills development for affirmative action appointees to obtain the necessary skills or qualifications required for a position in the particular workplace. There are two major concerns with enacting transformation of academic citizenship through this discourse.

The first pertains to the fact that a democratic government continues to rely on the very same racial categories, used by an apartheid regime to sow division and isolation, and stands in stark contradiction to a cultivation of a non-racial society, as propagated by the country's first democratically elected government. This suggests not only an inability to break from a race-based past but presents a palpable barrier to an anti-racist society (Davids, 2022).

It is for this reason, argues Ndlovu-Gatsheni (2021: 888), that 'African struggles for epistemic freedom often fell prey to the epistemologies and academic practices they set out to critique, largely because the immanent logics of colonialism always interpellated decolonisation'. Regardless of this irony, the explicit national discourse about what was described as an urgent need to radically change the demographics of the professoriate, assumed that the access of 'black' and/or female academics would equate to 'deracialisation and degendering of the academic workforce' (Belluigi & Thondhlana, 2019). Hence, explain Belluigi and Thondhlana (2019), as a seeming panacea for academic equality, various 'development' programmes were piloted from the early 2000's at several historically 'white' universities.

The models for these programmes were imported and funded by philanthropic organisations in the global north, tracing geopolitical ties with countries of democratic, capitalist leanings (Belluigi & Thondhlana, 2019). The programmes incrementally altered institutional demographics in stable ways and permitted access to a select few 'talented' individual academics, while not relinquishing existing constructions of quality (Belluigi & Thondhlana, 2019). These academics, according to Belluigi and Thondhlana (2019) were tasked, to varying degrees, with embodying or effecting transformation at an historically white university. Belluigi and Thondhlana's (2019: 955–956) found that the dominant discourses at the historically 'white' institutions where these academics were placed, were that of review ('process of 'evaluating existing conditions') and compliance ('transformation as a response to constitutional and legal requirements'). One of the academics in the study shared the following:

> I am looking forward to a time when Black people aren't so treated as *designated, but* they are seen as scholars in their own right and who do not require to be designated into certain groups. I am also looking for a time when everyone who sits in selection committees become acutely aware of the racial past which has perpetually disadvantaged certain people...If this becomes the case, we will employ the previously disadvantaged without the need for the whip of the law to force us into line (Belluigi & Thondhlana, 2019: 956).

The second concern relates to the fact that the Employment Equity Act (Department of Labour, 1998) was designed for the 'traditional' business employer, such as a company or factory. Portnoi (2003) clarifies that while the university is a particular type of employer, the challenges and constraints it faces are not, in many cases, comparable to those of standard business and industry employers. Additionally, the core business of higher education institutions requires high levels of skills, specialisation and qualifications for a majority of positions, both academic and technical or administrative (Portnoi, 2003). She continues that in the South African context, the divergence from other kinds of industries is exacerbated by the fact the functions of universities were created and shaped within the delimitations of the apartheid state apparatus.

Hence, universities are not only required to grapple with higher education employment needs in terms of employment equity, but must also confront their race based histories and try to reconfigure themselves in the new social, political and higher education environments (Portnoi, 2003).

Despite a flurry of reform policies, which include the Employment Equity Act (Department of Labour, 1998), and programmes, such as the 'Transformation Strategy Group and Transformation Management Group' (2015), the 'Transformation Strategy Group' (2017), and 'Grow your own Timber Programme' two sets of reports (DHET, 2008; and SAHRC, 2016) revealed that although public universities have complied with broad requirements, transformation has not only been slow and insufficient, but discrimination and exclusion remain prevalent.

According to the 'Report of the Ministerial Committee' on social cohesion and transformation (DHET, 2008), transformation in broad terms means that firstly, a general and narrow understanding of the term was presented where transformation was interpreted in terms of institutional compliance in response to constitutional principles and national policy goals and imperatives, including race and gender equity, skills needs, effective teaching and learning and financial sustainability. Secondly, a broader understanding emerged in which transformation was defined as more than rectifying the demographic imbalances of the past, and instead ensuring meaningful change in the academic, social, economic, demographic, political and cultural domains of institutional life (DHET, 2008).

Although these understandings were explicit in terms of policy and regulatory compliance, as well as epistemological change, as constituted by the curriculum, serious gaps and tensions presented in the citizenships of academics. On the one end, a 'black' female academic shares:

> Racism is prevalent on campus, as is male chauvinism. The perception is that this is an Afrikaner institution - for example, the graduation ceremony has not changed. It is assumed that it is a Christian institution... The numbers discussion is easier than the more substantive and deep issues relating to institutional culture... The cultural capital that whites take for granted is not the experience of black academics. There are also hidden codes. For example, I am referred to as professor even by senior black academics, while white academics assume equality (DHET, 2008: 60)

On the other end, a 'white' male academic states:

> What is the meaning of transformation? Equity legislation is all targeted at white men. The narrow agenda is anachronistic and white males will soon be extinct. Do students want the best lecturers or representative lecturers in terms of race and gender? Students will choose quality (DHET, 2008: 59).

Eight years later, another report, the 'Transformation at public universities in South Africa', undertaken by the South African Human Rights Commission (SAHRC, 2016), confirmed the same concerns highlighted in 'Report of the Ministerial Committee' (DHET, 2008). Specifically, that the lack of a common understanding of what transformation means has resulted in discrepancies and sometimes seemingly contradictory approaches to transformation amongst different institutions. In response, the Commission recommended a conception of transformation that aligned more closely with the preamble of the Constitution, and hence, reads as follows:

> [T]ransformation in the higher education sector will entail the creation of a system of higher education which is free from all forms of unfair discrimination and artificial barriers to access and success, as well as one that is built on the principles of social inclusivity, mutual respect and acceptance (SAHRC, 2016: 32).

Significantly, the Commission (SAHRC, 2016), also concluded that if the above understanding of transformation is accepted as correct, then it becomes apparent that issues of transformation are not only the concern of historically 'white; universities, but of equal concern at historically 'black' universities, which are confronted by other forms of prejudices and discrimination based on ethnicity, disability, nationality, language, culture, gender and sexual orientation, amongst others. Furthermore, transformation agenda must transcend beyond the preoccupation with demographics and must instigate changes in the cultures of institutions of higher learning (SAHRC, 2016).

Emanating from these two sets of reports, are the complexities involved in transformation discourses and processes. Specifically, that any movements towards change has to commence from an interrogation of the concept of transformation. Due attention has to be given to what transformation is and involves, how it might unfold and in the case of academic citizenship, what it might mean in relation to the employment and promotion of academic identities. Apparent from the discussion, thus far, is that when one set of race-based identities are given priority in terms of employment equity, by implication and inevitably, another group feels side-lined and threatened. The consequences of this kind of perceivably discriminatory process are dire.

On the one side, 'black' academics are seen as token appointments, or are not appointed on merit, and as such, are neither qualified, nor competent to assume a role in the university. These perceptions are not limited to how 'black' academics might be perceived by others. These might also be the impressions that 'black' academics have of themselves, considering how their appointments have been framed both by the Department of Higher Education and Training, with its numerous reform strategies, as well by individual institutions. In my own faculty, a few 'black' and 'coloured' academics have entered the academy via 'New Generation of Academics Programme' (nGAP) (DHET, 2015).

As a nationally coordinated programme, the nGAP (DHET, 2015) is positioned as a transformation mechanism to accelerate diversification of staffing current demographics by reserving up to 80% of new posts for 'black' and/or women academics. The programme adopts a phased development approach, with penalties for dropping out. Funding is allocated for salaries on a sliding scale over 6 years; for fees to complete doctoral or master's degrees; for mentoring; for participation in staff development activities; and for research costs and international mobility (DHET, 2017). Participants benefit from a reduced workload; working only 20% of what would have been their expected workload in years one to three; 50% in year four, and a full workload from year five onwards (DHET, 2017).

The Department of Higher Education and Training (DHET) specifies the duties of the mentors and that the mentors should be senior academics who are recently retired academics (DHET, 2017). In a context of slow transformation, an ageing workforce, as well as as relatively under qualified academic staff workforce' (DHET, 2015), the importance of programmes become clear and necessary. The problem, however, is that academics, who have been initiated into the academy under the banner of programmes, such as the nGap (DHET, 2017), find it very difficult to discard the label, and end up not being taken seriously as academics. On the other side, is a simmering discontent at perceivably being 'targeted' by an 'anachronistic agenda', which not only spreads insecurity and fear, but places 'white' academics in a juxtaposed position to transformation. These tensions, quite literally constructed along racial lines and divisions, very easily contribute towards a climate of mistrust not only among colleagues, but of transformation itself.

9.3 Academic Identities and Institutional Transformation

The mistrust that may arise from perceptions and experiences of transformation are often located in the ways in which universities position themselves in relation to academic citizenship. On the one hand, explains Henkel (2002), universities have power to shape the lives, relationships, and self-perceptions of academics. This is apparent in hierarchical constructions of designations, which at times, includes certain privileges, such as bigger offices, or offices with more windows. So, too, it has the power to shape how transformation is constructed and implemented, which, in turn, has consequences for how certain academics are perceived and how they perceive themselves. On the other hand, universities, states Henkel (2002) can also be distanced from academics, and hence, weaker forces for identification. In this case, if academics conceive of themselves as 'token' appointments, or if they are called this by colleagues, this might lead to a detachment from the university.

Concomitantly, if certain academics, who are already on the 'inside' perceive transformation as the university departing from its 'traditional' ways and values, they, too, might decide to distance themselves from the institution. Some academics, argues Henkel (2002: 7), might experience transformation as a 'breakdown of longstanding conditions for strong, stable academic identities, sustained internally by the structures and cultures of academic systems'. At the time of writing this book, many academics at my university have taken to social media to express their lack of support for the vice-chancellor, because of efforts to transform the university by implementing a more inclusive language policy.

Apparent from these comments, is that the more transformation attempts to take root at the university, the further away it is perceived to be slipping from its historical identity, which presents a serious dilemma for those academics, who wish to see that history retained. Certain academics struggle or resist transformation for moral or ethical reasons, and hence they see their overt opposition and rebellion as justifiable and right responses to the changes taking place in university, as well as the broader society (Ylijoki & Ursin, 2013). Although these two sets of perceptions and experiences—one from the 'outside' and the other from the 'inside' university—are ideologically irreconcilable, they can in the end translate into the same response and action, which, according to Henkel (2002: 141), leads the university becoming a target 'for opposition and a means by which academics consolidate their sense of professional identity through differentiation from the management of the institution'.

Amid the discourses of transformation, and faced with continuous changes, state Ylijokia and Ursin (2013), academics need to rework and redefine what it means to be an academic and what key values and moral commitments are associated with being an academic in these complex, multi-layered contexts. In other words, how academics contextualise their identities have an impact on the way in which they make sense of transformation and their universities. In this regard, no one can dispute the central role of teachers or academics in preparing students for a world, that is in constant need of deconstruction and reconstruction. A changing world, increasingly in crisis of one sort or another—whether through armed conflict, global warming, global pandemic, or poverty and starvation—means that the responsibility and responsiveness of universities remain incomplete. work of the university.

The extent to which students are steered towards an awareness of the world and their responsibility in that world, often depends on the kind of teaching to which they exposed. In other words, whether students are conscientized into a responsibility to the world and others, largely depends on the extent they are transformed through their education. Transformation does not only pertain to what happens externally, as in visual redress, diversification through representation of different races and

9.3 Academic Identities and Institutional Transformation

cultures, or through student massification. Indeed, the very idea of massification implies that greater attention should be given to diversity and how to engage with difference. In this way, universities ought to be a place of transformative experiences so that students develop the capacity for critical thinking, curiosity, and reflection. According to Giroux (2003: 196):

> [T]he university is about more than educating students in those bodies of critical knowledge and performative discourses that name and help to produce the events upon which any viable idea of democracy is founded. The university must also provide a public space that addresses issues of critical social agency and the responsibility of intervening in public life in order to struggle against 'the powers that limit a democracy to come'. How might the university be not just a place to think, but also a space in which to learn how to connect thinking with doing, critical thought with civic courage, knowledge with socially responsible action? Knowledge must become the basis for considered individual and collective action, and it must reach out beyond the university to join with other forces and create new public spheres in order to deal with the immense problems posed by neo-liberalism and all those violations of human rights that negate the most basic premises of freedom, democracy, and social justice.

On the one hand, states Giroux (2017), some academics claim that faculty should not address important social issues in either their research or teaching. To do so, he continues, is to run the risk of not only becoming incapable of defending higher education as a vital public sphere, but also of having no influence over the conditions of their own intellectual labour. Yet, without their intervention as public intellectuals, argues Giroux (2017), the university defaults on its role as a democratic public sphere willing to produce an informed public, sustain a culture of questioning, and enable a critical formative culture' that advances the power of the imagination.

To Giroux (2017), it is only through a formative and critical educational culture that students can learn how to become individual and social agents, rather than disengaged spectators or uncritical consumers. At the very least, students (and academics) should learn how to think otherwise, to engage from different perspectives, and to act upon civic commitments (Giroux, 2017).

For Giroux (2017: 189), if young people are to develop a deep respect for others, a keen sense of social responsibility, as well as an informed notion of civic engagement, 'education must be viewed as the cultural, political, and moral force that provides the knowledge, values, and social relations to make such democratic practices possible and connect human agency to an engaged notion of the civic imagination, social justice, and the politics of possibility'. This, then, provides what can be described as the external responsibilities of academics—that is, that regardless of their respective disciplines, there should be a shared commitment to cultivating a particular kind of student, who is equipped to live, be, and engage in increasingly pluralist societies. To this end, universities become embedded in transformative ideas and practices, and conceive of themselves in a perpetual state of deconstruction and reconstruction, continuously alert to a changing world and its demands.

On the other hand, academic identities, who academics are as individuals, hold a transformative potential, insofar that their very presence can bring into contestation the reproduction and legitimation of entrenched institutional norms and cultures. This is not to say that diverse academic identities necessarily lend themselves to diverse pedagogical and inclusive practices. Rather, that the broader the range of academic identities, in terms of race, culture, gender, ethnicity, religion or sexuality, the greater the chance for students to find points of resonance and understanding with those who teach, supervise, or mentor them.

Importantly, the educational benefits of diversity apply to all racial and ethnic groups in the academy, as well as to both students and faculty members; they inure to the entire academic community, rather than to only individuals of particular racial or ethnic groups (Alger, 1999; Gurin et al., 2002). From an educational perspective, asserts Alger (1999), 'white' students and faculty may have the most to gain from racial diversity on campus because, as members of a racial majority, they have lived in a culture where most people in positions of authority are also 'white'.

Here, my own experiences as a 'coloured', Muslim, female academic at a historically 'white' university might be of some educational benefit. I knew that the majority of students I was expected to teach, had never been taught by a 'coloured' individual, let alone by one who is Muslim. I quickly learnt to use my identity as a pedagogical tool in disrupting stereotypes. Admittedly, this was not easy. During my early years of being at the university, each new academic year commenced with the usual looks of surprises once students realised that the person standing in front of the lecture theatre, was actually the lecturer. Generally, they were polite and respectful, but as the lessons passed, their curiosity about me would lead to eventual questions about my identity and how I ended up teaching at 'their' university. It is important to know that up to about five years ago, my classes—up to 320 in a Postgraduate Certificate in Education class—was overwhelmingly 'white'. Any 'black', 'Indian' or 'coloured' students were hyper-visible because of their small number.

By using my own identity as a point of reference and conversation about stereotypes, I can open the way for 'safe' participation from minority and marginalised identities in my class. I know that my presence and role as their teacher has had a significant impact on several students over the past decade that I have been at this university. Students are generally wonderfully forthcoming about their opinions on lecturers in the annual student evaluations, and in my case, this always includes references to my identity, and a disjuncture between their initial perceptions of me, and what they actually experienced. There are inevitable vulnerabilities. There have indeed been times when I have been confronted by some resistance from a handful of students, resistance that had little to do with my teaching, but with who I am as a teacher. Experience has been helpful in this regard, but a greater dose of simply accepting that not every student's or academic's mind can be changed, is probably the best remedy.

Importantly, it is not only that the benefits of faculty diversity accrue both to students and to faculty members, but also, argues Alger (1999), that racial diversity among faculty members may be even more valuable than student diversity in breaking down stereotypes because of the perceived authority and expertise of faculty. When students are taught or supervised by diverse identities, these experiences provide a contradiction to certain stereotypes about certain identity groups. Alger (1999) explains that when students enter college with preconceived notions of intellectual abilities and interests based on race or national origin, these prejudices can be overcome by exposure to individuals who provide living demonstrations of the falsity of these race-based notions. Benefitting from diversity, however, requires universities to define its transformational mission in relation to its educational vision educational mission in part by considering the institution as a holistic learning environment, rather than simply appointing isolated individuals for the same of legalistic compliance (Alger, 1999; Gurin et al., 2002).

9.4 Key Considerations of Chapter

Transformation is as complex, as it is tiring and demoralising. It is looked upon with suspicion and fear, because if universities are expected to change and open themselves to new identities, new thinking, new knowledge, new values, there is a chance that other identities and their accompanying knowledge and values might have to give way. But transformation is not about replacements of individuals or renaming buildings. Transformation asks for an openness to critique that which is already in place. So, one can hold onto certain institutional traditions, or structures but there must be a willingness to step back and consider whether these traditions serve to exclude and marginalise, whether it brings discomfort, even alienation, or whether they are open and hospitable.

Without transformation, there can be no new considerations, perspectives, or growth. It is hard to imagine how a university might be responsive to its perpetual stream of students, an ever-changing world, or new academic identities, if there is a resistance to transformation. The very idea of a profession seeped in knowledge, research and thinking, demands a willingness to step out of what is already known and familiar into that which is yet-to-be known.

Transformation, therefore, sits at the very centre of new offerings, knowledge and values. While this chapter touched on the importance of transformation as external manifestations of inclusion and representation, it also highlighted the role of academic citizenship in relation to inculcating transformative pedagogies and cultures. The greater the diversity in this regard, the greater the chances of creating points of reference and resonance for students, as well as for colleagues, who have yet to step into a different worldview. Transformation, therefore, holds the potential to disrupt biases and stereotypes, as well who is presumed to hold knowledge, and hence authority and power; it also holds the capacity for awakening and preparing students and academics alike for a world beyond the university.

References

Adhikari, M. (2004). 'Not black enough': Changing expressions of Coloured identity in post-apartheid South Africa. *South African Historical Journal, 51*, 167–178.

Alger, J. (1999). When color-blind is color-bland: Ensuring faculty diversity in higher education. *Stanford Law & Policy Review, 10*(2), 191–204.

Badat, S. (2008). Redressing the colonial/apartheid legacy: Social equity, redress and higher education admissions in democratic South Africa. In *Conference on affirmative action in higher education in India, the United States and South Africa New Delhi, India* 19–21 March 2008. https://core.ac.uk/download/pdf/49241219.pdf

Badat, S. (2010). The challenges of transformation in higher education and training institutions in South Africa. Paper Commissioned by the Development Bank of Southern Africa. https://www.dhet.gov.za/summit/Docs/2010Docs/The%20Challenges%20of%20Transformation%20in%20Higher%20Eduaction%20and%20Training%20Institutions%20in%20South%20Africa.pdf

Badat, S. (2018). *On black professors, deracialisation and transformation.* http://www.thejournalist.org.za/spotlight/saleem-badat-on-black-professors-deracialisation-and-transformation/

Battersby, J (2005). Re-inscribing race and ethnicity in post-apartheid South Africa. In: P Gervais-Lambony, F Landy & S Oldfield (Eds.), *Reconfiguring identities and building territories in India and South Africa* (pp. 85–97). New Delhi: Manohar Publishers.

Belluigi, D. Z., & Thondhlana, G. (2019). 'Why mouth all the pieties?' Black and women academics' revelations about discourses of 'transformation' at a historically white South African university. *Higher Education, 78*, 947–963.

Cross, M., & Motala, S. (2020). Introduction. In I. Rhensburg, S. Motala & M. Cross. (Eds.), *Transforming universities in South Africa: Pathways to higher education reform* (pp. 1–19). Brill Sense.

Davids, N. (2022). *Out of place: An autoethnography of postcolonial citizenship.* African Minds.

Department of Higher Education and Training (DHET). (2008). *Report of the Ministerial Committee on social cohesion and transformation.* DHET.

Department of Higher Education and Training (DHET). (2015). *Staffing South Africa's universities framework: A comprehensive, transformative approach to developing future generations of academics and building staff capacity.* DHET.

Department of Higher Education and Training (DHET). (2017). *Standard operating procedures for the new generation of academics programme.* DHET.

Department of Higher Education and Training (DHET). (2019). *Employment equity policy.* Pretoria: Government Printers.

Department of Labour. (1998). *Employment equity act.* Government Gazette No 19370.

Du Plessis, P. (2021). Decolonisation of education in South Africa: Challenges to decolonise the university curriculum. *South African Journal of Higher Education, 35*(1), 54–69.

Fataar, A., & Fish, T. (2022). *The politics of visual redress at Stellenbosch University.* https://www.universityworldnews.com/post.php?story=20221024010337871

Giroux, H. A. (2003). Selling out higher education. *Policy Futures in Education, 1*(1), 179–200.

Giroux, H. A. (2017). Neoliberalism's war against higher education and the role of public intellectuals. In M. Izak, M. Kostera, & M. Zawadzki (Eds.), *The future of university education* (pp. 185–206). Palgrave Macmillan.

Gurin, P., Dey, E. L., Hurtado, S., & Gurin, G. (2002). Diversity and higher education: Theory and impact on educational outcomes. *Harvard Educational Review, 72*(3), 330–366.

Henkel, M. (2002). Academic identity in transformation? The case of the United Kingdom. *Higher Education Management and Policy, 14*(3), 137–147.

Hlatshwayo, M. N. (2020). Being black in South African higher education: An intersectional insight. *Acta Academica, 52*(2), 163–180.

Lange, L. (2020). Transformation revisited: Twenty years of higher education policy in South Africa. In I. Rhensburg, S. Motala, M. Cross (Eds.), *Transforming universities in South Africa: Pathways to higher education reform* (pp. 39–59). Brill Sense.

Le Grange, L. (2016). Decolonising the university curriculum. *South African Journal of Higher Education, 30*(2), 1–12.

References

Ndlovu-Gatsheni, S. J. (2021). The cognitive empire, politics of knowledge and African intellectual productions: Reflections on struggles for epistemic freedom and resurgence of decolonisation in the twenty-first century. *Third World Quarterly, 42*(5), 882–901.

Portnoi, L. M. (2003). Implications of the employment equity act for the higher education sector. *South African Journal of Higher Education, 17*(2), 79–85.

Rensburg, I. (2020). Global Africa: Nelson Mandela and the meaning of decolonising knowledge and universities—problems and opportunities. In I. Rhensburg, S. Motala, M. Cross (Eds.), *Transforming universities in South Africa: Pathways to higher education reform* (pp. 60–73). Brill Sense.

Soudien, C. (2010). Some issues in affirmative action in higher education in South Africa. *South African Journal of Higher Education, 24*(2), 224–237.

South African Human Rights Commission (SAHRC). (2016). Transformation at public universities in South Africa. https://www.sahrc.org.za/home/21/files/SAHRC%20Report%20-%20Transformation%20in%20Public%20Universities%20in%20South%20Africa.pdf

Transformation Strategy Group and Transformation Management Group. (2015). *A transformation barometer for South African higher education*. Universities South Africa.

Transformation Strategy Group. (2017). Transformation barometer framework. *Universities South Africa*. http://www.usaf.ac.za/transformation-strategy-group/

Waghid, Y. (2002). Knowledge production and higher education transformation in South Africa: Towards reflexivity in university teaching, research and community service. *Higher Education, 43*, 457–488.

Ylijoki, O., & Ursin, J. (2013). The construction of academic identity in the changes of Finnish higher education. *Studies in Higher Education, 38*(8), 1135–1149.

Chapter 10
Stories as Reclamations of Knowledge

Thus far, I have focused extensively on the intersections between identity, citizenship, and vulnerability, followed by arguments for the criticality of unlearning, relearning and curiosity, and hence new forms of knowledge. This leads us to the inevitable question of how. How should academics and universities foster curiosity about the other? How can academics unlearn that which might be misplaced, even harmful, if these views are never brought into question?

The emphatic leaning on theorisation in the university carries its own preconceptions of what qualifies as knowledge, and what does not. More problematically, theory is often used to reify norms, when what academics should be doing is to interrogate these norms. If academics conceive of themselves as citizens of the universities, then there are certain implications for citizenship itself, specifically, knowing who they *are* as citizens. Academic citizenship must start with academics wanting to know about one another, how they conceive of themselves, and how they conceive of themselves in relation to others.

Stories assist us in doing this. It provides us with knowledge, not only of experiences, but of emotions, intuitions, and vulnerabilities. Stories provide us with untapped insights into the lived histories and realities of individuals. As such, they offer platforms of engagement that hold potential for profound mutual sense-making, unlearning, and relearning. What kinds of knowledge might be gained from recognising and valuing stories as integral to academic citizenship, and hence to universities? This chapter, therefore, draws on the voices and experiences of academics, situated in various geopolitical contexts. Their lived experiences offer profound insights into their nature of their academic citizenships, assigned to them by their identities. More importantly, their stories help provide us with the knowledge, necessary for the awakening of new kinds of academic citizenship.

10.1 Why Stories Matter

Having the opportunity to talk about one's life, explain Lugones and Spelman (1983: 573), is to 'give an account of it, to interpret it, is integral to leading that life rather than being led through it …' It is necessary, therefore, to capture what is lived, not as told from the vantage points and parameters of others, but from direct, first-hand experiences. Particularly evident in knowledge production as personal, explain Sium and Ritskes (2013), is the fact that storytelling is agentic and participatory. Indeed, to Lugones and Spelman (1983: 574), part of human living and experience is talking about it—'the articulation of our experience is part of our experience' state Lugones and Spelman (1983: 574).

In telling the stories of their lives, says Fivush (2008), individuals revealing who they are and share their worldview. They do not just tell what happened, they explain how and why these events happened, how they felt and how they reacted to them. In this way, stories allow individuals to make sense of their experiences and create meaning, allowing them to reinterpret, re-evaluate and reconstruct their experiences (Fivush, 2008). In turn, 'the cultural stock of stories' offers academics a means to come to terms with, and orient themselves amidst, a variety of changes taking place in their work environment and higher education in general (Ylijoki & Ursin, 2013).

While stories are necessarily complex, state Ellis et al. (2011: 274), they are also 'constitutive, meaningful phenomena that introduce unique ways of thinking and feeling and assist individuals in making sense of themselves and others'. As such they hold the potential, on the one hand, to 'sensitise readers to issues of identity politics, to experiences shrouded in silence, and to forms of representation that deepen our capacity to empathise with people who are different from us' (Ellis et al., 2011: 274). On the other hand, stories can be 'disruptive, sustaining, knowledge producing, and theory-in-action. Stories are decolonization theory in its most natural form' (Sium & Ritskes, 2013: ii).

By telling our stories, explain Sium and Ritskes (2013: iv), 'we're at the same time disrupting dominant notions of intellectual rigor and legitimacy, while also redefining scholarship as a process that begins with the self'. Storytellers, for instance, have never been silent in the face of colonial violence that subverted and neutralized various other forms of resistance (Sium & Ritskes, 2013). Instead, they are central to the exercise of agency and renewal, they shape communities through the spoken and written word, and 'are not only agentic and individual but they are communal sharings that bind communities together spiritually and relationally' (Sium & Ritskes, 2013: v).

By recognising the critical role of stories in capturing the lived experiences of academic citizenship, this chapter takes the form of an offering of stories from eight academics. Their invitation to participate included the following brief: the seemingly homogenous descriptor of academic citizenship has yet to be peeled back for interrogation. While some academics stand inside of the institutional culture their universities and its power dynamics, others do not. There are certain unexplored discriminations about what it means to be a citizen of the academy, which are not

10.1 Why Stories Matter

only shrouded in the silence of unspoken experiences, but which speak to an exposure of vulnerabilities.

This book seeks to bring into question the idea of academic citizenship as a homogenous and inclusive space. Among its objectives is not only to delve into who academics are, and how they come to embody their academic citizenship, if at all. It is also about stepping into the unexplored constructions of how knowledge and research are used in the deployment of valuing some forms of academic citizenship, while devaluing others. As such, the project plans to draw upon the direct accounts or stories of academics, located at institutions in different geopolitical contexts.

Ten academics, in various phases of their academic careers, from various geopolitical contexts, were invited to participate in a research study on academic citizenship, identity, knowledge and vulnerability. Criteria for the research participant sample was limited to permanent employment as an academic at a university; diverse identities; and different geopolitical contexts, which include South Africa, the USA, Hong Kong, and the Philippines. The research sample was deliberately constituted to ensure a predominant group of female academics. Although there is agreement that women's experiences must be made visible as an authoritative and unmediated source of knowledge, women's lives, stories and experiences, as feminism seeks to accentuate, have largely been excluded, reduced or invalidated (Davids, 2022).

While all ten (seven females and three males) academics initially accepted the invitation to participate in the study, responses in the form of a completion of Google survey and questionnaire were received from only eight participants—seven females and one male. Participants were given ten weeks to respond to ten questions. Typically, participants took between 60 and 90 min to address the questions. Some added that the questionnaire took longer than expected, because they had never given any prior thought to what it meant to be a citizen in the academy.

The responses to the ten questions have been captured and synthesised within the following five themes:

- Participants' understandings of academic citizenship
- Dominant forms of knowledge, institutional norms and cultures
- Diversity and transformation
- Identity and vulnerability
- Re-imagining inclusive academic citizenship.

Considering the profoundly different experiences of academics, because of their specific identities—as has thus far been discussed in this book—participants were invited to reveal how they identified themselves in terms of race and gender, if at all. To ensure anonymity and confidentiality of the participants, they have each been assigned a pseudonym. Their respective universities are not revealed; instead, their universities are differentiated based on the country in which they are located. Four of the participants are based in South Africa, their respective universities are identified in terms of their provincial locations. To preserve the authenticity of each story, I have presented the data as shared, and presented these in line with the five indicated themes. Any additions or amendments, as presented in the parentheses, are purely for the sake of clarity.

10.2 Academic Citizenship as Lived and Storied

Jess

Jess, a 'coloured' female academic, has been in the academy for nineteen years. She is currently employed as an associate professor and Head of Department of a Language Department at a historically 'white' university, in the Western Cape in South Africa. She has been at this institution for nearly five years. She describes her university as fairly diverse but still predominantly 'white'. There are a few efforts to ensure a pluralist, diverse institutional culture, but change is very slow. One still experiences micro aggressions as a black womxn.

My understanding of this concept [academic citizenship] is it is the way in which one serves the collective (the institution, one's department, one's chosen academic community, other colleagues at other universities, and one's colleagues) for benefit of the entire community (international, national, institutional and departmental). It is about a vision for a collective intellectual and pedagogic project where one sometimes sacrifices one's own needs in order to advance the collective.

I have practised and benefitted from academic citizenship. I practice citizenship through mentoring students and more junior colleagues, running writing workshops, participating in professionalisation workshops for our postgraduate students, taking up the position of Head of Department of a large department, acting as external examiner for a undergraduate and postgraduate department of another South African university over three years, examining MA and PhD theses as an external examiner, reviewing as a peer reviewer for accredited international and national journals, presenting research and writing workshops for postgraduate students, and serving on various faculty committees such as the staffing committee and Humanities Transformation Committee. I have also benefitted from others' mentoring and guidance as they have enacted their own ideas of academic citizenship.

I think being in a position of leadership naturally lends itself to being asked to do more citizenship. One leads through academic citizenship. Some academics feel a larger responsibility than others to be active in citizenship, especially people of colour and women, as we want to "lift while we climb" through the ranks of academia. In other words, as we take up more senior leadership roles, we wish to empower others to step into leadership, especially women of colour and other populations which have been marginalised historically at SA universities. I am highly active because I want to see other junior scholars succeed in a difficult, challenging environment. Unfortunately, I see other more senior academics not interested in citizenship and avoiding it as much as possible.

Without inclusive academic citizenship, higher education is highly elitist and conservative by nature. The academy has always been discriminatory and biased toward the mainstream majority and men, the able-bodied, and so on. Research that is inclusive is better research. Likewise with teaching and administration. All people stand to benefit from inclusion in higher education including the broader society which should gain from the work of academics. I think barriers exist as the level of

10.2 Academic Citizenship as Lived and Storied

citizenship what one can give often depends on one's seniority in an institution of higher education.

The more junior one is, the less citizenship one can give, as one has to focus on publishing, teaching, and balancing research and teaching. One needs to be a bit more selfish as a junior academic entering a position. This is a barrier to citizenship, but a necessary boundary. Precarious employment practices such as contracting out teaching also leads to barriers to citizenship, as one is not motivated as a precariously positioned worker to serve others through performing citizenship. Mentoring, for example, comes from experience and thus lack of experience can also be a barrier.

There is a tendency by some academics to shirk duties of academic citizenship, as they take away from research time, which is most valued at our institution. On the other hand, citizenship activity is necessary for confirmation of probation and promotion. We strive to mentor emerging faculty to cultivate a balance of service/citizenship and research, with teaching. Research is, however, most valued at our university and is the main component in promotions.

I am not sure what pluralist forms of academic citizenship are, but they are not really valued at my institution. There is activist work in developing black staff, for example, outside of formal structures, and is often frowned upon and actively criticised by non-marginal staff members.

I think certain intersectional identities have a lot more to negotiate in the university. Being 'black', being a woman, being a 'black' woman, being disabled, being gender non-binary—these are still vulnerable identities which need support and protection, in my view. This is why I live out citizenship, to assist and promote such identities, because I know how difficult it has been for me as a 'black' womxn to get ahead in academia in South Africa. The only reason I have a job is because of the 'RhodesMustFall' and 'FeesMustFall' student movements. Their call for decolonial scholarship and pedagogy created a space for me in South African higher education.

Before these protests, no-one was interested in my research or found it valuable. I had more offers abroad but could not find a job in South Africa. This personal story demonstrates the vulnerability of being of a marginal group, trying to do research centering marginal groups. We are not valued as people and our research on people like us is not seen as valuable either. It is only the student movement's insistence on decolonisation that has given us a certain status in academia recently.

I believe collegiality and trust are critical for an inclusive academic citizenship. To lead a department or programme, for example, one needs to be collegial and trustworthy. One needs the respect of one's colleagues. Without this, citizenship is virtually impossible. To mentor younger colleagues and graduate students, one must be respected, trusted, and trustworthy. One must be seen as an expert, and successful, in order to be viewed as having any knowledge worthy of imparting. It is very important to have 'black' people ('Indian', African and 'coloured') and specifically 'black' womxn in positions of power and authority. They can understand the barriers other 'black' people face (including junior colleagues and postgraduate students). We are invested in their success and from my own observations, we will go the extra mile to nurture, protect and enable other black colleagues to thrive. We want to see our institutions diversify; we want to retain our talented young 'black' academics. We do not want them to experience the same violence we have gone through to find a space in academia.

Michael

Michael is a 'coloured', male academic. Of his six years in the academy, he has spent five years at a historically 'white' university in the Free State, and more recently took up a new post at relatively new university, established in post-apartheid South Africa in 2014. He is a senior lecturer in the School of Education.

At my previous institution, there were several barriers in place so as not to disturb the system. The university was only interested in preserving the predominance of 'white' academics and holding onto historical structures of 'white' culture and tradition. 'Black' academics were simply invisible and had no role in the structures of the university. I am currently at a new university, which is more representative of South Africa's diverse population.

For me, academic citizenship entails offering academic service to the broader university community and the wider community. The service to community is presumed to be a mutually beneficial engagement. But it could also be peer support, mentoring, and reviewing. I have engaged in it at community level (outreach community work like talks at schools, radio); institutionally (mentoring, moderating, committees, etc.) and in my discipline (reviews, or serving on professional bodies). Mostly it is tiring and time consuming, and difficult to accommodate because it competes with one's formal workload. If it is not credit bearing, academics don't bother to engage. If it is not mandated by the institution, they decline the task when approached. Universities do not encourage all types of academic citizenship.

For example, outreach is discouraged unless it shows potential to generate money or third-stream income for the university and enhances the institutional image. All academics do not experience the same citizenship. Certain institutional cultures still persist to exclude. The big issue here is the lack or slow pace of transformation. In some disciplines where outreach is part of the program offering, there is no acknowledgement for the work and investment academics make. It is not counted as academic citizenship.

Collegiality is important, but it can also have negative effects, when certain groups are only collegial with the 'in-group', and deliberately try to marginalise or exclude others. It is not only that the contributions by 'black' academics are ignored. The reality is that they are simply ignored. There are no attempts to create an inclusive environment. Collegiality might work in other university settings, but in broken systems like the South African higher education system and others, this is simply not possible.

Huda

Huda, a 'coloured' female academic, has been employed at a historically 'white' university in the Western Cape, South Africa, for the past 21 years. She is a full professor, with a specialisation in educational psychology. She describes her faculty as diverse in terms of race but not ethnicity.

The nature of academic citizenship in cross-cultural situations, gives focus to developmental areas, and where a high degree of consensus is found even if it is only in one's perception—this give way to inclusiveness. My lived experience is often ignored. I often feel as though my views are the last resort. I do not feel included in my institution's culture. Certain types of citizenship are matched to certain disciplines, and people. If you are 'white' you are seen to be part of the dominant group, and you therefore are entitled to have opinions. For those who are not 'white', the experiences are very different.

Furthermore, my experience has been that, because our programs are linked to the caring professions, requests to engage with communities and provide psychological support or counselling are more likely to be referred to our department, than to others. Academics are inundated with requests from communities that the university refers to us, but not necessarily supports and provide resources for. Universities often engage with service to the community as a marketing strategy, and as a photo opportunity when an academic with institutional clout is involved. Much more visibility is given to individuals that the university wants to showcase, rather than due to wanting to serve or bring about change in community.

Service learning as a pedagogy allows one to bring academic scholarship and academic citizenship together. However, in my experience there is no institutional infrastructure to support and encourage it. All the administration and liaison work rests with the lecturer, and becomes a logistical nightmare when classes are big or administrators dictate a mode of delivery that clash with the pedagogy.

My university's identity is very different from what it was a few decades ago, and that is reflected in its structure and governance. Scholarship does not seem to be its core business anymore. The institutional culture is driven by competition and individualism which I think works against values such as collegiality, mentorship, and peer learning. The value of an academic is not determined by the quality work she delivers to her students and the scholarship she helps advance in academia; rather the academic's value is determined by what she is worth for the institution, in monetary terms.

Transformation at my university is a complex process. Transformation cannot be brought about by strategically placed, or high-profile individuals only. Transformation entails population and intellectual diversification. The drivers for transformation could be a combination of policy, systems change and buy-in by the whole higher education environment. Without safe spaces and trust the transformation will be cosmetic only. Higher education remains a deeply unequal space. Historically advantaged institutions are well resourced and capacitated. However, they have lost the plot! If academics can model academic citizenship in all its forms in the institution (mentorship and peer support) and the disciplines (collegiality) and in collaboration with community through outreach, meaningful difference to society is possible.

Anna

Anna, a 'black' female, is an early career academic, and attained her PhD in 2018. She was appointed as a lecturer at a historically 'white' university in the Eastern Cape, South Africa, in 2020.

My university continues to struggle with issues of whiteness in how it expresses its culture. They university is committed to continued delivery of teaching and learning amidst world pandemics and the worst blackouts South Africa has seen. With such a dedicated focus on academic output, I imagine there is not a lot of time to come together to reimagine how the university might function. The members of the department are diverse in terms of race, religion and language. However, I don't have any examples of concerted efforts to unite the members within the department or a particular ethos that has become apparent to me within the 2.5 years that I have been a member of the department.

A citizen is someone who lives within particular boundaries, bound by certain rules and regulations, and with an expectation to part-take within the community. A citizen of academia might have particular experiences as a member of this global community, which I imagine is referred to academic citizenship. I don't know if working in academia constitutes 'owning' citizenship. When joining the university, as full-time lecturer, I suppose that made me an academic citizen. Though, for an early career academic, if one does not understand the rules of the game, you can't play the game properly. It has been a tough time figuring out what the expectations are, who acts in the university space, when do they act, how do they act, why do they act.

Issues of power and empowerment prevail among academic staff members in higher education spaces and is also evident where I work. I have spent a lot of time observing, listening, and questioning to make sense of myself within the university space. If you ask me if I feel as if I am an academic citizen, I'll answer 'no'. I do not feel 'at home', empowered, as if I know the rules of the game, or as if I belong. I am not the only who feels this way. Other early career academics, regardless of their race, also feel isolated and unsupported. However, I do love teaching and have an inexhaustible passion for all things education.

To me 'playing the game' in higher education, firstly, requires understanding the game. To understand the higher education game various factors have impacted my experience—the lack of a supportive community, mentorship within the faculty, and collaborative learning. In general, there is not a culture of collaboration in our faculty, which is deeply unsettling to me. I feel that true participation as an academic citizen is expressed in your publication list. Participation in academic citizenship might be expressed in the level of outputs that the academic produces. I have learnt that this is what counts in academia. Therefore, the powerful are those that produce publications. Institutional systems are hierarchical and there are many systems that I am not included in due to my lower position as lecturer and short time in higher education and the university. Maybe in the lecture hall or the classroom—this is the predominant space that I feel I can express myself most and feel most as a functional part of the university and where I can contribute to education.

Although my faculty has more female than male academics, males still dominate the space, especially in meetings, where female voices are often ignored. There is a strong culture of masculinity and its association with power, competitiveness and success. As a female, I am struggling to navigate the higher education, I have spent many hours unpacking why without fully understanding yet. But it might be that I truly don't yet understand the space and how it operates and therefore do not understand how to express myself within it.

I agree that relationships of trust and collegiality play a critical role in academic citizenship. You don't become a citizen if you are isolated and are expected to operate on your own. Citizenship is possibly accomplished when there are connections of trust and care amongst the members of the community. Maybe if we all are allowed to express our identities authentically and safely, that could be a starting point to understand each other to work and live together—allow more authentic expression, not academic identities which has been residing in higher education since ancient times, but newer expressions of who academics might look like and act like.

Miriam

Miriam, a female 'Palestinian-American', has spent 16 years in the academia. She started her career as an assistant professor and was promoted to associate professor. Currently, she works as a researcher and director of a centre at a university in Washington D.C.

My academic institution is diverse in student body but not among faculty and administration. Efforts were declared to diversify the staff but that did not materialize yet. I specifically joined campus wide committees examining and addressing racial and ethnic diversities and controversial issues on campus. I was always on the outside, no matter how much I tried. Being an immigrant, a Palestinian, with an accent, in a faculty kept me outside the circle of the college I served in. My citizenship became limited to working with international students and faculty who are interested in global education issues. During the Obama campaign, I was blacklisted as a faculty member who supports the Palestinians (which was portrayed as a bad thing those days and till now). My citizenship focused on advocating for international students and those who are a minority (African American and Latinos) as well as creating alliances for those voices that are silenced.

In the United States, at least the universities I am aware of, academic citizenship is specific to one issue that a faculty cares about. If it's gender, then they focus on that. Few of the faculty I have worked with have the awareness that citizenship is about making connections and that many of the issues related to equity and justice are interrelated. They aim to be politically correct but do not take the route of self-study and examination of their own biases and prejudices. I think in my context (The U.S.), it's very typical unfortunately. There are too many hidden agendas and people play it civilized but also dirty when someone threatens their territory. I learned professors are very territorial.

Serving on tenure and promotion committees and having power is one of the goals of many senior faculty and they abuse that in some instances. There are 'clicks' in the schools of education, I experienced. Some faculty try to bring up the issues of inequities in representations on major committees but not successfully. This happens because the administration in many instances is in the hands of the same profiles of faculty. In schools of education the deans and staff at the top are 'white' males while the faculty are women and some minorities.

Collegiality and trust are necessary, but I am not sure this can be obtained because of the structure of academic promotions in the United States. The tenure track and the promotion process itself, puts people on a trajectory of compliance and passive engagements with faculty because of fear of retaliation. You see that even in students' evaluations and how faculty 'bribe' their students to rate them highly. Academic citizenship can begin to take shape, if scholarship of professional learning and individual transformation are encouraged. The discourse of what counts as scholarship should change.

Several of my colleagues were denied tenure because of their race, and research on culture work does not count as scholarship. Encouraging projects that engage faculty in identity work and dialogues that are considered fit for scholarship should be prioritised. This is of high importance as students look up to role models and to go through a process of learning and personal transformation, students need to feel someone is there to support them. Increasing students' sense of belonging to the institution is in large in the hands of the faculty, the advisors, and staff of the university.

Mel

Mel, a 'white' female academic, obtained her PhD in 2009. She is currently a full professor at a university in Hong Kong, where she has been employed for the past two years. She describes her institution as somewhat diverse. Maybe 15% of faculty are international and among students and staff there is a split between Mainland and local Chinese, who have different cultures and languages. There are concerted efforts to ensure a pluralist and diverse ethos. I lead a 'Diversity, Equity and Social Inclusion Research Group' and the 'Women Researchers in Education Network'. There are other similar groups, and some academic staff are tasks with focusing on diversity, equity and inclusion in their research and at the institutional level.

I don't have a strong sense of the term [academic citizenship]. But I guess it is like service and it would relate to a sense of citizenship as having to do with belonging, responsibilities, and rights and privileges. I know from my own work that there are many different senses of citizenship in relation to different country priorities and different views of nationalism as ideology and as a scholarly study of nation-states and related entities. I guess views of academic citizenship could vary in parallel to debates in those broader fields.

There is a sense that everyone should contribute to the greater good and benefit from the collective work that is done. This can be in academic societies and in your institution at University/Faculty/Department levels. I've found it hard to grapple, honestly. I'm often encouraged to serve and as a woman I am often pressured and made to feel like something is wrong with me if I don't want to serve heavily. However, I don't like to serve heavily, and I often feel the work is invisible labour. Some people are doing the invisible labour while others (older, majority men) are benefiting from their obliviousness and their lightened load.

Even diversity work falls more on the diverse who must defend their belonging and status against a political majority who is often ignorant about their challenges and the inequities in the system. I resent those who seem to only benefit from the system, and I feel frustrated that I have to do so much service which takes away from my ability to work as a scholar in the intellectual domain. I think that for some the barriers are that they don't even realise they should be contributing more and feel like their job should just be research and teaching. Meanwhile for others, they are taught implicitly that they are expected to engage in heavy service, and they are treated with resentment and intolerance if they do not. I see recognition as a relational and interpersonal experience. People recognise each other across different types of work groups, units, interdisciplinary and thematic teams, friend groups, through awards based on excellence and caring in different domains, through awarding people with formal titles for service work in committees and coordination work, etc.

I see vulnerability as a good thing, but some people are expected to be more vulnerable than others. Some people fail to get the opportunity to cultivate vulnerability while others are never given the opportunity to have influence and authority. Without collegiality and trust people feel isolated and cannot recognise or be recognised in their community effectively. Actually, people would rather feel trust that colleagues see them as important in order to participate than anything else. Leaders and those with influence, authority and power at all levels need to challenge the status quo and be open to challenges to the status quo from diverse members of the community. They need to not leave the 'diversity' work to the diverse, but instead engage in self-learning and improvement. The script needs to be flipped; the experts on diversity and equity are at the bottom; they need to belong and be recognised. Only in this way can all people transform and grow for the better as individuals and as an institution.

Without inclusive academic citizenship, higher education is highly elitist and conservative by nature. The academy has always been discriminatory and biased toward the mainstream majority and men, the able-bodied, and so on. Research that is inclusive is better research. Likewise with teaching and administration. All people stand to benefit from inclusion in higher education including the broader society which should gain from the work of academics.

Judith

Judith has been in the academy for 23 years and is currently employed as an assistant professor at a university in Manila, Philippines.

My current institution has a good male/female gender balance, also good diversity in terms of age ranges, as well as ethno-linguistic diversity in terms of intra-Philippine diversity. Not much diversity in terms of non-Filipino diversity but I'm not sure what the statistics are like in comparison to the larger population. Not much religious diversity because it is a Catholic institution in a majority-Catholic country (although employees don't need to be Catholic to be hired). In terms of students, we have one of the highest numbers of foreign exchange students and inbound study abroad students in the country, so we are relatively diverse in terms of nationalities, compared to other universities. No concerted effort for diversity per se, except in terms of trying to recruit more foreign exchange and inbound study abroad students, for ranking purposes.

I'm not familiar with the phrase academic citizenship. This is the first time I've heard of it. Because of this question, I did look it up and it seems to be equivalent to what we call 'service and outreach' in my country. If it is, then this would include tasks expected of faculty members outside of classroom teaching and research. This would include, for example, university administrative work, involvement in professional societies/associations, and disseminating expertise to the wider community. I'm not sure if that's right though. If my understanding of the phrase 'academic citizenship' is right, then I have a lot of experience of academic citizenship, because I have been working in academia for more than 20 years.

When I was a junior faculty member, much of my university service involved department-level administrative work and committee work, but over time, my responsibilities broadened to school-wide and then university-wide work, including representing the university to outside parties. I have, for example, held roles in university-level committees, such as our Committee on Standards and our Committee on Discipline. My 'outreach' work has been of two types: those related to my teaching and research, and those not. This has included active participation in professional/learned societies related to my field and working with the wider community in areas related to my fields. I have, for example, given workshops to non-academics in areas related to my research. I would describe my experiences as varied. Some of it has been enriching and fulfilling. Other times, the work has been bureaucratic and full of red tape.

In terms of university service, more outspoken, extroverted academics whose views are generally aligned with the dominant views within the university seem to be noticed more, and tend to get assigned to committees, possibly because they are more quickly remembered by leaders choosing committee members. Those who show leadership skills or who have shown good organizational skills also seem to be assigned to committees more quickly. In my experience, 'homegrown' academics—those who have spent part of their own studies at the same university also seem to be at the top when being assigned to committees. Academics who show collegiality, who get along well with colleagues, seem to be elected more frequently.

In terms of outreach or academic citizenship beyond the walls of the university, involvement is more dependent on the academics' initiative; some academics choose to be very involved in this kind of work, whereas others don't. There are some barriers to involvement, however; some academics have financial situations or family responsibilities that hinder them from being active in professional societies.

I think there are some fields/disciplines where there are more gender imbalances, and therefore where gender may have an impact on access to academic citizenship. For example, philosophy is a field that is heavily dominated by men in the Philippines. Although there are women leaders in the field (chairs of departments, for example), the professional associations in the country tend to be very male dominated and there have been barely any women presidents of the large national associations in the field. Many women have also reported experiencing sexism at conferences, which have made some women more hesitant to attend such conferences, which in turn have made them less likely to be very involved in the associations that organize these conferences. There are also other fields which are very female dominated, but

I do not know whether this has an impact on men's access to academic citizenship in those fields. Furthermore, I think if someone's gender is other than cisgender, more negotiation is required. At my institution, although I have not observed nor experienced it myself, I do imagine that someone who is trans might feel the pressure to dress more androgynously, for example. At my university I also think that some disabilities require more negotiation.

I think different universities have different cultures and dominant forms of ethos, which may affect the access to academic citizenship of its faculty members. For example, the Philippines has many Catholic universities. I do think that in some Catholic universities, faculty members who share in the particular kind of Catholic ethos explicitly espoused by such a university tend to form the 'inner circles', in that they tend to become the leaders who stay in leadership beyond one or two terms, and progress from department-level leadership to school-wide and university-wide leadership.

In the Philippines, the push for universities to become more research-focused also means that those with PhDs tend to be preferred for leadership positions. Accreditation policies imposed by the national government and quality-assurance associations make it harder for those without PhDs (including those with professional higher degrees). National immigration policies create barriers for non-Filipinos. Outside of the Philippines, academia in the Global North also often has practices and policies that make it harder for academics from the Global South to be included. Visa restrictions and differences in income make it very difficult, for example, for academics in the Global South, to participate in conferences that are located in the Global North. I imagine that as a result, so-called 'international' societies located in the Global North tend to have very little representation from Global South academics.

There has also been progress in terms of diversifying the university through the appointment of different identities. For example, our university recently enacted a gender policy which explicitly commits to gender inclusivity and gender safety. I think that this may have the effect of creating more gender inclusivity for academic citizenship among faculty members as well, although I do not know what indicators can be used to measure this. There is less space for pluralism in terms of religion. Although the university accepts faculty members regardless of religion, the Theology Department of the university is a Catholic theology department, and within that department, religious discussions are largely either Catholic or related to Catholicism (for example, interreligious dialogues between Catholics and Muslims). I imagine that hypothetically, a theologian whose specialty is not in Catholicism might have more chance of joining the philosophy or sociology departments rather than the Theology Department.

Academics with minoritized or non-dominant identities might speak out about the vulnerabilities they experience, which others in the institution might be blind to. This can be the starting point for building a more just institution. Because justice matters. Also, if higher education is committed to knowledge production, then failing to make academic citizenship inclusive would mean that knowledge inequalities and knowledge injustices would be perpetuated.

Rose

Rose, a 'white' female academic, joined the academy in 2011 as a lecturer. She is currently a full professor at a historically 'white' university in the Northern, Cape, South Africa.

My institution remains a very phallocentric and conservative institution. Although the institution does initiate things like 'Gender Awareness Week' among staff and students, a mostly monoculture remains where men occupy management positions and people of colour are only included as a 'political symbol' but are often silenced. I understand academic citizenship as scholar-activism. There is no uniform academic citizenship, each is uniquely embodied and embedded in their own socio-historical contexts. There is a direct influence of the academic space, namely our higher education neoliberal institutions filled with competitive and individualistic performativity cultures.

Academic citizenship also involves who we are as persons in our nature and being (for example, as more caring, aggressive, deliberative). It also involves the scholarship we profess as academics and how we choose to profess this knowledge with (not to) our students and colleagues and even our management. I have often been ostracized because of my gender, race, and age.

Being a 'white' woman in a field that wants to unlock social justice issues is often regarded as paradoxical. My age has always been a defining factor. My ideas are often questioned because of my lack of experience (in years) and not growing up in a pre-1994 dispensation when exclusion and discrimination were rife. So, what would I know about social justice issues being a young, 'white' woman? I often have to navigate my way through alternative pathways (like specific intercultural research teams) to have my voice heard.

The neoliberal, performativity culture of universities dictate how academics can access and participate in their academic citizenship. Funding streams: the natural sciences receive more funding that the social sciences. This excludes some while advancing others. Universities are businesses. They are a capital machine that operates in ways that suite their financial models and operations. So, the same kind of citizenship cannot be assigned to all its academics. Spaces of and for recognition of pluralist forms are available at my institution at a micro level. For example, as academics we are not challenged in how we teach (we are challenged in terms of what we teach as this must align with the university vision and mission). But how we teach, is not 'monitored'. In this space we can express pluralistic forms of academic citizenship.

When academics are scholar-activists they are critical of the neoliberal space of universities. It is about challenging different forms on consensus and conformativity through dissent. For Maistry et al. (2021: 216) 'dissent as an ethical act counteracts any a priori ethical rules or guidelines so that dissent is immanent in the activities humans engage with, and immanent to being and becoming. Dissent is immanent to human becoming, such as the becoming of human activities or organisations. Moreover, dissent is rhizomatic in the sense that we will never know what it will or could do'.

An inclusive academic citizenship should matter because academics differ. They come from various gender, culture, race, class, religion and knowledge backgrounds. An inclusive academic citizenship supports a decolonised and affirmative ethics ethos. It does not colonise academics into being the same for purposes of performativity measures, for example. Being inclusive will invigorate the much needed 'difference' that my university lacks. as Mouffe (2000: 19) proffers about pluralism: 'It is taken to be constitutive at the conceptual level … as something that we should celebrate and enhance … (It) gives a positive status to differences and questions the objective of unanimity and homogeneity, which is always revealed as fictitious and based on acts of exclusion'.

10.3 Key Considerations of Chapter

Unsurprisingly, the various understandings of academic citizenship, as revealed in this chapter, are closely tied to academics' identities. There is a very explicit connection between who academics and the type of citizenship they embody. The more centred and aligned certain academic identities are, the greater the chance of enjoying a 'full' citizenship of equal opportunity and recognition. The more academics differ from the dominant, or the more complex the layers of diversity—as found in Miriam, a Palestinian-American—the more there is to navigate and negotiate to find any measure of inclusion, however fleeting. Academic citizenship, therefore, does not unfold in a vacuum, instead, it is influenced, in a complex way, by academics' biographical background, professional trajectory, employment and working conditions, among other factors (Galaz-Fontes et al., 2016).

Also apparent from the stories are marked differences between the experiences of senior and early career academics. While senior academics have greater latitude in terms of what they choose to do as an enactment of their citizenship, early career academics seem to be left to their own devices, with very little support not only in terms of their roles and responsibilities, but also what exactly is understood by being an academic citizen. These experiences substantiate Höhle and Teichler's (2016) view that while professionals in other professions might be considered to be fully qualified already and their career paths have stabilised, academics in many countries are still viewed as building up their competences along possibly productive work. They posit that there is hardly a single academic profession.

On the one hand, the views and activities of academics at teaching-oriented institutions have little in common with those research-intensive institutions. On the other hand, junior or early career academics might not be viewed as being the followers of the university professors, but rather as significantly distinct during this career stage from university professors, as they are being socialized during another period of time (Höhle & Teichler, 2016).

As a closing remark, all the stories shared by the participants in this chapter reveal some vulnerability. If not in terms race and gender, then in as a novice or immigrant academic. It is hard not to notice the uncertainty of how *to be* as an academic or how to fit into the university. There seems to be a detachment from it all, couched in a silent recognition, that a full sense of belonging or acceptance as an academic citizen might never come to fruition. At the same time, there is also a yearning to be part of the collective 'in-group'—again, whether this defined in terms of race, ethnicity, gender or religion. The stories, while only able to offer fleeting insights, are nevertheless profound in capturing the complex nature of academic citizenship, and seems to confirm, that for some academics, citizenship might remain an elusive state.

References

Davids, N. (2022). *Out of place: An autoethnography of postcolonial citizenship.* African Minds.
Ellis, C., Adams, T. E., & Bochner, A. P. (2011). Autoethnography: An overview. *Historical Social Research, 36*(4), 273–290.
Farber, D., & Sherry, S. (1995). Telling stories out of school: An essay on legal narratives. *Stanford Law Review, 45*(4), 807–855.
Fivush, R. (2008). Remembering and reminiscing: How individual lives are constructed in family narratives. *Memory Studies, 1*(1), 49–58.
Galaz-Fontes, J. F., Arimoto, A., Teichler, U., & Brennan, J. (2016). Biographies and careers throughout academic life: Introductory comments. In J. F. Galaz-Fontes, A. Arimoto, U. Teichler, & J. Brennan (Eds.), *Biographies and careers throughout academic life* (pp. 11–30). Springer.
Höhle, A., & Teichler, U. (2016). Career and self-understanding of academics in Germany in comparative perspective. In J. F. Galaz-Fontes, A. Arimoto, U. Teichler, & J. Brennan (Eds.), *Biographies and careers throughout academic life* (pp. 241–270). Springer.
Lugones, M. C., & Spelman, E. V. (1983). *Have we got a theo*ry for you! Feminist theory, cultural imperialism and the demand for 'the woman's voice.' *Women's Studies International Forum, 6*(6), 573–581.
Maistry, S. M., Blignaut, S., Du Preez, P., Le Grange, L., Ramrathan, L., & Simmonds, S. (2021). Towards a counter-narrative: Why dissent/agonism might have appeal in a neoliberal higher education space! *Alternation, 28*(2), 211–237.
Mouffe, C. (2000). *The democratic paradox.* Verso.
Sium, A., & Ritskes, E. (2013) Speaking truth to power: Indigenous storytelling as an act of living resistance. *Decolonization: Indigeneity, Education & Society, 2*(1), I–X.
Ylijoki, O., & Ursin, J. (2013). The construction of academic identity in the changes of Finnish higher education. *Studies in Higher Education, 38*(8), 1135–1149.

Chapter 11
Responsibility and Being *Other*-Wise

Although situated and framed in discourses of intellectualism and the academia, the responsibilities of universities, as Derrida (2004) reminds us, 'cannot be purely academic'. There are privileged responsibilities, which accompany the production of knowledge, which demands that universities, and hence, its academic citizens, turn their gaze beyond the certainty of what is already known, and consider what might be other and otherwise. Pondering on the strangeness of others, allows us is to slip away from pre-existing ways of seeing and being in the world (Levinas, 1988). The capacity to step into the strangeness of others is not something unfamiliar to us. As social beings with stories, we are already entangled with others. We are always already in conversation with the world in which we find ourselves even when we are unconscious of those around us.

It is up to academics to accept the responsibilities pertaining to that which is not 'purely academic', and to see the value of turning towards others, not only for the purposes of knowing about the other, but to become wiser about the worlds which constitute others. This turning is necessary for the cultivation and support of new formations of academic citizenship—formations which are averse to othering and marginalisation. For universities, the benefits of cultivating an academic citizenship of responsibility and being *other*-wise, include discarding inscribed binaries between different kinds of knowledge, and more importantly, between different kinds of people.

11.1 That's How the Light Gets in

In this place we call 'university', writes Barnett (2022: 160), 'rhythm is a pool of rhythms, flowing across each other, with deep forces at work, producing great currents that wash through university life. These deep forces take many forms, some more apparent than others, manifesting at times in knowledge, values, curricula, research, pedagogies, other times in dissent and protest. The university is never quite one thing, or one space. It shapes around discourses and cultures, absorbing memory after memory as academics and students move through its corridors. At time it is bold in its stance, offering much needed wisdom to those around it, basking in the glory of its epistemological prowess.

Other times, it is subdued by resistant voices, urgently in pursuit of something more, more than what the university is prepared to give. The university is at once the pinnacle of dreams realised as it is symbol of lost opportunity. All the while, no matter how old, or how historical the architecture or the traditions, the university is never quite what it seems. This is because it lives in 'a pool of rhythms', at the beck and call not only to those within it, but also outside of it. If society is under siege and instability, so is the university. If the world is full of cracks, then, so too, is the university.

The cracks are crucial, because as Leonard Cohen sings in his well-known and haunting song, 'Anthem', 'that's how the light gets in.' If education is what the university does, then every single crack or crisis opens possibilities for renewed ways of thinking and living in this world.

Crisis, states Arendt (1968: 170), 'tears away facades and obliterates prejudices'; it forces humans back to the questions themselves and requires from them either new or old answers, but in any case, direct judgements.

When the world was plummeted into a submissive retreat by a global pandemic in 2019, the crack was severe in its swoop of deaths and isolation. But it also reminded human beings not only of their vulnerability, despite their social, scientific, technological and medical advancements, but also of their inter-connectedness, and hence inter-dependency. This is because crisis 'tears away facades and obliterates prejudices—to explore and inquire into whatever has been laid bare of the essence of the matter…' (Arendt, 1968: 180). The light shone through in every act of compassion and outreach, highlighting human resilience. And in the face of social isolation and immobility, the need for human connection intensified.

Determined to keep the educational light going, universities were quick to transition and transmit their knowledge across virtual platforms—beaming lectures and tutorials into the safe havens of students' homes, single-mindedly focused on ensuring that the academic year remains on track. While mostly satisfactory in achieving its goals of virtual teaching and learning, the university, yet again, showed how lithe and responsive it can be in the face of crisis and adversity. It also reminded us that universities, and by implication, academics, and teachers, are 'always educating for a world that is or is becoming out of joint, for this is the basic human situation, in which the world is created by mortal hands to serve mortals for a limited time at home' (Arendt, 1968: 180).

It is crucial for universities to be responsive to the 'out-of-jointness' of the world—whether this involves global pandemics, political turmoil, economic depressions, or the crises of global warming. It also crucial, however that even when these crises might emanate from 'outside', the university is never immune to the effects of these crises—much like was found in the case of a global pandemic. Other times the 'out-of-joint' world emanates from the university itself, as is the case with student protests against exorbitant fees, student exclusion, or gender-based violence. These protests often spill over into surrounding communities of universities, thereby drawing society into university conflicts.

Other times, university campuses are brought to a standstill because of disputes regarding academic freedom, and who should be allowed to speak on campuses and who should not. But of course, careful considerations of these crises will reveal that although the crises are seen to start on campuses and by students, at times, the origin of these crises lives in the world. If students on campus are raising concerns and demanding action from universities to deal with the scourge of gender-based violence, or student food insecurity, as two examples, then it is highly likely that these same dilemmas will be found in the society of the university. In other words, the university is as much in the world, as the world is in the university, meaning that the 'great currents that wash through university life' (Barnett, 2022), are often a convergence of what is happening in the university as it finds itself in the world.

At the time of writing (and not for the first time) a few universities in South Africa are in turmoil in the face of serious allegations of corruption and bringing the university into disrepute against vice-chancellors and councils. At one institution, both the vice-chancellor and council chairperson have resigned before disciplinary proceedings could unfold. At another, it was found that the university's management and council had failed in executing their mandate, resulting in widespread practices of maladministration and tender irregularities, as well as governance failures. These findings, as well as the investigations or commissions appointed to investigate mismanagement at universities are not atypical to higher education. It is also very common in the world of these universities.

Yet, as these findings are made public, and some individuals decide to vacate their positions, it allows the light to come through and shine a light not only on the missteps, but also on what is necessary to correct and set right. To Arendt (1968), it is the responsibility of education to preserve newness—that is, to think about matters anew when faced with crises. Crises and cracks, therefore, are necessary to jar us out of complacency, and assumptions of functionality and normativity, it forces us to pause take stock of what we know, what we value and what needs to be reconsidered or renewed.

11.2 Responsibility and not Being 'Purely Academic'

If we accept that the university is in the world, and the world is in the university, then it follows that academics and academic citizenship are not separate from the world or its daily rhythms. What happens in the world should be of as much of concern to academics as what happens within the university. McNiff (2023) contends that academics can do much to challenge and change the situation; it is their jobs to use words meaningfully and vigorously for the purpose of improving the quality of life for the planet and the living forms it supports. As such, explains McNiff (2023), the task or responsibility of an academic is to engage both in scholarly thinking work and in the kind of practical other-oriented work that will influence democratically cooperative developments in the social world, and use their knowledge in the service of human and non-human others for the future of the planet.

In turn, Derrida (2004: 91) proffers that to think of responsibility, is to equate it with 'a summons requiring a response' (Derrida, 2004: 91). Implicit in this description is an understanding of responsibility as an obligation to which academics must respond. The fact that academics consider themselves as educated, scholars, or intellectuals, means that they have the capacity to think and deliberate on certain topics, but it also suggests that they have a deeper and wider grasp of the world and how it functions. It is not only that academics should assume responsibility. To Derrida (2004: 148), it is also a matter of finding 'new ways of taking responsibility'.

Finding new ways of responsibility means a preparedness to step into unfamiliar zones, it also infers the possibility of rethinking certain views and positions, and recognising that the more academics claims to have, as well as to produce knowledge, the greater the responsibility. For example, some academics might hold the view that it is not their concern to ensure that students feel included in their teaching. They might argue that their job is to teach the content, and how the student comes into the learning of that content, is not the academic's concern. So, too, academics might have little interest or care in the personal stories of students, maintaining that it is not their job to help students with accessing funding, or finding accommodation, or when there are at risk of dropping out because of domestic responsibilities. In sum, their interest in students is limited to transmitting the academic project, and not the whole development or wellbeing of the student.

But it might be, that because of engaging in dialogue with these same students, or with colleagues who conceive of academic citizenship in a different way, these academics reconsider and adjust their views and approaches to taking new responsibility for students, and for their own relationships with students. They might even begin to take responsibility for their responsibility—after all, responsibility can only take place through a responsible individual. For this reason, Derrida (1995: 25) conceives of responsibility as a self-reflective concept:

> And let us not forget that an inadequate thematization of what responsibility is or *must be* is also an *irresponsible* thematization: not knowing, having neither a sufficient knowledge or consciousness of what being *responsible* means, is of itself a lack of responsibility. In order to be responsible it is necessary to respond or to answer to what being responsible means. For if it is true that the concept of responsibility has, in the most reliable continuity of its history, always implied involvement in action, doing, a *praxis*, a *decision* that exceeds simple conscience or simple theoretical understanding, it is also true that the same concept requires a decision or responsible action to answer for itself *consciously*, that is, with a knowledge of a thematics of what is done, of what action signifies, its causes its ends, etc.

For academics, this calls for a deep reflection on their own sets of histories, identity formation and socialisation, what they hold as true and valuable, and what not. It is through this kind of self-reflection, that academics might become awakened to who they are, what they know, as well as what they stand for and what they are prepared to take responsibility for, and act upon. Importantly, these responsibilities, argues Derrida (2004), 'cannot be purely academic'. If these responsibilities are difficult to

11.2 Responsibility and not Being 'Purely Academic'

assume, or precarious, he continues, 'it is because they must at once keep alive the memory of a tradition and make an opening beyond any program, that is, toward what is called the future' (Derrida, 2004: 149).

Hence, being an academic cannot only be defined as a set of responsibilities in relation to particular disciplines or assigned teaching loads. To be an academic is to step into the entirely of a responsibility, which, at once, is concerned with and responsive to, what happens inside as well as outside the university. Moreover, by understanding that academics' responsibilities 'cannot be purely academic', comes a recognition that things cannot simply be left as they are, and this includes relationships with others, whether colleagues or students. Academic citizenship, as has been laid out in this book so far, can be fraught with power tensions, and clear lines between those who are on the inside, and those who are not—not unlike the experiences of students.

Although notions of academic citizenship are associated with being in the academy, the responsibility of the university has always been looked at as having to extend beyond the immediate functions of the academy. And this means that academic citizenship, too, has to make imprints on the world outside of disciplines, faculties and the university itself. This includes recognising responsibilities in relation to speaking out against injustice or responding to crises. But, often, because of fears of not attaining tenure, or not being promoted, or simply not wanting to be seen as being 'controversial', most academics shy away from issues, which they deem as separate to their professional identity, or because they are unaffected directly, they remain quiet or complacent. Yet, the university itself (and by implication, the world) is never without crises or controversy, so if the objective is to avoid controversy, it simply is not possible.

Most recently, for example, Jansen (2023), in his book *Corrupted: A study of chronic dysfunction in South African universities*, reveals how easily corruption oozes into universities, not only in South Africa, but globally. Since the country's transition to a democracy in 1994, there have been no fewer than 20 interventions by government into 15 of South Africa's 26 public universities. To Jansen (2023), visible signs of chronic dysfunction include: never-ending stakeholder conflicts, ongoing student protests, violent confrontations, occasional burning of buildings, police presence and campus closures. Some of the consequences are a loss of teaching time, funder withdrawal, research delays, the departure of top academics and students, a drop in staff morale and government intervention with the appointment of an administrator. While Jansen (2023) acknowledges the role of historical inequity and inequality in the continuing dysfunction of some institutions, he also identifies the lack of governance and managerial capacity combined with a lack of academic integrity, as key factors.

The bigger picture might not always be clear or known regarding the extent of corruption at higher education institutions. But academics might see evidence of this in departments, faculties, senates or council meetings. They might also see evidence of preferential acceptance of students into programmes when they do not necessarily qualify. They might even witness the use of racist language by colleagues. None of these issues are definitively 'academic', but they say something about the academic citizenship and the university. And yet, most academics remain silent, preferring to adopt a blinkered approach to their environment, preferring 'not to get involved' and refusing to accept and act on the responsibility that comes with being an academic.

But non-involvement is not only an indication of shirking responsibility, it also lulls the university into an assurance that things can simply be left as they are. To Derrida (2004), the problem with not holding the university to account, is that, indeed, things will not only be left as they are, but might even get worse. By not calling out sexism, sexual harassment, or certain initiation practices which involves copious amounts of alcohol, for example, means that these cultures and traditions will simply be reproduced.

While the appeal from Derrida (2004: 91) to think about responsibility as 'a summons requiring a response', can be interpreted as an invitation for academic activism, this is not necessarily the case. This might be true, if one understands academic activism as embodying a willing acceptance of responsibilities that extend beyond teaching, learning, research, and writing, and which are critical to the development and sustenance of any healthy democracy (Davids & Waghid, 2021). Whether one chooses to frame the responsibilities of academics as activism is up for debate.

Barnett (2020), for example, explains that the 'public intellectual is a justifiably hallowed form of such activism', who, for decades, 'have spoken truth to power and sometimes with terrible consequences, being incarcerated in prison or worse'. But he questions whether their actions are forms of academic activism, or civil actions, meaning that the public intellectual is not so much an academic activist but a citizen activist bringing the resources of her intellect into the two public arenas (Barnett, 2020). For Barnett (2020), the public intellectual justifiably crosses the line between the academic life and the wider society. This debate, however will not detract from the fact that having knowledge, which places academics into positions of trust (as teachers, supervisors, mentors, reviewers, examiners and assessors), creates expectations of a wider social and societal reach, commentary, critique and response.

To the point of the central thesis of this book, to act on this responsibility, will depend on academic's identities, as well as the extent to which they are prepared to make themselves vulnerable. Speaking out against nepotism, or calling out institutional racism, demonstrates courage, but it also places academics in a vulnerable position. A dual process of responsibility unfolds.

On the one hand, the academic assumes the responsibility of calling out racism at an institution, and on the other hand, the onus of providing evidence of this racism falls onto the academic—thereby pitting the academic against the institution. In turn, the academic might find herself alone in assuming this responsibility, because those of who might have offered support and encouragement for her to speak out, might be less inclined to walk alongside the same path of responsibility. So, in her courage to enact her responsibility she makes herself vulnerable, while also revealing the strength of her convictions. Notably, her vulnerability may be temporary, but her position and voice will last long enough so that others might find assurance in her responsiveness.

Moreover, and perhaps most importantly, while academics associate themselves with specific universities, with some of these associations, being seen as offering scholarly prestige, it remains imperative for academics not to attach themselves to these universities so that their freedom to act or speak autonomously, is constrained. In other words, whatever attachment is held to institutions, needs to be flexible enough to allow for unconditional academic freedom, so that opinions are not held captive by universities. Being an academic citizen, therefore, should not be conflated with being a university citizen—the two designations are neither the same, nor should they be.

11.3 Epistemic Bubbles and (Dis)entanglement

Derrida's (2004) contention that the responsibilities of the university, and hence, academics, 'cannot be purely academic', can also be interpreted as a reminder to academics to turn their attention and gaze to that which is unknown and familiar. The certainty with which academics function in their professional identities is not necessarily extended into their collegial relationships, where less might be known about certain individuals. When something or somebody is unknown or unfamiliar, we are left with particular scenarios. This includes remaining disinterested, which involves a particular opinion of the person, regardless, because there has to be some way of justifying our reasons for our non-interest.

So, justifications might go along the following lines: 'I don't know her, because I have never had the chance to talk to her'; or 'I don't know her, because she has never made an effort to talk to me'; or 'I don't know her because I don't think we have anything in common'. Other times, justifications rely on preconceived perceptions, which feed into a perpetuation of stereotypes, which can, in turn, manifest as a fear, threat, or dislike, and hence, remain, unfamiliar, foreign, and unreachable.

Breaking these scenarios or patterns of what is essentially dis-engagement, is a complex process, because it involves a willingness to step out of comfort zones and into unfamiliarity, even inconvenience. Sometimes, remaining in ignorance can be comfortable, and knowledge can be complicated. It is easier to live with pre-existing ideas and in an epistemic bubble or echo chamber, than to bring those ideas into question, with the possibility of renewed understandings or beliefs.

Although interrelated, clarifies Nguyen (2020), epistemic bubbles and echo chambers are two distinct social phenomena, different in their origins, mechanisms for operation, and avenues for treatment. According to Nguyen (2020: 141–142), both reinforce ideological and are structures of exclusion, 'but epistemic bubbles exclude through omission, while echo chambers exclude by manipulating trust and credence'. He continues, an epistemic bubble is a social epistemic structure in which some relevant voices have been excluded through omission; they can form without ill intent, through ordinary processes of social selection and community formation.

For example, close friendships might gradually dissipate as different parties enjoy different interests. Relationships change because of marriage, divorce, death, geographical relocation or social mobility. In the same way, a PhD student might enjoy a close relationship with an academic and might in the nascent years of her career share many of the arguments propagated by her supervisor, whether in her writing or presentations. But as she becomes more established, this relationship might shift so that there is no longer a shared academic interest. The point in epistemic bubbles, other voices are merely not heard; is there is no conscious intention to actively undermine or exclude anyone (Nguyen, 2020).

By contrast, an echo chamber, says Nguyen (2020: 142), 'is a social epistemic structure in which other relevant voices have been actively discredited'. Members of an echo chamber share beliefs, which include reasons to distrust and actively isolate those outside the echo chamber (Nguyen, 2020). By discrediting and actively excluding outsiders, explains Nguyen (2020), echo chambers leave their members overly dependent on approved inside sources for information. To Nguyen (2020: 143), 'echo chambers prey on our epistemic interdependence', which means that in some circumstances, echo chamber members do not have full epistemic responsibility for their beliefs—'Once one is trapped in an echo chamber, one might follow good epistemic practices and still be led further astray'.

For example, it is not unusual for 'white' South Africans, including academics, who lived during apartheid to express incredulous views on the dehumanising effects of apartheid. They will argue that 'it could not have been that bad', or more problematically, that apartheid was never meant to oppress anyone, it simply intended to propagate a segregated citizenship.

Ironically, my very presence as a faculty member at a historically 'white' university is used as evidence for the argument that 'apartheid could not have been that bad'. I encounter the same kind of rhetoric among my 'white' students, when they try to explain their ignorance about apartheid on their 'friend circles', that they have never come into contact with anyone who has experienced apartheid. Importantly, as Nguyen (2020) points out, the distinction between epistemic bubbles and echo chambers is conceptual; a community can practice both forms of exclusion to varying degrees.

Academics, for example, on the one hand, might actively undermine and exclude peers on racial or ethnic grounds, and in this way rely on existent normative structures, which construct minority group academics as 'equity' tokens', and hence, 'incompetent'. By only engaging with academics who look and think like them, they construct an echo chamber in which the presence and voices of others are intentionally held at bay and devalued. On the other hand, academics might try to be inclusive of all groups by not actively undermining or excluding them, but contributions from these groups are not necessarily heard.

Consider, for example, how ideas or suggestions from female academics in faculty meetings unacknowledged. But when a male makes the very same suggestion, it would be received as if the female academic had not already made it (Reeves, 2015).

The problem of epistemic bubbles and echo chambers notwithstanding, as human beings we are already entangled with others. Ahmed (2002: 559) asserts that, 'It is through particular encounters we have with this other, as the one whom I am presented or faced with, that we open up the not yet, as the possibility of being faced by other others'. It is violence, declares Ahmed (2002), to assimilate difference into a category of sameness, or to seek to appropriate or contain that otherness as a way of establishing one's own identity. Hence, it is ethical to celebrate otherness:

11.3 Epistemic Bubbles and (Dis)entanglement

[I]t is by attending to the particularity of *this other* that we can show that which fails to be grasped in the here and the now, in the very *somebody* whom I am faced with. In other words, we can open up the 'not yet', as that which fails to be grasped in the present, not through giving up on the particular and finite, but by attending to the particularity of others. To negate or give up on the particularity of others would involve its own violence: the transformation of others into the figure of the other involves its own betrayal of the future, as the possibility that others might be other than 'the other' or as the possibility of being faced by other others (Ahmed, 2002: 560–561).

Ahmed (2002) is appealing for an approach to the particularity of the other that does not assume it is simply present on their body or face. In this way, we should not assume that someone is different because of what we see in terms of race, gender, culture, ethnicity, or sexuality. For her it might be necessary for us to rethink the very notion of what it might mean to face an other, to face her face, to be faced by her. Because 'to name her as particular in this face-to-face encounter is in danger of reifying the very moment of the face to face…' (Ahmed, 2002: 561).

On the one hand, Ahmed's (2002) appeal contests our inclination to see others as we wish to see them, so that they are assimilated into our predefined frameworks and ideas about the world. As such, academics, for example, might already have specific ideas of how other academics should act or speak, without 'seeing' and 'meeting' them as they are. On the other hand, Ahmed (2002) taps into the preconceived and predetermined ways that individuals or academics come into the presence of others—often already jaded by epistemic bubbles and echo chambers, which prevents the encounter of unfolding openly and without bias. In this way, some academics are already blocked as 'different' or 'exotic' because of his accent, or her dress code.

Like the attempts to assimilate others into a normative culture and discourse, the de facto presumption of particularity acts as barriers to truly meeting, encountering and engaging with others. The particularity of the meeting is therefore 'bound up with a notion of generality, with a movement outwards, and towards other others, who are already implicated in the face-to-face' (Ahmed, 2002: 561). Instead, by thinking about the relationship between ethics and difference, states Ahmed (2002), then we can examine differentiation as something that happens at the level of the encounter. For example, she continues, rather than thinking of gender and race as something that this other has, which, in turn, would thematize this other as always gendered and racialized in a certain way, we can consider how such differences are determined at the level of the encounter. To this end, maintains Ahmed (2002), the immediacy of the face to face is affected by broader social processes that also operate elsewhere, and in other times, rather than simply in the present.

These broader processes can include the intersectionality of identities, as well as the social context of the university, which might not be inclusive and hospitable to all identities. Following Ahmed (2002), there seems to be a call for consideration of a simultaneous process as the encounter is opened: on the hand, to put aside what is physically seen—that is, not to go on 'face-value'—so that the encounter is not pre-decided or biased towards generalised understanding of particular characteristics, such as race or gender. On the other hand, she calls for a consciousness of the contextual influences of the encounter, so that there is an awareness of how these broader processes, such as power dynamics, shape the encounter.

Yes, sometimes, how we encounter or address someone, is quite simply a way of speaking to or about someone. But, explains Butler (Yancy & Butler, 2015), a mode of address may also describe a general way of approaching another such that one presumes who the other is, even the meaning and value of their existence. We address each other with gestures, signs and movements, but also through the broader processes of media and technology (Yancy & Butler, 2015). Assumptions about who the other is, are made all the time: this is someone; this is someone I avoid, to the extent, states Butler (Yancy & Butler, 2015), that the other may well be someone whose very existence makes cross to the other side of the road.

Coming into encounters with others, and moving from the unknown to the familiar, is hard. It is not simply a matter of seeking to know or making oneself to another. It also a process of questioning the epistemic bubbles and echo chambers in which all of us live and function. The confrontation of the truth of who the other is, is potentially also a disruption of the echo chamber, whereby it might become apparent that the knowledge of the other is not only misinformed, but harmful. And while the complexities of these encounters can be evident in the daily processes of the academy—where academics sit in meetings, with whom they collaborate, or who they greet and acknowledge—the point remains that the others are strangers only insofar that they do not meet what has been reduced as knowable and desirable entities of identity. Academics can become *other*-wise, when they respond to the summons of their ethical responsibility for the other (Levinas, 1988).

11.4 Key Considerations of Chapter

While filled with vibrancy and the continuous potential for innovative thinking, renewed possibilities and the production of new forms of knowledge, the university can also be a space fraught with tension, upheaval and questionable norms and cultures. In this way, the university is not only a reflection of the world in which it finds itself but is as much in the world as the world is inside of the university. Central to this chapter is a recognition that cracks and crises—whether internal or external to the university—are critical for jarring academics into responding to the responsibility of their professions.

These responsibilities, following Derrida (2004) 'cannot purely be academic' and extend not only beyond the confines of the university, but also into relationships with other academics. Remaining loyal only to that which is already known and familiar, and dismissing others and their way of life, whether intentionally or unintentionally, creates epistemic bubbles, which, in turn, sustain echo chambers. As a result, for all their knowledge, academics can operate in a chamber of ignorance about others. In response, the chapter argues for the necessity of encounters in which others can be met as they are, and not as distorted by preconceived judgements and stereotypes. Inasmuch as it is difficult to question certain understandings of the world and perceptions of others, doing so is critical not only for the deepening and broadening of academic citizenship, but also for the university, who can never shirk its responsibility and responsiveness to the world.

References

Ahmed, S. (2002). This other and other others. *Economy and Society, 31*(4), 558–572.
Arendt, H. (1968). *Between past and future*. Penguin.
Barnett, R. (2022). *The philosophy of higher education: A critical introduction*. Routledge.
Barnett, R. (2020). Academic activism: Justifying the unjustifiable. https://pathes.org/wp-content/uploads/2020/08/Barnett.pdf
Davids, N., & Waghid, Y. (2021). *Academic activism in higher education: A living philosophy for social justice*. Springer.
Derrida, J. (1995). *The gift of death*. Trans. G. Collins. Verso.
Derrida, J. (2004). *Eyes of the university: Right to philosophy 2*. Trans. J. Plug, & Others. Stanford University Press.
Jansen, J. D. (2023). *Corrupted: A study of chronic dysfunction in South African universities*. Wits University Press.
Levinas, E. (1988). *Totality and infinity*. Trans. A. Lingis. Kluwer Academic Publishers.
McNiff, J. (Ed.). (2023). *Representations of the Academic: Challenging assumptions in higher education*. Routledge.
Nguyen, C. T. (2020). Echo chambers and epistemic bubbles. *Episteme, 17*(2), 141–161.
Reeves, A. N. (2015) Mansplaining, manterrupting & bropropriating: Gender bias and the pervasive interruption of women. Yellow Paper series. https://research.umich.edu/wp-content/uploads/2021/12/manterruptions-bropropriation-and-mansplaining-2-yellow-paper-series.pdf
Yancy, G., & Butler, J. (2015). What's wrong with 'All Lives Matter'? https://archive.nytimes.com/opinionator.blogs.nytimes.com/2015/01/12/whats-wrong-with-all-lives-matter/

Chapter 12
Concluding Reflections: Academic Citizenship, Collegiality, and Trust

Although some might disagree, others hold that collegiality is at the heart of the university. There is a certain taken-for-grantedness that when academics assume positions within universities that they not only align themselves with specific universities and their cultures, but with their colleagues. Seemingly their love for knowledge and research binds them in an implicit collegiality. Collegiality creates certain expectations of a shared professional identity, mutual regard, responsibility, and trust.

But as this book has set out to show, these presumptions are misplaced. Instead, different identities experience different forms of academic citizenship, and consequently, are subjected to different kinds of vulnerabilities. It follows, therefore, that if academic citizenship does not provide a consistent or equal frame of inclusion, recognition and belonging for all academic identities, then presumptions about presence or practices of collegiality are questionable. It also follows that if some academics experience vulnerability, which stems from marginalisation or suppression, there would be little motivation for co-operation, collaboration, or trust.

The matter of trust is an especially delicate one, considering the implicit risks should the trust be broken. Of course, one can self-trust, which speaks to yet another strength and enhancement of vulnerability—that is, the idea of believing and acting in one's own best interests. Trust demands a certain standing, a certain worthiness of being trusted—rendering it incapable of existing without the involvement of others. The relationality of trust implies an immediate vulnerability: there is a risk that this trust could be betrayed. As a concluding chapter, it is apposite to consider the importance and vulnerability of trust within academic citizenship. Specifically, how can trust be conceived and enacted as both a condition and consequence of academic citizenship? How might trust be (re)prioritised as an institutional ethos and basis of academic citizenship?

12.1 Collegiality

On the surface, the notion and expectation of collegiality seem almost out of place with being an academic. As made apparent and discussed throughout this book, how academic citizenship is conceived and experienced is incredibly heterogeneous, which explains why Macfarlane and Burg (2018: 3) opt to describe it as 'a set of attitudes and activities connected to internal and external service work', rather than attempting to capture all the various roles and responsibilities academics are required to adopt in various institutions.

Others like Nørgård and Bengtsen (2016: 4) describe it in broader terms as 'the intertwining of participation in, engagement between, and mutual responsibility of, universities and society', which echoes the discussion in Chap. 11. And while it is possible to associate certain virtues, such as responsibility, trust, benevolence, care, compassion and empathy with academic citizenship, these are sometimes overshadowed by the sheer volume of roles: writing, teaching, peer review of manuscripts, serving on appointment and promotion committees; peer evaluation of teaching and research, serving on editorial boards, conference presentations; applying for research grants, serving as conference programme chairs, mentoring of junior colleagues, student supervision consultation, serving on an array of university, faculty and departmental committees serving as departmental chairs and fulfilling administrative responsibilities, serving on national regulatory bodies, networking and engaging with industry and professional bodies.

The word 'serving' comes up frequently in this list, which by no means is exhaustive. Depending on whatever crisis may have unfolded at the university, academics will be roped in to constitute and serve on even more committees, or 'working groups'. The more the university massifies and diversifies, the more the social and service demands on academics will increase. Yet, contends Macfarlane (2005: 299), 'in the conceptualisation of academic life, the role of service has been, by and large, overlooked or trivialised as little more than 'administration' rather than essential to the preservation of community life'. Missing, but centrally embedded however, is the term 'competition'. Competition, not only in terms of vying for promotions, research productivity, teaching awards, or international recognition, but also by virtue of the fact that academics are continuously invited to review and assess the performances of their peers, whether this involves reviewing a journal article, a conference abstract, or examining a PhD thesis.

The competitive culture within universities and cultivated within academic citizenship, ties in with 'academic capitalism', which, according to Slaughter and Leslie (1997), refers to ways in which universities have adopted neoliberal tendencies, to the extent that higher education policy is treated as a subset of economic policy, particularly in the pursuit of income. Slaughter and Leslie (1997) explain that engaging in 'academic capitalism' results in an increased income for universities, while also enhancing reputation and esteem, since competitive grants are secured from prestigious organisations.

12.1 Collegiality

In the kinds of contexts and conditions described here, one has to ask whether collegiality is at all possible or desirable in higher education institutions. Firstly, however, what do we understand by collegiality? Like academic citizenship, collegiality means many different things in different contexts. Despite its historical roots in the governance of medieval collegiate universities in Europe and the UK, states Kligyte (2023), over time, collegiality has gained many additional meanings and interpretations, and is at the heart of the academy's collective endeavour. She describes it as central to how we think about academic governance structures, academic cultures, as well as the norms guiding academic work. Collegiality continues to be viewed as a fundamental feature of academic identity and is associated with academic structures, cultures, ideals, values, and norms (Kligyte, 2023).

Tapper and Palfreyman (2002), identify three institutional arenas within which collegiality expresses itself. The first is the college itself and, although colleges are not necessarily collegial institutions, it is within this context that the idea can find its fullest and purest expression. The second is the collegiate university—collegiate universities have federal systems of governance and federalism suggests the possibility of a fluctuating power balance between the centre (the university) and the periphery (the colleges). The third arena is very broad and includes all those institutions of higher education that have incorporated aspects of the collegiate tradition as identified within the colleges and the collegiate universities (Tapper & Palfreyman, 2002). In turn, Kligyte and Barrie (2014) distinguish between three kinds of collegiality: collegiality as a governance and consensual decision-making structure; collegiality as allegiance to disciplinary knowledge communities; and collegiality as a behavioural norm.

Although it is possible to describe what collegiality entails and looks like, experiencing and practising it suggest a very different impression. I have already touched on the intensity of roles and responsibilities bundled into the concept of academic citizenship, which has a significant influence on collegiality. There is the additional matter of how new as well as early career academics are socialised into the academy. On the one hand, if senior faculty, for example, adopts an instrumentalist approach, which prioritises the achievement of mandated performance metrics over academic citizenship activities, state Beatson et al (2022), then this will set the tone of collegiality for newer faculty. Concomitantly, if junior faculty are not sufficiently mentored and developed from the outset, their academic careers will be inhibited due to an inability to publish in highly ranked journals, thereby placing the career paths at risk.

On the other hand, if collegiality, as expressed through support, co-operation and shared responsibility is not made visible to new and early career academics, they would be inclined to forge a similar kind of citizenship. Furthermore, Macfarlane (2005) posits that hierarchical authority has always been present in universities, but collegiality no longer plays such a strong balancing role. He elaborates that while hierarchy is about vesting decision-making authority in designated leadership roles, as might be commonly found in many business organisations, collegiality works based on members having an equal authority in decision-making processes, the results of which must be respected by all—a process which has been in decline at faculty and departmental levels.

It is evident, that in the face of rising trends of academic discontent, erosion, or disengagement, as discussed in Chap. 2, as well as the struggles that both early and more senior academics experience in navigating departmental and faculty spaces, that collegiality is critical not only for academic citizenship, but academic well-being. If understood as a relationship based on respect, co-operation, and shared responsibility towards a common goal within a particular setting, then collegiality can play a significant role in strengthening academic citizenship. The dark side of collegiality, such as taking on heavy service loads, doing favours for senior colleagues, poor leadership or tolerating inconsiderate bad behaviour, explains Spierling (2023), does not negate its potential as a positive force in others. Every story of unkind, disrespectful and marginalising conduct by colleagues, can be outweighed by the guidance and support of others.

To Lixinski (2022), the romanticised image of the solitary academic toiling away on their next great discovery is increasingly outdated, as it becomes clear that interdisciplinary work is required to solve society's most pressing problems. Even university teaching has become a collective process drawing on experts from different fields to create engaging courses (Lixinski, 2022). He cautions, however, that the subtle power of collegiality should not be taken for granted nor underestimated. It is often built in indescribable and unexpected ways, via informal hallway conversations, serendipitous encounters that lead to a shared coffee or meal, or that bond-forming chitchat about everything and nothing before and after a committee meeting (Lixinski, 2022). And, as has been detailed in Chaps. 7 and 8, the formation of potential relationships, knowing about others, learning, unlearning and relearning stems from curiosity—that is, recognising that there is something missing in what is already known, and having a desire to know.

What collegiality offers is not simply a relationship of familiarity, as opposed to disinterest and ignorance, but a soft-landing space in a professional environment that holds great capacity for agonism, discomfort, self-doubt, as well as isolation. As such, collegiality can begin to take shape by simple expressions of interest and regard. While the seniority of academics might matter with regard to offering mentoring and leadership, it should not serve as a barrier to inviting all academics into a space of equal regard, care and hospitality. Collegiality resides in showing support not only to new academic appointments, but when academics are under pressure both professionally and personally. This relies on having knowledge of peers, their families, their pathways to the institution, and their hopes for themselves. This is not about prying into colleagues' lives.

Rather, it is about knowing *about* who we work with, so that there might be some connection and recognition of them, their work, their achievements, and their challenges. At a very practical level, collegiality is evident when academics offer their support in reducing another's teaching or administrative load when needed, extending warm wishes on the attainment of certain milestones, or project funding, or simply asking about their wellbeing or that of their family. The more academics are seen and recognised by their peers, the more they feel supported and included, and the greater the opportunity for cultivating collegiality.

12.2 Trust, and Trustworthiness

To Levi and Stoker (2000: 476), 'trust is relational; it involves an individual making herself vulnerable to another individual, group, or institution that has the capacity to do her harm or to betray her'. It is also seldom unconditional; it is given to specific individuals or institutions over specific domains (Levi & Stoker, 2000). For example, when students confide in their supervisors, or when academics share personal details about themselves with colleagues, they will do so on a basis of trust—that is, they believe that they and what they share will not be misused or betrayed.

Trust is a fragile emotion or attitude and is clearly not without vulnerability. When we believe that we can trust someone, it is because that person has made us feel that it is safe to do so. Inasmuch as one might trust, so, too, one might distrust, based on nothing more than a gut feeling or a hunch. It is not uncommon for individuals to just have a sense of another, often captured in a phrasing, 'I don't know what it is, but I just don't feel like I can trust him…' D'Olimpio (2018: 193) maintains that 'to be considered worthy of trust, as an individual or an institution, one must do the right thing at the right time for the right reasons, and the action should have its intended effect'.

While trusting someone emanates from a sense of safety and connection, distrust sits at the opposite end of the continuum and can be accompanied by vigilance, or in more extreme cases, a complete severing of the relationship (Levi & Stoker, 2000). It might be that academic X confides in academic Y about certain difficulties related to her teaching or her writing, thereby making herself vulnerable to academic Y in that he knows something about academic X, which can potentially be harmful or humiliating to her. The vulnerability arises from the fact that academic X takes a risk by believing that academic Y is indeed trustworthy.

In some instances, says Levi (1998), the risk may be so low that we tend to use the label confidence instead of trust, while in other instances, the risk is so high that we consider the truster gullible. To Levi (1998), the actual extent of risk and the extent to which the truster is taking a 'sensible' risk are variables—'They are always partially and often largely functions of the trustworthiness of not only the trustee but also those on whom the truster relies for information and sanctions against a trust-breaker'. Trust is, therefore, a relational and rational, although not always fully calculated, action (Levi, 1998).

If academic X finds out that academic Y had in fact revealed what had been confided to him, the trust is broken. In this case, whatever trust and sense of security that academic X had with academic Y is quickly replaced with distrust—that is, that she is not safe with academic Y, and that he is, in fact, untrustworthy. There is something, therefore, in the other (a colleague), which leads the individual to arrive at an assessment that the colleague can be trusted, that he is trustworthy, or that he cannot. Levi and Stoker (2000: 476) describe this as the 'trust judgement', which reflects beliefs about the trustworthiness of the other person (or group or institution). Behaviourally, argues Levi (1998: 79), 'the more trusting an individual is the lower the personal investment she will make in learning about the trustworthiness of the trusted and in monitoring and enforcing his compliance in a cooperative venture'. Importantly, maintains Levi (1998), the emphasis in on trusting *behaviour*, not its outcome, meaning that someone can trust mistakenly.

Like trust, trustworthiness is also relational but in a more limited sense (Levi & Stoker, 2000). To be trustworthy means that one can be counted or relied upon. An academic, therefore, can be trustworthy in terms of always being honest and keeping her word, but she can also be trustworthy in that she does not betray the trust that is placed in her. Even when there is no call for trust, continue Levi and Stoker (2000), a person or institution can possess the attributes of trustworthiness, which assure potential trusters that the trusted party will not betray a trust. These attributes fall along two dimensions:

> The first involves a commitment to act in the interests of the truster because of moral values that emphasize promise keeping, caring about the truster, incentive compatibility, or some combination of all three. When we call someone trustworthy, we often mean only this commitment, but there is in fact a second dimension, namely competence in the domain over which trust is being given. The trustworthy will not betray the trust as a consequence of either bad faith or ineptitude (Levi & Stoker, 2000: 476).

Why does trust and trustworthiness matter to academic citizenship, if at all? As already hinted at in this chapter, while possible and appealing for some, the sentimental idea of the solitary academic is not only increasingly outdated (Lixinski, 2022), but it does not serve the cultivation and flourishing of academic citizenship. This is not to say, that academics should not work in solitude, or not seek out extended periods of aloneness, as might be the case with sabbaticals, which can allow academics the much-needed time and space to write without interruption. What I am saying, is that the establishment of academic citizenship rests on the nurturing of social relationships, as fostered through curiosity, dialogue, and making oneself vulnerable through the sharing of stories.

As social and political beings, asserts D'Olimpio (2018), we are able to flourish only if we collaborate with others. And importantly, successful collaboration with others requires trust (D'Olimpio, 2018). To D'Olimpio (2018: 193), deciding when to trust others and being trustworthy are virtuous character traits—'To be considered worthy of trust, as an individual or an institution, one must do the right thing at the right time for the right reasons, and the action should have its intended effect'. For academics, this means being honest, sincere, and authentic in their relationships with their colleagues and their students. It means not gossiping or listening to gossip about colleagues and students. Trust relies on commitment: to colleagues in terms of honouring responsibilities and workloads; to students in terms of being prepared, informed and open in communication; to oneself by being honest and open when a mistake has been made. Trust therefore is made visible when academics show themselves as being reliable and open to accountability.

In order for academics to come together as a collective, with intentions of a common purpose, and endeavours towards shared responsibilities, there have to be both trust and trustworthiness, or a discourse of trust. Academics can only trust their colleagues if their colleagues present and prove themselves as trustworthy. It is not only a matter of being able to trust colleagues with certain bits of information, but rather a matter of being able to trust in colleagues not to act in a harmful or corrosive way. A discourse of trust implies acting in a way which always give the other the benefit of the doubt, so that the professional environment is free of gossip and suspicion, as well as free from mistrust of others because of physical or assigned attributes.

An academic might for example, from the outset, decide to mistrust a colleague because of her gender, ethnicity, or accent. These kinds of perceptions and actions stem from an echo chamber, which serve only to constrain and strain academic citizenship, and should be unlearnt, not only so that all colleagues can be trusted (until they suggest otherwise), but so that all colleagues can be deemed as trustworthy. In other words, when an academic opts to mistrust a colleague because of preconceived biases about certain groups of people, that academic renders herself as untrustworthy—that is, she cannot be trusted to judge individuals on merit and who they are.

Amid the complexities of diverse identities, knowledge, and knowledge production, as well as the embedded and unspoken vulnerabilities, we need a renewed ethos of trust in academic citizenship. An ethos, which not only gives precedence to who we are, rather than what we do, but is fundamentally opposed to the kinds of mistrust which inform ideas and practices of othering and marginalization. This would mean cultivating an academic citizenship, which is open, curious, vulnerable, and trustworthy. More importantly, it would establish academic citizenship as a desirable space of belonging, opening possibilities for yet-to-be-considered intellectual and social contributions and thought. In a world increasingly turned against, rather than towards each other, the responsibility of the university must be one, which places human regard above that of innovation, and a restoration of trust that offers a vulnerable, yet strong foundational starting point.

12.3 Key Considerations of Book

The interest of this book was never only to draw attention to the myriad roles, responsibilities and services which constitute academic citizenship—although these are adequately highlighted and unpacked throughout the chapters. There are certain unexplored discriminations about what it means to be an academic citizen, which are not only shrouded in the silence of unspoken experiences, but which speak to an exposure of vulnerabilities, which are, perhaps, unprecedented in other professions. When left alone, and unconfronted, the university can become a deeply hostile, inhospitable and toxic space, which not only keeps certain identity groups at bay, but prevents them from fully coming into their professional identities, and potential achievements.

The primary intention of the book, therefore, has been to bring into question the idea of academic citizenship as a homogenous and inclusive space, and highlight that even when academics occupy similar positions, or hold similar professional standings, their citizenship and implied notions of participation, inclusion, recognition, and belonging are largely pre-determined by who they are personally, rather than what they do professionally. As a result, not only do academics experience different kinds of citizenship, but they live through different sets of vulnerabilities.

Despite its sustained focus on the potential barriers and pitfalls which reside within the experiences of academic citizenship, the book never loses hope in the capacity of academics to rethink and reconstruct their relationships with others (colleagues and students) and in relation to the university. It is apposite, therefore, that I conclude this book with a focus on collegiality and trust, not only because both are desirable attitudes for academic citizenship, but because beyond the frames of academic designations and titles, are the profoundly more critical questions about who academics are as human beings. Being seen as non-collegial and untrustworthy, does not only reflect a professional disposition, but also speaks to the identity and values of that academic.

Hence, for academic citizenship to be restored, as might be the case in some faculties and departments, or nurtured, requires a close reflection by individuals on who they are and what they can bring as human beings, rather than only as academics, and what they can do.

References

Beatson, N. J., Tharapos, M., O'Connell, B. T., De Lange, P., Carr, S., & Copeland, S. (2022). The gradual retreat from academic citizenship. *Higher Education Quarterly, 76*, 715–725.

D'Olimpio, L. (2018). Trust as a virtue in education. *Educational Philosophy and Theory, 50*(2), 193–202.

Kligyte, G. (2023). Collegiality as collective affect: Who carries the burden of the labour of attunement? *Higher Education Research & Development*. https://doi.org/10.1080/07294360.2023.2183940

Kligyte, G., & Barrie, S. (2014). Collegiality: Leading us into fantasy—the paradoxical resilience of collegiality in academic leadership. *Higher Education Research and Development, 33*(1), 157–169.

Levi, M. (1998). A state of trust. In V. Braithwaite & M. Levi (Eds.), *Trust and governance* (pp. 77–101). Sage.

Levi, M., & Stoker, L. (2000). Political trust and trustworthiness. *Annual Review of Political Science, 3*, 475–507.

Lixinski, L. (2022). The art of collegiality and why it matters. https://www.timeshighereducation.com/campus/spotlight/art-collegiality-and-why-it-matters

Macfarlane, B. (2005). The disengaged academic: The retreat from citizenship. *Higher Education Quarterly, 59*(4), 296–312.

Macfarlane, B., & Burg, D. (2018). Rewarding and recognising academic citizenship. *Leadership Foundation for Higher Education*. Southampton: University of Southampton.

Nørgård, R. T., & Bengtsen, S. S. E. (2016). Academic citizenship beyond the campus: A call for the placeful university. *Higher Education Research & Development, 35*(1), 4–16.

Slaughter, S., & Leslie, L.L. (1997). *Academic capitalism: politics, policies and the entrepreurial university.* Baltimore, MD: The John Hopkins University Press.

Spierling, K. E. (2023). Collegiality helped me endure a rough ride from a columnist. htttps://www.timeshighereducation.com/blog/collegiality-helped-me-endure-rough-ride-columnist

Tapper, T., & Palfreyman, D. (2002). Understanding collegiality: The changing Oxbridge model. *Tertiary Education and Management, 8*(1), 47–63.